HASLEMERE

being

Haslemere in History
and
Haslemere 1850-1950

Wm. BRIDGER, the first bandmaster of the new band in 1837—from an
old painting.

HASLEMERE

being

Haslemere in History

and

Haslemere 1850 ~ 1950

G. R. ROLSTON, O.B.E.

PHILLIMORE

1978

Published by
PHILLIMORE & CO. LTD.,
Shopwyke Hall, Chichester, Sussex

Haslemere in History
was first published in 1956

Haslemere 1850–1950
was first published in 1964

Mrs. M. E. Rolston, 1978

ISBN 0 85033 309 1

Printed in Great Britain by
UNWIN BROTHERS LIMITED
Old Woking, Surrey,
and bound at
THE NEWDIGATE PRESS
Dorking, Surrey

HASLEMERE
IN
HISTORY

G. R. ROLSTON

CONTENTS

LIST OF ILLUSTRATIONS

Wm. Bridger, the bandmaster   *Frontispiece*

Between pages 54 and 55

Piperham Farm, about 1865

Old Farm at Critchmere, circa 1880

Plan of Haslemere 1600–1700

Haslemere High Street, 1865 or thereabouts

View up Haslemere High Street, mid-nineteenth century

Plan of Haslemere Borough 1735, by William Morley

Thursley End, circa 1900

Haslemere House (now Humewood), before 1820

Lythe Hill Farm House

Imbham's Farm and Pond

Plan of Haslemere Borough 1775, by H. Cotes

Goodwyns, prior to 1880

Lane End Farm, 1875

View from Cherriman's, 1857

View from Shepherd's Hill about 1800

Haslemere Windmill, before 1870

Haslemere High Street, circa 1870

View over Haslemere, circa 1885

PREFACE

In writing this story of a small country town, I have deliberately avoided the usual method of assembling information. It has always seemed to me that History, whether of countries or places, is like the continuous production of a loom. A cloth is being woven by many hands contributing each their thread of importance or interest. The resulting pattern is guided by events beyond the control of the individuals, who however contribute their own life quota of colour or strength. Even the pattern may change or develop as generation succeeds generation.

In such a small town as I describe, the threads of the pattern are largely homespun; few silk or gold threads will be found, and in its whole length the changing patterns will scarcely merit admiration.

But we may trace development from very simple sacking to serviceable cloth, with hints in latter days of the development of armorial tapestry.

In this record is a recognition of Tradition which often is regarded as stuffy, but it is well to recall—

> "Tradition is a thing inherited that it may be carried on and is concerned with the future. We English, who almost pride ourselves that our memories are short, too early forget that memory is the custodian of the future." EDM. ESDAILE.

G. R. ROLSTON.

Crofts,
  Haslemere.

1956.

ACKNOWLEDGEMENTS

I wish to acknowledge here, valuable help from various sources. Chief among these has been the Haslemere Educational Museum, its reference libraries, news cuttings, old diaries and its always helpful staff.

The Woods Collections, housed in Godalming, have been a vast mine for local information.

The illustrations are from photographs made available by the Haslemere Museum, and of water colour paintings belonging to Miss Bridger—Petworth Road, Miss Bridger—Sandrock, and Miss Booker—Longdene Road.

The volume by Swanton & Woods, "Bygone Haslemere," has been of great general help, though I have mined, wherever possible, my own ore from original sources.

HISTORY OF SURREY — *Manning & Bray.*
HISTORY OF ENGLAND — *Trevelyan.*
HISTORY OF ENGLAND — *Oman.*
VICT. COUNTY HISTORY OF SURREY.
SURREY ARCHÆOLOGICAL SOCIETY AND RECORD SOCIETY.
SUSSEX ARCHÆOLOGICAL SOCIETY AND RECORD SOCIETY.
HISTORY OF KIRKBY STEPHEN — *Sowerby.*
GOTHIC ENGLAND — *Harvey.*
HASLEMERE PARISH REGISTERS — *Penfold.*
PRIORY AND MANOR OF LYNCHMERE AND SHULEBREDE — *A. Ponsonby.*
JAMES L. OGLETHORPE— *Ettinger.*
RURAL LIFE IN HAMPSHIRE— *(Capes).*
RECORDS OF CHICHESTER — *Willis.*
HISTORY OF ENGLISH PEOPLE — *Mitchell.*
GROWTH AND DEVELOPMENT OF ENGLISH PARISH — *Wray Hunt.*
MISCELLANEOUS — *D'Israeli.*
PLACE NAMES SOCIETY'S VOLUMES, SURREY AND SUSSEX.

I wish also to acknowledge great help from my wife, in the ultimate fashioning of this record; to the Committee of the Haslemere Educational Museum for their encouragement to publish, and to Mr. F. O. Meddows Taylor for much help in production.

All illustrations are from photographs by Colin G. Futcher, Haslemere.

G.R.R.

CHAPTER I

Prehistory and Early Settlements

PREHISTORY — EARLY SETTLEMENT, ROMANS,
SAXONS, NORMANS, PIPERHAM BURGAGES —
MARKET AND FAIR GRANT

THE PARISH OF HASLEMERE occupies the extreme south-west
of Surrey, and the town stretches to the adjacent Sussex and
Hampshire borders. The high street of the town of Haslemere
forms a watershed of the Wey and Arun Rivers, beneath the
bleak but sheltering Hindhead and Blackdown hills.

It is not surprising therefore to find a store of interest under
its present simple country town appearance, and a history which
stretches back to earliest hunting man.

If you had visited the district 10,000 years ago, you would
have found on the hill-tops various clans of hill-top inhabitants.
These folk were mainly hunters, and have left traces of their way
of living, chiefly in their hunting and fighting tools, together with
occasional flint knapping and dwelling sites, and burial mounds.

These earlier so-called Stone Age inhabitants were later
over-run by the New Stone Age tribes, who were the primitive
and outflung waves of a civilisation developed in the Eastern
Mediterranean lands. To all these people, the hill-tops around
the future Haslemere were a safe living area and refuge from
the wild beasts of the forests below. Having some knowledge of
land cultivation, weaving, and making pottery, these New Stone
Age people made small fields on sheltered slopes in which to
grow their simple crops, and kept small herds of sheep.

The next people who came to live nearby had learned the
art of making and using bronze tools, weapons and vessels. They
were thus able more readily to extend the cultivated areas
farther into the lowlands.   Traces of their occupation of this
countryside have been found on the lower heaths around
Haslemere, though little trace has been found of the finer work
of their craftsmen.

About a thousand years later a further wave of invaders from North West Europe, called Brythons, arrived in Southern England, bringing iron equipment and knowledge of iron smelting. These last folk also left a little of their speech in such place names as Wandle, Wey, Marley, Critchmere, Camel.

Scarcely any trace of their occupation has yet been noted in this area. They were, however, great sheep farmers, and lived chiefly on the chalk hills, to the South and East and West, where we can still see and wonder at their huge defensive earthworks.

Various other North European tribes, chief among them the Belgae, crossed to Southern England, bringing later ideas of urn burial, and vastly increased hill-top defence works. It seems likely that one or two families of these last may have found their way to the Haslemere district.

In the first years of the Christian era there would appear to have been a large farmstead, or as we would later say, Manor House, at the upper end of the present town of Haslemere. This farmstead, of which no trace has yet been found, is evidenced by the discovery of 27 burial urns, each with accessory vessels, in 1903-5, and expert opinion has fixed their date as between 40-80 and 80-120 A.D. The family who lived there were probably Britons who had close contact with the Roman civilisation then spreading over the English countryside.

As to why a settlement occurred early in Haslemere, we may surmise that there was a large pool*, fed by springs convenient for water supply, under the Hindhead hills, perhaps originally the western end of a great Wealden lake. When, over geological time, the water level fell, what is now Haslemere High Street became a watershed, dividing the sources of the Arun and Wey rivers, as well as holding back the last remains of the pool, which was still in evidence in 1859.

As earlier stated, the hill-tops and slopes had been the living sites of the local tribes, which, as the countryside became more cleared and developed into areas of family influence, felt more content to live at the lower levels, nearer the springs.

---

* This pool probably covered most of the area between High Street and Derby Road.

Hence, in course of time, and by the date of the first Roman invasion, we find the nucleus of the later town in the farmstead near the present Grayswood Road. A little further light on the early settling of the Haslemere Romano-British site has recently been granted. The nearest similar settlement was on Pockford Farm, Chiddingfold, where in 1883-8 the remains of a small villa were uncovered. It had also been thought that the nearest Roman Road was the Stane Street (Chichester-Pulborough-Dorking-London) with its branch towards Guildford, from Rowhook. However, four years ago, study of air photographs of the country near Milland, six miles west of Haslemere, showed the presence of a Roman marching camp, and further examination revealed the line of a Roman road which has since been described in Sussex County Magazine for October, 1951. This road came up from Chichester over the Downs at Linch, and so, near Iping, where in the 19th century Roman urns were discovered under the Church. Then on to Milland, where further burial urns had been discovered under the site of the old Tuxlith Church. The further course northwards of this road is not yet established*, but may well have continued to the large pottery factory, of which many traces have been uncovered in the Goose Green part of Alice Holt Forest, near Farnham. It is interesting to realise that the potteries of that neighbourhood were working over a period of 400 years, while one writer has even suggested that when the works were in full blast, that area must have resembled our present day Stoke-on-Trent. More recently still, in 1951, a burial urn of about 200 A.D. was dug up from a depth of 2ft. near Passfield Common, a fact which suggests the presence of another villa in its neighbourhood. This urn may be seen in the Haslemere Museum, as also representative pieces of the original Beech Road find.

So, for 8,000 years, the Haslemere district had received and nurtured one new group of people after another, each the fine adventurous section of an Eastern civilisation, impatient of domestic restrictions. We may compare them to the early settlers in the British colonies—where toughness of health and character were of more importance than the elaborate but decadent culture of the home country. We may, therefore, be proud of our local inheritance.

---

* Recently (1956) proved to be making for Silchester.

The coming of Roman civilisation brought a centralised order and discipline which continued for four hundred years. However, the sudden recall of the Legions to home defence in Italy left England unprotected against the growing raids of the Saxon tribes. When the Saxons found England without a home guard, their desire for more and better lands brought more and greater parties of raiders, who, as they conquered, became settlers. For 250 years these raids continued, striking farther inland; halted for a generation by such a notable patriot as King Arthur.

There is no trace of the Saxon battles in these highlands, the raiders probably following the Roman highways so that the Haslemere uplands were, possibly, again a refuge area. Gradually the kingdoms of South Saxons, West Saxons and others developed and, by the time of Alfred, various other villages and towns in the neighbourhood must have come into being, e.g., Haslemere, Godalming, Eashing, Cocking, Lurgashall, Thursley and Witley. There are names in the Haslemere area which may date from this time — Dallingwick* (possibly the site of the Roman farm), Piperham, Crookedham*, Imbhams, Prestwick. We may feel certain that these farms were cleared and cultivated by early Saxon settlers. Of these, Piperham appears to have been the most important, for in later years this name is found as a farm name, as the name of the first local church, and as a family name.

Before these later developments, the Danes, in their turn, came marauding over the eastern half of England. The Danish bands raged over the English countryside from their ship bases, as had the Saxons 300 years earlier. They probably made use in a similar way of the Roman roads, for their forced marches. We are, therefore, not surprised to find their traces in the neighbourhood of Haslemere. In 894 the Anglo-Saxon chronicles record that the Danes were camped between the mouth of the Thames and Appledore in Kent, and that they sent out raiding parties all along the Weald. Having collected much booty, they were turning north to cross over the Thames to reach another of their depôts in Essex. However, King Alfred's forces outrode the Danes and met them in battle at Farnham. The Danish army was completely routed, and all the booty recaptured and the escaping Danes fled on over the Thames.

---

* Dallingwick, Crookedham, were properties near Pound Corner.

Again in 1001, in these same chronicles, it is recorded that everywhere the Danes raged and burned, so that they advanced (from Southampton area) till they came to the town of Alton. But there they were met by the men of Hampshire, who fought against them. The battle was inconclusive for, though many more Danes were killed than English, the Danes remained in possession of the battlefield. We find on the south of Haslemere, above Fernden School, that there is a Dane's Copse, and although a number of field names in the Fernhurst area to the south appear Danish in origin, this is almost certainly fortuitous.

In the famous year 1066, the Normans, in their turn, coveted the green and rich countryside of England and, helped by hordes of mercenaries, made the last successful foreign invasion.

William the Conqueror imposed a new governing pattern in the form of strict feudal discipline; a system of land tenure, where freehold began in the King and radiated down through his Barons to the Villein, the lowest grade of possible freeholder.

All such freeholders owed military service to the King, and all others were bound with their occupation lands to their over-lord. This system proved a good fighting weapon, when the King was strong. Here should be mentioned that Haslemere, in Queen Elizabeth's reign, claimed the status of a borough as from time immemorial. It is on record, even so early as 1370, that Haslemere paid town or burgess rent to the Lord of the Manor, and the inhabitants claimed and maintained the special privilege of Ancient Demesne. Both these privileges are usually found to antedate the Norman Conquest, so that considerable grounds exist for the claims of Haslemere to have been an ancient borough.

But to return to Norman times again: Haslemere appears first in history as the Chapel of Piperham, which in 1180 was stated to belong to the Church of Chiddingfold. At this date there was in Chiddingfold a family named Heysulle, whose name died out with the marriage of an heiress in the 14th Century. We can now offer a reasonable derivation of the name Haslemere; as the mere or boundary of the land of the Heysulle family.

Forty years later, in 1221[1], the sheriff of Surrey received the Royal Command to grant to Richard, Bishop of Salisbury[2], the Manor of Godalming, and the Market of Haslemere. So that quite early in the reign of Henry III there is evidence that

---

[1] Earliest mention of name of Haslemere.
[2] Bishops of Salisbury remained Lords of Manor until Dissolution of Monasteries.

Haslemere had become a market town. We also gather from the Royal order that these properties had been in the ownership of the Broc family for about 100 years. This market status of Haslemere was another coveted privilege, and its grant antedated the markets of most of the towns and villages in the neighbourhood.

From this date onwards there is an increasing number of deeds, which give us personal names and place names in the long reign of Henry III. In 1230 a deed grants land near Clammerhill and Imbhams, and among the names mentioned are Jocelyn de Meadfield, William de Longhurst, Edward de Gostrode, Godwin de Haslemere, Thomas Dunscod, Peter de Heysulle, and Luke the clerk. This last man may well have been a local curate, while Peter de Heysulle was a member of the Chiddingfold family who, as previously suggested, may have given their name to Haslemere, generations before.

Of the other names, Meadfield is a 40-acre farm estate today; Gostrode is a farm to the south of Chiddingfold; Duncecod was a small property near Collards, somewhere along the Petworth Road. Fifty years later another deed describes how Robert de Prestwick makes a grant of two acres of land called Northdown, where Highlands now stands—not far from the Holehurst or Holvast property. Among the witnesses to this were Peter de Heysulle, Nicholas de Meadfield, Nicholas de Godley (Chiddingfold), Robert de Chiddingfold, John de Haslemere, Luke the clerk of Haslemere, and Robert the butcher of Prestwick.

Gradually we are beginning to know the little community; at this date, however, only from the more prominent inhabitants.

Here is a more homely reference, and yet one which proves that burgage property existed in 1279 in Haslemere. Julia and her husband, Adam Pokgele, sued her widowed mother, Eva Chyrk, for the house in which Eva lived. The suit failed on a technical point of law, viz, the form was wrong in an area within an Ancient Demesne. Thirty years later, in 1306-7, Adam and Julia granted to their son Herbert, at an annual rent of 5/-, a certain burgage which lay between Adam's house and the house formerly occupied by Herbert's grandmother, Eva.

Among the witnesses to the grant were Richard de Heysulle, William le French, Thomas de Piperham, Nicholas Duncecod, Richard le Taylor. In this deed is the first mention of the Piperham family.

CHAPTER II

Mediæval Records

EARLY FARMS AND THEIR OWNERS — 14TH AND
15TH CENTURY, NEWS FROM MANOR COURTS,
CONSECRATION OF BURIAL GROUND, CONFIRMA-
TION OF FAIR — POACHING

AT THE BEGINNING of the new century we have note from
various sources of quite a number of settlers in the neighbourhood. Stotely, Hazelhurst, Imbhams, Medefields, Haslemere,
Longhurst, Prestwick, Piperham, and others were the names of
farms in the area near the town and gave name to families who
lived there. Within the town itself other folk lived, some of
whose names appear on a taxation list nearer the next century.
In trying to visualise the Haslemere of 1300 we should be correct
in seeing two parallel roads one on either side of a marshy valley,
which itself is bridged by a hard raised Causeway*. It is along
this bridge that the small cottages, perhaps half-a-dozen on
either side, have been built and which forms a nucleus for the
market granted nearly 100 years before; a sheltered spot, a
healthy spot in a very bleak and wild area full of new holdings,
almost a frontier town, but a good halting place with fresh water
springs.

A few years later, in 1315, there was a severe and widespread famine in Europe, and in 1349 the Black Death reduced
a population which was increasing faster than sanitary knowledge
could support, and incidentally began the redistribution of
Feudal powers. The half-century of the reign of Edward III,
1327-77, was further marked by a series of mainly unsuccessful
wars.

It is true to say, however, that much artistic development
occurred during this period, reaching a climax in the reign of
Richard II, who was another clever but inconstant King.
Ordinary folk by the new century had learned their worth, but

---

* High Street.

they also began to measure their worth by a money standard
which lost them their stake as practical landowners.   Their
standard had been taken from that of their overlords, for cultured luxury had been the motto of the master, while money for
luxury was the aim of the man.

In Piers Plowman, William Lackland reflected the disgust
of the ordinary man for the jobbery and deceit, widespread in
all classes, while Chaucer, who lived at the end of this period,
reflected in his poetry the outlook of decent cultured folk, and
we may almost recognise some of the Haslemere inhabitants, in
the procession of characters in the Canterbury Tales.   We had
no local knight or esquire here, but there were several yeomen,
in coat and hood of green, armed with a longbow.   A hunting
monk might not infrequently be seen on the outskirts of Haslemere from Shulebrede Priory or Waverley Abbey.   Friars might
be met anywhere in the countryside and were often thorns in the
flesh of the orthodox local priest.   The poor parson himself, such
as John the Clerk of Haslemere in 1343, no doubt was "in
adversity full patient."   For "wide was his parish and houses
far asunder, but he wotted not for rain or thunder, in sickness
nor in mischief to visite the furthest in his parish—much and
light upon his feet, and in his hand a staff," and perhaps it was
this staff which led to trouble, for in the year 1343 John was
charged at Godalming Court with some unspecified offence and
fined 4d.   Probably, like the Parson in the Tales, he had
"snybben sharply for the nonce, an obstinate parishioner."

On fair days and market days might sometimes be seen the
Summoner, an official of the Archdeacon, seeking wrongdoers,
and the Pardoner, selling like hot cakes his pardons just come
from Rome.   There was also a lively Prioress, who lived not far
away at Easbourne, who enjoyed fine living and no doubt
hawking round Henley Hill; receiving thereby rebuke from the
Bishop.

Others, such as the buxom Housewife, the Miller, Carpenter,
Tailor, Weaver, Dyer and Ploughman would all have been seen
in the little town, and in Chaucer's sure hand each is etched
for our study.

With the death of the cultured king at the end of the
century, the mainspring of the arts, painting, architecture,

poetry and music was lost. Having now a background for the 14th century, we will return to Haslemere in 1330 and see who is living there.

In an assessment levied on all who had more than 5/- worth of goods, we find twelve families assessed for tax in Haslemere Parish, and many names still present today are found for the first time. Robert de Stoteley, Roger Hazlehurst, Alice de Puckshott, Richard le Steed, Mathilda and Richard Whatman, Richard Piperham, John le Turner, Richard le Rodgate, William le Taylor, Richard and Agnes Pokgele, William Hondeleys*, are found for Haslemere, and others in the country around, as Grayswood, Stillwell, Chitty, Brooker, Hunt, Sturt. We can now be certain of a small settled community forming the Town, and many of the names just mentioned are those of persons or places still known here.

That other folk lived here besides these chief townsfolk appears from the Godalming Court Rolls of a few years later, when we read the names of Smith, Boxfold, Thrull, Johnson, Page, Cock, Burghurst, Gace, Stoke, Caesar, Marchant.

In 1339, Richard de Piperham granted an area of land round the present day Foundry Cottage to a newcomer called Nicholas de Wakener. There was considerable fuss at the manor court over the transaction, which had evidently been made without previous permission of the Lord of the Manor. The grant, however, was registered and the name Wakener has clung to that collection of fields and little farmhouse ever since.

In the following year, Richard de Puckshott was tithingman for Haslemere, and his name remains attached to the old house and farm near Keffolds, overlooking the Grayswood valley.

At this time there seems to have been fresh building operations in the Haslemere area, as witnessed by several lawsuits, at one of which John Arrowsmith was accused of unlawfully cutting and removing timber from Grayswood. Also, at a certain wood called Wilfore (probably just by Coombeswell), other men were accused of incendiarism, but this may only have been in order to clear partly felled trees. The following recent discoveries at Coombeswell may have been in connection with an early iron works, for pieces of slag have been picked up and charred earth observed in some newly cleaned land.

* Houndless.

At every court, numerous townsfolk were fined for breaking the excise regulations relating to the manufacture and sale of ale and bread.

At this time John Aleyn was tenant of Imbhams, but as the area was noted, even then, for the size of its oak trees, and exceptionally heavy soil, his farm must have been chiefly a pig farm, dependent on the acorn harvest. It would have taken a tough man to clear the big oaks and cultivate the heavy land.

The Black Death of 1349 received no direct mention in any local Haslemere records, but it is unlikely that the town escaped scot free. Certainly, some of the farms which were noted at the beginning of the century received no further mention. But at Shulebrede Priory, three miles distant only, a document from the Bishop of Chichester in 1358 remarks "that many of the serfs and coloni of that priory have been taken off in the last wonderful pestilence."

By 1352, a Richard Burghurst was living at and farming the land where the Manor House now stands at the bottom of Three Gates Lane, and John Goodwyn was tenant of land adjoining the High Street. John lived in, probably, and may have built, the old house which still bears his name, next to Well Lane. It was subsequent to the Black Death that a needed improvement was granted to the local Piperham Chapel. Until 1363 there was, it seems, no local burial ground. It was to the Mother Church at Chiddingfold that all must make the last journey. Such a journey, except in the height of summer, must have been difficult, and the cause of much lamenting, when anyone was unkind enough to die in mid-winter. For in spite of frequent prosecutions at the local courts for blocked and undug ditches, the nuisance of drowned roads persisted.

In 1363 the Rector of Chiddingfold, Thomas Quarreour, petitioned the Bishop of Winchester on behalf of the parish, that Haslemere Chapel should be consecrated and dedicated, as also the land round the Chapel, for a burial ground for deceased parishioners. The Bishop appears to have raised no objection, and issued a licence for the performance of the consecration.

In 1378, the records of the Godalming Court reflect a good deal of social unrest, e.g., Johanne, a servant, raised the hue, i.e., made some complaint against John Gase, and John Gase also made complaint against Walter atte Fanne. Here it looks as though John and Walter had some boundary dispute and Johanne, an employee of Walter, may have objected to John Gase's tactics.

Then Dionysia, the daughter of John Arrowsmith, made complaint against a certain Robinson, while William Gase attacked and drew blood unjustly from William Robinson. Once again we seem to have the eternal triangle, but history does not relate which of her two beaux the lady finally chose.

In another case, Mathilda Boxfold was accused of diverting a watercourse at Boxfold to her neighbour's damage; unfortunately, we have no exact knowledge as to where Boxfold was : a guess would suggest where was afterwards Hunt's Farm.

Coming now to 1380, we find that there were 26 heads of families, who paid the Poll Tax levied by Richard II, and from the list can be reckoned that there were 62 persons, male and female, over the age of 15 years in the Parish of Haslemere.

In the following year occurred the great peasant revolt, ending in the death of Wat Tyler, but the Godalming Court rolls for that year are non-existent. Those for the year 1382 show no departure from the usual run of offences, e.g., neglect of ditches, fences and ale laws.

We may feel that Haslemere was too far off the map to be concerned with what was a Peasant uprising.

A few more place names which occur about this date are Kuttelane, Streetes Lane, Holvast and Coomsfold, these two last being known today as Holdfast and Coombeswell. There is also in 1383 news of an interesting lawsuit, when William Cardemaker of Guildford sued Richard atte Rodgate (whose grandfather had been Tithingman of Haslemere). William Cardmaker claimed 16d. for a parcel of cards which Richard had detained without due payment.

In 1393 Richard II confirmed and granted the five-day fair at Haslemere, together with the weekly market on Wednesday, to John Bishop of Salisbury. King Richard must have needed money, and one way of taxing a community was to remind them that the original charter of privilege was (a) out of date, (b) lost, and (c) much stronger if confirmed.

Before we finish with this century, let us not forget that architectural development had just achieved the nave of Canterbury Cathedral, and that French had largely given place to English in the Grammar Schools and Law Courts.

At the beginning of the 15th century England was ruled by a new King, Henry IV, who had reached the throne by the conquest and deposition of Richard II. Henry could not free himself from the helping hands of those who had put him in power, and when at last he seemed settled on the throne as master, he fell victim in 1408 to leprosy. His son, Henry V, succeeded to the throne in 1413 and waged a series of successful battles in France for some years, till early death robbed him of the fruits of his inspired efforts.

Henry VI, only a minor, on his accession to the throne in 1422 was a good but weak character, which led fatally to the Baronial wars. Through much of his life and that of his successor, Edward IV, was waged the struggle between the two parties of York and Lancaster. These ultimately were by battle exhaustion cancelled out, and paradoxically, like the phœnix, rose again to united power in the marriage of Elizabeth of York with the Lancastrian Henry of Monmouth after the Battle of Bosworth, 1485.

For country folk, and such small towns as Haslemere, this century was in the main a time of development and prosperity, in spite of famines, plagues and the general disorder of the Wars of the Roses. Enclosures of land were made on an increasing scale by both master and man, usually by adjustment and the exchange of strips on the commonfields, or from manor waste, to form medium sized or larger farms. Some landowners needed cash for their military business, and were prepared to sell, or at least rent, more of their demesnes or woods for clearing.

Another factor which made for prosperity was the spread of sheep-farming, even to small farmers, and the coincident cloth weaving in the homes of poor folk all over the countryside. Hops were now grown on a general scale, and the manufacture of beer began to take the place of the old English ale, which, being made from malt without hops, had no keeping quality. By the end of the century, instead of a feudal community under an overlord of a few freemen, some tenant farmers, and a number of labourers all having rights in some land, the village would consist of men farming areas varying in size from small holdings to over 100 acres, some of whom followed other trades; and lastly, a number of paid but landless workers. The working man had freed himself from being bound to a locality and had gained a wage, but in so doing had lost his land and must perforce work whole time for a living wage under an employer. There is evidence at this date that the countryside was becoming favoured for retirement by some of the merchant class of larger towns; men enriched by the wars, at home and abroad.

There seems to have been little disturbance of the quiet growth of Haslemere. The little history of this century, which has come to us from the Godalming Courts, is of day to day local troubles and never hints at the foreign wars, or the Barons' War at home. So that we read in 1412, Alice Goodwyn became tenant of Meadfields and paid the usual entry fine and did fealty for the tenancy.

It may be inferred that either her husband or her father had died, and that she was performing her customary duty to the Lord of the Manor. We find also that a William Yaldwin had recently died, leaving apparently no heirs; in his case, the Bailiff was ordered to take charge of a certain garden which had belonged to William. Two cases of trespass were reported : a certain farmer, John Godegrome, had allowed ten ewes and ten lambs to trespass over the Lord's Croft. Secondly, Richard Haselhurst had broken down a small oak tree belonging to the Lord of the Manor at Clammer Hill Strete.

Some years later, in the summer of 1438, a certain Walter Bedyll, one of Henry VI's Court, was granted the lease of the Manor of Ashurst or Frillinghurst, which lay between Witley and Grayswood. When, however, he went to collect the rents and revenue of the Manor, he met with obstruction, allegedly "vi et armis," by members of the Hussey family, who owned Hascombe. John Kilby was one of the obstructing party and probably lived at Burghurst (Old Manor House), and farmed Holdfast and perhaps Imbhams estates. Further lawsuits followed, leaving Walter Bedyll with a definite grip on his royal grant.

As usual, a great deal of the Court business at Godalming consisted of cases of infraction of the ale assize and the various other taxed or priced commodities such as Tannery and Butchery. We find names of new people appearing on the Haslemere lists, who settle and carry on for many generations. Hunt had as one of his occupations that of brewing, in which he upset the law; Robert and John Tanner the elder and the younger, all tanners, as their name signified, were fined for selling their goods at excessive rates.

The Prynce family also appears for the first time in a gallant attempt by Agnes, wife of John Prynce the younger, to rescue her husband from arrest by Thomas Lonecock the bailiff. She did not appear at Court as required, and her pledges were fined 2d. each in consequence; in addition, she was accused of having stolen some woollen thread, presumably for weaving, and was fined a further 6d. Billinghurst and Wakeford appear also for the first time.

Thomas Haselhurst, of Bunch Lane, like many other careful folk, had his own fish pond which proved too much of a temptation to some of his neighbours. Two of these, Nicholas Hunt and Thomas West, were each fined 2d. for poaching the said fish pond, which was quite probably the present Inval pond.

At this time the stream which flows between King's Road and the railway line seems to have been called Britton's water, and there is record also of a mill near by, though whether water or wind is not stated.

The appointment of Night Watchmen was part of the legal duties of the townsfolk, but at the middle of the century both Haslemere and Chiddingfold were fined for omitting this reasonable burden. We may safely conclude that our local townsfolk were, in the main, well-behaved and that national unrests had not unduly contaminated our forbears.

The unfortunate Agnes Prynce does not seem to have learned wisdom from her earliest court experiences, for in 1448 she was fined for being an eavesdropper under the walls of her neighbours' houses.

Even in those days there was a strong clannish tendency among the townsfolk, and a reluctance to obey outside authority, which is illustrated by the following record: The Bailiff of the town in 1452, Henry Stede, was set upon by John Tanner and beaten with a staff, in an attempt to rescue a friend from arrest; while Thomas Lonecock, Bailiff of the Godalming Hundred, lost a cart of lathes, which he was trying to impound from Thomas Benyt by way of distraint, and furthermore was assaulted with a stick by Isabella, wife of John French, and again by Richard Churcher, while carrying out his duties. Evidently, even in those days, the policeman's lot was not a happy one, though naturally we hear only of the court cases and not of those which might have been settled happily out of court by a suitably timed gift.

Poaching, as usual, was a much patronised art, or should we say, craft, the extent of which we can only guess at, for only gross offenders were caught. But John Lyte, a miller, and Richard Colpays, labourer, were each fined 12d. (no small sum) for keeping ferrets and nets, and taking rabbits on the lands of their neighbours.

It was in this year, 1453, that Henry Piperham, owner of the house and lands called Piperham, north of Haslemere, died; and his brother and heir, John Piperham, became owner on paying customary dues to the Lord of the Manor. Four years later he let this property, described as being near the Church of Haslemere, to John Boxfold, no doubt a member of the Thursley family, at a yearly rent of 33/4. The Boxfolds continued to hold the property first as tenants, then as owners, until 1707.

We have no further news of life in Haslemere till we find in 1487 a list of names of Taxable families, of which there were 24, in the Haslemere Parish. A few new names are found in the list, such as Farnden, Court, Pope, Madjwyk, Colin, Mylle. From other deeds of this date, we learn that the land to the north of Pound Corner, where, of course, there was still no through road to Grayswood, was known as Northlands and Princes, Holemore and Bridgehall, that there was a farm called Chounsams to the immediate east of the southern half of the High Street; and beyond that, to the East, a farm called Sopers. Land on the east of the mid-section of the High Street was farmed as Pope's Farm, and to the west was Halland.

By the end of the century the leading families were those of Boxfold, of Piperham and Northland; Gace of Halland, Barfield, and Chounsams; Wakeford of Houndless Water; Penycode of Old Manor House (i.e. Burghurst), Holdfast and Skitredons; and Aylwin.

CHAPTER III

The Tudor Period

WHEN THE YEAR 1500 opened the effect of the new Broom was evident in the English countryside. The broom had been Henry Tudor, grandson of a Welsh Squire and Henry V's widow, who had taken the crown of England from Richard Crookback at the Battle of Bosworth fifteen years before. Henry was ruthless to his enemies, and adopted the policy of strengthening the crown by all and any means. He had found a willing ally in his Chancellor Morton, a precursor of a modern type. Morton was the inventor of the well known dilemma, extravagant living manifested wealth, while a retired mode of living suggested much saving, so that he found excuse to fleece both types of taxpayer.

Parsimony was a fine art with Henry Tudor, his aim being to amass sufficient wealth in his private treasury in order to buy off trouble without resort to Parliament. Fifteen years of this policy brought, however, a settled country and great improvement in trade.

Furthermore, there was a stir in the air—the known world was enlarging. Portuguese ships had made voyages to India round the Cape of Good Hope in 1489 and had brought back tales of incredible wealth. In 1492 Columbus had discovered America, as he thought, Amerigo Vespucci in 1499 had sailed to Brazil and returned with news of further wonders, and incidentally left his name to the new continent. John Cabot had sailed from Bristol to Nova Scotia and Newfoundland, where he found seals and salmon and cod.

In Italy, Greek refugees from the Turkish invasion of Greece had initiated an intellectual resurgence. Italy was learning Greek culture, and scholars from all over Europe hurried to Italy to study Greek literature and philosophy. Medical practice in England received a new birth when Linacre translated the works of Galen. Dean Colet proclaimed a practical religion based on his study of the Greek gospels, with their exposition of the life of Christ, which resulted among other benefits in his foundation of St. Paul's School.

France and Spain were then the great world powers. England was only beginning to recover from the disastrous Wars of the Roses, which had removed by death the flower, as well as the scum, of English nobility.

The merchants, as usual, had made a useful profit from these military operations, which in the main had not disturbed the towns or the work of the countryside.

This is what a contemporary preacher said : "Look at the merchants of London; and ye shall see when and by their honest vocation, God hath endowed them with great abundance of riches, then can they not be so content but their riches must abrode in the country to buy farms out of the hands of worshipful gentlemen, honest yeomen and pore laboring husbands."

The development in use of wool, and its price, led to enclosure of small farms, many of which were decayed already owing to lack of money or labourers. These enclosures made large sheep runs which proved at that time more profitable than agriculture, but only served to swell the ranks of unemployed labourers. By 1514 a petition to Henry VIII went so far as to state, that where there had been in a town twenty or thirty divers houses, they be now so decayed, ploughs and all, and all the people clene gone and decayed, and the church down, no more parishioners in many parishes but a neatherd and a sheepfold in the stead of 60-80 persons.

Haslemere, it would appear, escaped most of the hardships of this time. The reasons I would suggest are, that evidence exists for its borough status even then, and the yeomen farmers of the neighbourhood seem to have held a near freehold estate within the Godalming Manor. Lastly, it was part of an ecclesiastical manor and without considering Christian principles no Bishop would willingly alienate the tenants of his manors, and so lose support in the struggle which loomed near.

Henry VIII had succeeded his father in 1509, and after the economical, astute political opportunism of the father, aiming at supremacy of wealth, England trembled at first with joy, then admiration, and lastly with fear, under growing dictatorship

of the son. Both father and son had the enviable and priceless
gift of selection of good servants. Morton had been top executive
for Henry Tudor, and similarly Cardinal Wolsey and later
Cromwell for Henry VIII.

Owing to the dissolution of the Monasteries in 1536-39 there
was a great mass of labourers thrown out of work—a writer of
the time said "such poverty reyneth everywhere that few men
have so much to spare as they may give anything to repair of
highways and bridges." Prices from 1540 of all goods and
commodities were rising rapidly, though there was plenty of
corn, grass and cattle of all sorts. More expensive tastes were
developing and more money came into England from the new
trade abroad. Greed for wealth led to debasing of the coinage,
so that by 1551 the shilling contained less than 1/7th of the
pure silver of 1527. Prices of foodstuffs rose, a fact which helped
established corn farmers, and in Haslemere there seems to have
been as much agriculture as sheep farming.

The second half of the century after the unhappy but
fortunately short reigns of Edward VI and Mary saw the
development of a quiet revolution which had begun much
earlier. This revolution had three main points, religious, leading
in England to the development of an English Protestant Church,
distinct from and owing no allegiance to Rome; an intellectual
revival, not confined to England, leading to the literature of
Shakespeare, Spenser and the like; and territorial, resulting
from the discoveries of brave seamen of all the leading nations.
In the countryside the Lords of Manors had lost some of their
power, partly because the new men barely understood their
powers, but chiefly because of the creation by Tudor kings of
Royal officials, called Justices of the Peace. The work done by
them was under direct supervision of the all-powerful Star
Chamber, of which the King was head. So the germ of centralised government had appeared. Part of the duty of the
Justices was to control thieves, beggars and the poor. The
break-up of the Feudal system, the enclosures and the dissolution
of the monasteries had been responsible for a vast increase in
vagabonds. Inflation was well under way and there was little
attempt to control prices. As, however, Elizabeth's reign progressed, national confidence was restored, and gradually a
reciprocal confidence based on mutual respect between Elizabeth

and her government allowed the people's will to be more often expressed. This was in marked contrast to the early part of her reign, when Elizabeth had kept her own counsel. To a petition in regard to her marriage she replied : "Were I to tell you that I do not mean to marry, I might say less than I intend, and were I to tell you that I do mean to marry I might say more than is proper for you to know. Therefore I give you an answer—answerless."

The struggle for world power continued throughout Elizabeth's reign, with Scottish intrigues round the person of Mary Queen of Scots; Ireland the refuge and hope of plotters; and most anxiously and continuously with Spain. But in this latter contest, crowned by the defeat of the Armada in 1588, Elizabeth had anticipated her opponents' moves and usually struck her blow first. By 1600 Spain was just a shadow of the former terror and England was left mistress of the seas.

Elizabeth closed her reign in splendour at home and triumph abroad, thanks to her own skill and the daring and devotion of her worshippers, but the last years of her life were those of a lonely woman out of touch with the new national spirit which she had fostered.

We have now surveyed the century in the spirit of a time voyage, and we will now focus on a small corner of the picture. In our approach to Haslemere let us begin with a bird's-eye view of the countryside. We should see very large areas of heathy common land, patterned by occasional rivers and so-called roads, and broken at intervals by woods of various sizes. The trackways as they dipped into the valleys might cross one another, and there we might see a collection of houses watched over by a church tower or spire. Around this collection of houses would be seen the gardens, and stretching farther out towards the commons we should see acres of cultivated ground; in some places the long narrow shape of common fields, and in others enclosed fields already in being. Trees, such as oak, elm, ash, beech, holly and so forth will be dotted about on the land-scape, with enormous stretches of woodland in the further distances.

Dropping nearer to Haslemere, we see that there is a main North-South street, with 6-8 larger houses on either side. The street is crossed at either end by an East-West road, that at the

North turning at each end ultimately towards London; that at
the South East to Petworth; and South to Midhurst and Portsmouth.   A few interlacing tracks will also be seen, deepening to
lanes on softer ground, or on the lower slopes of the hills around.
In the countryside round the little town will be seen a church
to the North West, and scattered farm-houses surrounded by a
greater or less amount of cultivated lands.

Descending closer to the town we shall see the cultivated
crops, wheat, barley, oats, peas, hemp; cattle and many sheep
and the usual farmyard denizens.   Round about also we shall
see smoke rising from the numerous iron forges.   Down near the
bottom of the town is probably the Town Hall, a half-timbered
building of uncertain date, and a little farther up the street is
the old town pond or Wyer pond, flanked by the stocks, pillory
and ducking stool for various classes of local offenders.   At the
upper end of the street is the Town Pound* for stray cattle, while
away to the North East, near the London road, are the Archery
butts, practice at which was insisted on by an act of 1538.

If now we drop down into the Town square, about the
middle of the century, we are at once aware that it is a Wednesday.   Our noses inform us that there is an all pervading
smell of cooking fish and our eyes tell us that it is market day.
An early act of Queen Elizabeth ordered that Wednesday, as
well as the previously ordained Fridays, Saturdays and all holy
days were to be fish days, so that there were at least 200 such
fish days in the year.   To meet the great demand for fish, fresh
and salt eels to the value of nearly £1,600 were imported in
1559.   Elizabeth's ardour for fish was, I am sure, not entirely
spiritual; she wished to encourage home fisheries and the new
fishing fleet of Newfoundland.   "Let the old course of fishing
be maintained by the straitest observation of fish days, for
policy's sake; so the sea coasts be strong with men and habita-
tions, and the fleet flourish more than ever."   (Cecil.)

The weekly market was an old standing event, and our ears
are probably deafened by the many voiced baa-ing of the sheep,
the lowing of cattle, and the grunting and squeaking of pigs
which seem to be everywhere.   On one side of the timbered

---

* It was at Pound Corner and is now commemorated by a wall plaque.

Market House towards Haste Hill is the Butter House or Cross; towards Pilewell, stalls are erected in the street for farm produce, and the fish house or crosse is possibly a little to the north of the Market House. Facing the west side of the Market House is the Swan Inn, not as we see it today, but a small, half-timbered building owned by one of the Wakeford family. The George Inn is just over the way to the south, but we will step into the Swan, to escape the noisy street for a while.

As usual in a British Institution we walk into a party of good old grumblers. "What a pack of mad loons are the Government, to bring they green plants into the country. What good do they be, nasty coarse-looking stuff. They be called cabbage and I heard tell that Master Ashley saw them in Holland and said they was good to eat."

Well, I can tell you my good fellow that it cost the Queen £157 16s. 8d. to buy them for the country, and it'll do more good preventing winter scurvy than importing £178 worth of babies. But do not be alarmed, for in those days babies was the name for dolls. And so on go the arguments and grumbles; nothing new there.

> The Farmer will never be happy again
> He carries his heart in his boots
> For either the rain is spoiling his grain
> Or the drought is destroying his roots.
> In fact when you meet the unfortunate man
> The conclusion you come to is plain
> That nature is just an elaborate plan
> To annoy him again and again.

These lines were written by an author who probably valued his life, for he has remained anonymous.

At the beginning of this century the most successful farmers in the parish were Chandler, Penycode, Billinghurst, Wakeford and Aylwin, each of whom farmed 100 acres or more. In the middle of the century we hear more of Quennel, Gase, Stede, Farnden and by the last quarter Boxold, Humphrey, Miles and Bridger. The larger farms averaged 70-100 acres, such as Piperhams, Huntes, Shoelands, Black Stroud, Lythe Hill, Houndless Water, Imbhams and Whatmans. Others, 30-50 acres, such as Courtshill, Wakeners, Brittons, Bowlands*, Stedlands, Chownsons and Meadfields.

---

* Later Half Moon Inn.

The average price per acre was about £1 and the rent varied from 4d. to 6d. per acre per year according as the land was open or enclosed.

As I have said, cabbage was a novelty introduced by Sir Anthony Ashley, turnips were a kitchen root to boil or butter, while potatoes only became known later in Elizabeth's reign, when Sir Walter Raleigh returned from a voyage to America. He, of course, popularised another weed, the tobacco plant, which rooted freely in its new climate, not however in the fields, but in the mouths of the people. Tobacco had been brought back from America by Sir John Hawkins in 1565, and was cultivated in this country from 1570-1782.

Looking at the gardens, around and behind the houses, we should not see many rose plants. The damask rose was only introduced into England in 1524, while the cabbage rose did not arrive until about 1596. As to fruit, a few lines from a writer just after the close of the century will have to suffice : —

" The Persian peach and fruitful quince; and there the forward
    almond grew
With cherries knowne no long time since—the winter warden,
    orchard's pride.
The Philibert that loves the Vale
And red Queen apple, so envied of school boies passing
    by the pale."

(PEACHAMS " EMBLEMS " 1612).

Currant and orange trees were also novelties in this century.

While sitting in the Inn, we see the sign of the George hanging over old William Billinghurst's house.

Further up the street on our side we might notice the sign of the Angel Inn, and towards Pilewell we should find ale on tap at "The Bell"; there were probably other dispensers of drinks, but they have left no record. Having noticed the number of ale houses, and even making due allowance for the fact that Haslemere was a market town, our surprise is lessened when we learn that licensing of Inns was a pleasant and sought-after privilege, granted by the Crown to distinguished personages. Sir Walter Raleigh actually issued at least 1,000 such licences, and not all in Haslemere; but he may have been aware of the existence of Haslemere, for his son, Cary Raleigh, was in 1649 elected M.P. for Haslemere.

On the subject of inns—the poet Crowley at mid-century wrote : —

> " And, lightly in the country, they be placed so
> That they stand in man's way, when they to church should go
> And then such as love not to hear their faults told
> By the Minister that readeth New Testament and Old
> Do turn into the Alehouse and let the church go."

Well, having already turned into the alehouse, we may seem to merit a share in the poet's censure, but it's market day after all, and we will make amends later. Meanwhile, the Market House stands fronting us, and we should give it respectful consideration when we remember that at the date of our visit the market has been held for over 300 years. In fact, it was noted, in a transfer of manor ownership as already in use, in 1221. There is no direct evidence of a Market House until 1626, but in that year, at a Godalming Court, an order was given to the Haslemere burgesses to provide a rail upon the stairway adjoining the Market House. Presumably, therefore, there was such a building where the Burgess Courts were held annually, even from a much earlier date.

CHAPTER IV

Around The Old Town

LOCAL GOVERNMENT, BURGESS COURTS, CONTINUATION OF LOCAL SURVEY, MUSITIONERS — ESAU AND JACOB, LYTHE HILL FARM

HERE LET US DIGRESS to understand how Haslemere was governed. Haslemere parish and borough was part of Godalming Manor. Up to the dissolution of the monasteries the Bishop of Salisbury was Lord of the Manor and held his courts in Godalming by his Steward. The Crown bought the manor and were overlords for the last sixty years of the century. The parish had to take their complaints, introduced by the Tithingman and Aletaster, to the court at Godalming. The first named of these gentlemen was elected annually at the court leet and was a sort of headman or constable, whose duty was to summon juries, collect penalties of the courts, and try to preserve the lord's peace. The Ale Conner or taster was appointed at the same court to keep an eye, or should we say palate, on the brewing of beer, and baking of bread. The Reeve was a manor official whose duty was supervision and care of all arable lands, and he would usually be one of the better local farmers. In fact, the position grew to be associated with certain farms, which were called Reevelands. One of his duties was to receive the burgage rent for the Borough, which was collected by the Bailiff from the individual burgage holders; this latter sum amounted to 12/0¼. A little later we hear of officials called Searchers and Sealers of Leather; who were, of course, the Inspectors of the numerous local tanneries.

There were other more interesting courts, for Haslemere people, in the Burgess courts. Now, having mentioned the words Borough and Burgess, perhaps a little explanation of these terms applied to Haslemere is due. A Borough was originally a town endowed by a royal charter with certain privileges—later it included any town entitled to send representatives to Parliament. A Burgess was a householder in an ancient borough, who held his tenement from the King or other great Lord at a certain fixed rent. His tenement was then a Burgage holding, and the rent was Burgage rent. This burgage rent was a sum paid yearly to the overlord in settlement of all feudal services, and consequently was of ancient origin, and the tenancy was practically a freehold tenancy. In some boroughs, the youngest son would inherit his father's house and lands; while in others descent was to the eldest son or the widow. Again, in some boroughs, it was customary that a man could will his property in the borough to his next of kin, without the form of surrender to the Lord of the Manor, and the taking back again after payment of a fine, the fine being an early form of death duty. Haslemere, in fact, paid 12/0¼ consolidated annual rent for the burgages, and there are instances of yearly rent in 1504 and 1517 accompanying transfer of certain burgage property in the town, called Brembylgarden, and Burningfold, but no fine or relief was paid, thus bearing out the fact that the inhabitants maintained their privilege as burgesses. One of the borough officials must have been a swordbearer, who is referred to 200 years later; but the sword has disappeared, and it is hoped that one day it may be found, as was the case in Guildford.

Haslemere, as I have said, paid 12/0¼ annual rent to the Manor Lord, and elected from the number of burgesses in the borough, possibly twelve, a bailiff, also a constable, ale conners and searchers and sealers of leather. Even before Queen Elizabeth's charter of 1596, which after all was only a doubling of fair days, a re-grant of Market privilege, and a recognition of the fact that Haslemere burgesses had sat in Parliament at an earlier date, and we know of two in 1584—Haslemere was a borough town. These burgess courts, previously mentioned, sat in 1504 and 1517 and the borough status is specifically mentioned.

Now for a glance round the town. From the Swan we find no sizeable house till we reach the Angel, beyond the stream flowing west from the Wyer Pond. Above it is Walter Gase's home, a building now incorporated in the present Georgian Hotel. Walter was a pretty warm man and later, in 1596, was bailiff of the borough during the charter year. A little further up the street his uncle, Thomas Gase, might still have been

living in the Tudor cottage. Above Pathfields is the old farmhouse, now Heath Edge, but then lived in by John Quennell;
and the farm for some generations was known as Quennells. It
was on one of the orchards of this house that Town House was
later built, and no doubt John Cobden of Houndless Water was
already casting longing eyes on this, to him, desirable site for
his new house. Across the road at the end of the street, but
standing in the Manorial Wasteland, was the Lord's pound for
safe keeping of stray animals—another little source of income.
South from the pound was John Boxall's house, known as the
Burgage House and now the Museum. John Boxall, during
Queen Mary's reign, was Secretary of State—later Archdeacon
of Ely, Prebendary of Winchester, York, Salisbury and St.
Paul's, also Dean of Norwich and Windsor. One of the sons
of John Boxall of Bramshot, yeoman, he had been educated at
Winchester and New College, Oxford. At Queen Elizabeth's
accession he was stripped of his church dignities or acquisi-
tions, and after a spell of confinement at Lambeth Palace, was
released and lived in retirement. People who knew him spoke
of him as a man of great modesty and learning, and one of the
cleverest debaters at his University. We have no certain
knowledge of his living in Haslemere, but soon after his death
in 1570 his property was inherited by a nephew, Robert, whose
ownership continued till near the end of the century. Robert
seems to have retired to his Bramshot estates, and he transferred
the High Street property about 1604 to John Shudd of Thursley.
Another house called Okes, now represented by a Bank, stood a
little nearer the town, where Thomas Billinghurst, a clothworker,
lived. This was probably an old house, for by 1612, when
Billinghurst died, it was already divided into two tenements.
An old house, now 2-3 cottages, called Goodwyns, lay nearer the
south, bordering on Well Lane; and had been owned about the
end of the century by a member of the Gase family, though it
was possibly Aylwin property earlier: a Thomas Aylwin was a
tanner in 1548. But there had been a Goodwyn family in Haslemere in 1340, and there are still some of the name in the
neighbourhood. Opposite what is now the Georgian Hotel, there
was demolished in 1720 a very old house, which was apparently
owned from the mid-sixteenth century onwards by members of
the Billinghurst family, who often were maltsters. Below this
was the Wyer Pond, flanked by the Wyer Croft, a field in which
in 1572 William Haslegrove (clothworker) had built himself a

house. This later became the Crown or White Hart Inn and was pulled down to make way for Pink's Stores. We next come to the old three-gabled house now a chemist's shop, which a hundred years after our period was known as the Red Lion Inn. The Red Lion was the badge of John of Gaunt, who had died in 1399, and it is possible that this old house may have been first built about 1450. Glass quarries having Henry VIII's coat of arms upon them were in a rear window till last century; three of these only have survived, and may be seen in Haslemere Museum. Glass foundries, which could easily have produced the glass, were scattered all round the Chiddingfold parish to the east of Haslemere. It is a thought that the glass may have come from the old church at the Reformation, when, as we shall hear, beauty was considered to be the chief weapon of the devil and was therefore outcast. The last house on this side of the street was, in all probability, the house of the farm called Chounshams, which stretched away to the north-east.

Early in the 16th century this had been property of old John Gase, and was now, mid-century, being farmed by the Mellersh family. It is very likely that the corner houses of Mr. Welland, and a part long since pulled down, but in 1750 spoken of as ancient and in decay, may have been the core of the old Chounshams.

Turning east, we come to the Town's End at Collards, which was owned by a Billinghurst about 1540—the porched house now gone which stood nearer the town may have been called Brick-hill Farm. Dunsteds was, in my opinion, what is now the Green Frog*, after having passed through a period of being a Red Cow in the 18th century, and in the early 16th century was owned by an Aylwin. Across the road at the Town's End was a cottage, where is now Uptons, to which Thomas Chalcroft, a Chiddingfold farmer, had retired near the end of the century.

Turning back again to the town centre, we pass an old house where Jonas Port, a fyner from Lynchmere, had gone to live at the end of the century (now occupied by Mrs. Shelton). A little farther towards the town we may find a White Horse Inn, for in the middle of the next century it was transferred as a house lately known by the sign of The White Horse. Coming to the south-east corner of the town square we find the George Inn, occupied in the second quarter of this century by Mr. Billinghurst, later by a daughter, Maud, and her husband.

---

* Book shop.

Going towards Pilewell, we should find in all probability only two houses on the north side. The land to the south was at this time Manorial Waste, or in Thursley Parish and not yet developed. However, we should find the Bell Inn and beyond it, near the edge of the Pilemarsh, another Billinghurst House. There is evidence of several cottage properties in and around Pilemarsh, at the mid-century; and this is due probably to association with the tanning industry and dyeing of cloths, all of which needed flowing water, or its proximity, for use in tubs. Hence we find the known tanners and clothworkers all in turn settling by and competing for position near the streams of Haslemere. Tanner, Gase, Billinghurst, Bradfold, Cobden, Mitchell come and go along the water edge.

Turning up Hallane, we find a tannery, where Oaklands Hotel now is, established towards the end of the century by the Bradfold family, who had come into Haslemere from Chiddingfold a quarter of a century earlier. They came in on a rising market, and their family did well for over a hundred years. Walking up the slope of the lane to the north-east early in the century, we should see the little church guarded by its new tower, on the rise of land above a great pond. Beyond the church is the old Piperham Farm, an ancient half-timbered house, owned till 1505 by Thomas Piperham and his family for generations before. He was the last of his line locally, and had farmed a hundred acres or so in this parish, with other property in Chiddingfold. He was no doubt proud of the fact that the church had been the Church of Piperham for the previous 300-odd years, and may well have been initially the private family chapel. There is evidence that the family had owned considerably more of the parish 200 years before.

Nearby on the south of the church stretches the Halland property, much of the land of which, for many years, was associated with the owner of Oaklands. However, in 1510 Hallands belonged to John Gase, father of the Walter of whom mention was made in the borough.

It is unknown when the substantial brick house by the church was erected. But there is in 1589 a reference to a small newly-built cottage near the church, which I take to be the stable-cottage* portion of the present brick house. Certainly Robert Lusher, in his will of 1633, refers to the great old Chest, and the cupboard in the parlour, and his son Robert, in his will of 1671 refers to the great old chest in the churchyard chamber of his house, i.e., the large brick house, and the cupboard in the parlour. It seems fair to assume that both pieces of furniture stood in the same house, and a fair inference would be that the brick house was built between 1590 and 1630. (Probably between 1601 and 1630 after Sir G. More got possession of the Manor).

Farther afield, we should find Billinghursts at Puckshott Farm and at Haslehurst for most of the century. At Weydown Farm, only developed in the last quarter of this period, one of the Penycod family from Chiddingfold was doing a good job of reclamation.

Down near Stoatley Green stood the tragic farmstead called Huntes, the lands of which stretched down the lower slopes of Farnham Lane, and the valley below it, to the south as far as Brittons Water, as the stream below King's Road seems to have been called. Tragic, I said, for in 1548 the farmer John Boxall and eight of his household all fell victims to the plague. We recently saw the story unfolded in the Haslemere Pageant. John realising his approaching death was carried out near an oak tree, where his friend, George Lusher, sat. There George wrote down his friend, John's, spoken will. George Lusher had some difficulty later on in getting the will proved, and it wandered about in higher courts, but eventually one John Billinghurst, who had married a niece of the dead farmer Boxall, acquired part ownership. But by the end of the century, the whole farm was in the hands of the grandson of the writer of the will.

A stretch of common land, crossed by the Shottermill road, interposed between Huntes Farm and Brittons Water, and on crossing this stream and climbing the slope we come to Wakeners Farm, where late in the century was an iron foundry. Here is a tale of it : Walter Court, then owner, wished to mortgage some of the property. I think he must have had expensive tastes in his family, for he was always raising mortgages, but on this occasion the tenant, Henry Wheeler, was a limpet, and as sit-

---

* Recently, 1954, reconverted into a dwelling-house; during alterations a tile was found with the date 1522 deeply incised.

ting tenant clung on. However, in 1589, the new owner, Robert
Miles, passed over the £30 for the 30 acres, and in order to give
Robert a clear title, Walter Court entered upon Henry Wheeler,
expelled him and delivered seizin of all the premises to Robert
Miles. I hardly suppose Robert Miles really wanted to use the
property, for he was a tailor, and probably had only sought a
sound investment. It also appears that he is described as a
musitioner. So that nearness to an iron foundry would not be
his idea of heaven, though while practising scales, his neighbours
might wish him at the foundry, or worse. Henry Wheeler
appears to have resumed occupation after the legal battles, for
in 1609, in the parish register, an entry runs : Buried. Richard
Bartholomew of Wheeler's Hammer.

Coming up over the hill we reach Courts Hill Farm, which
was occupied by the before mentioned Walter Court and wife,
Juliana. Little remains of their house, but a small building in
the drive of Courtsmount is almost certainly a fragment.

Strangely enough, Walter raised another mortgage, in 1590,
from a John Boxall of Bowlhead; this time on Courts Hill Farm.
This John Boxall is described also as musitioner, while a few
years later a mortgage on Lilleys Garden, or Fleur de Lys, over
the hill to the south, was transferred by Robert Miles aforesaid
to one John Launder of Haslemere, musitioner. So we find that
Walter Court moved in musical circles, and may even have
taken some part himself. In 1639 another musitioner, one
Thomas Kent, was living in Lower Street in a recently built
house belonging to one of the numerous John Billinghursts. This
one, however, was a weaver and the Parish Clerk. It is more
than likely that these musitioners made music for the parish
church service. They must have met somewhere for mutual
enjoyment, and possibly for entertainment of friends, and I
should like to think the Swan was their meeting place. Musicians
have, at least in the past, been notoriously thirsty souls, and an
old Dutch sign board carried this inscription: "The reason why
so many alehouses in town and country have the sign of the Swan
is because that bird is so fond of liquid." Another sign-board in
Ireland carried "This is the Swan, that left her pond to dip her
bill in Porter, Why not we as well as she, Become a regular
toper." Lastly, a "swan displayed" was the badge of the
Musicians' Company.

Well, enough of these digressions on Swans, but at the foot of Courts Hill we shall pass the Bell Inn on our way to the Market Place. There were many Inns, so called, in Elizabethan times, when a German traveller could write : "The English are vastly fond of noises that fill the ear, such as firing of cannon, beating of drums and ringing of bells, so that it is common for a number of them to go up into some belfry and ring the bells for hours together for the sake of exercise."

On the east side of Haslemere, in 1505, we should find Thomas Pope at Popes Farm—one field of which, still Popes Mead, lay below the Georgian Hotel. Beyond, to the east, is Meadfields, owned for many years by the Mellersh family, who also leased in the last half of our century the Piperham estate. This latter farm was, for most of the period, farmed by Robert Chandler, father and son. Robert Chandler, senior, died about 1560, and in the Chancery Court a year or so later his will came into dispute. It appears that some years before, the eldest son John had proposed marriage to Agnes, the daughter of William Greyshott (the occurrence of this name is of interest, for it antedates any other mention of that place name by 300 years)*. In order to endow his son sufficiently, old Robert Chandler promised the reversion of the lease of Church Hill Farm and the marriage took place.

However, in his last weeks, Robert Chandler, senior, was prevailed on by his younger son to make over The Church Hill Farm lease to his favour, and only when the old man was actually dying was Robert, junior, made aware of this treachery. A dispute followed between the sons over their father's deathbed, which resulted in a promise by the father of benefits to Robert at least the equal to those which he was losing by his brother's double dealing. The Chancery case was brought to enable Robert to recover these promised benefits. But as is so often the case, the final arbitration is not forthcoming, and we may guess the result. We know, however, that John continued to farm the land.

Round the hill at the Manor House was the house of the Penycod family, who had acquired the property about 1520, and were there for the remainder of the century.

---

* More recent research has found the name Grayshott in 1185 (Pipe Rolls) and 1200 (Ecclesiastical Records).

Imbhams is partly out of our district, but in the last half of the century there grew up an iron foundry, the pond being made for storing the water necessary in working the hammers and bellows. For a great part of the century the farm and manor associated with it were in the hands of the Covert family, but towards the 1580's the Quennells of Lythe Hill Farm bought more property and early in 1600 became lords of the Manor of Imbhams, and so remained for three-quarters of a century. Lythe Hill farmhouse in the early 1500's was only the long arm of the L-shaped building that we now see. The south-east wing would appear to have been added about 1570-80.

If we knock on the door, Master Quennell will be delighted to show us his house and talk about the building. Up to the middle of the century most medium-sized houses would have been built of a strong timber frame, the beams mainly straight, but variously decorated or carved according to purse or whim, with daub or plaster filling the intervals. With the later buildings the framework would be filled in by smaller spars or laths, often curved, bedded in plaster, daub, or in some cases brickwork. The roofs were relatively steep and the upper floor tended to overhang the ground floor in the older building. Thatched roofs were common, Horsham stone being a novelty, introduced later with flatter roofs. The smaller type of house consisted of a great hall, where all sat and fed and cooked, flanked at one end by parlour, kitchen and staircase, and at the other end might be another one or more rooms. Such a house had a large central roof, with perhaps gables to one or two slightly projecting wings. The staircase led to bedrooms for the family, but in early days the farm hands slept in the hall.

The simplest type of house was a simple parallelogram, of one room down and one up and a winding staircase to one side joining the two floors. Farm hands had just begun to live away from the farmhouses, in cottages.

> Of one bay's breadth, god wot, a silly cote
> Whose thatched spars are furred with sluttish soote
> A whole inch thick, shining like blackmoor's brows
> Through smoke that down the headlesse barrel blows.
> At his bed's feete feeden his stalled teame
> His swine beneath, his pullen o'er the beame
>
> (BISHOP HALL, 1574-1656).

As the century aged, a new moneyed class developed and began building in bricks and mortar. Floors were made of Horsham stone or rammed earth, and strewn with rushes to collect dirt and to facilitate its removal. Furniture was of heavy timber, again decorated to suit purse or taste. Many utensils were of wood, e.g., bowls, jugs, spoons, cups; with pewter or silver for the more well-to-do-yeomen—in two local wills a brass pot is considered important enough to mention, also feather beds, which were treasured possessions, one with most careful disposition made of it and the bed which it overlay, as to its future use. About the middle of our period, an old writer notes that pillows came into general use, which had heretofore been used among ordinary folk only by women in childbed.

CHAPTER V

On Dress, Manners and Men

Dress — The Parish Church, a Local G.P.
— Trades and Amusements, Charter of
Queen Elizabeth — The Mores of Loseley

As to dress and appointments prior to Henry VIII, men wore
long hair and were clean shaven, but he reversed this procedure
and polled his head and wore a short beard. However, by
Elizabeth's reign men had taken to wearing long curls trailing
on their shoulders.

The fashion for women's patches seems to have arisen from
the skill of a foreign lady in covering a wen on her neck. In
Henry VIII's time square-toed shoes were the fashion, and an
order had to be made that no-one should wear shoes above 6ins.
square at the toes, but with the reign of Elizabeth picked pointed
shoes became fashionable. The ladies under Elizabeth wore large
hoop farthing-gales, while the men wore enormous breeches,
stuffed out with rags, feathers, etc., till they resembled wool-
sacks. Neck ruffs grew to such dimensions that an act forbade
the depth of the ruff to exceed one yard, and the rapiers worn
by men were also not to exceed one yard.

Queen Elizabeth had in her earlier days, we learn, worn
cloth stockings, but after receiving the present of some black
silk knit stockings, and after due trial, she reported : "I like
the stockings so well because they are pleasant, fine and delicate;
I will wear no more cloth stockings". Silk stockings had seldom
been seen before, although Henry VIII occasionally had a
pair and Edward VI, we hear, also. Until Elizabeth had been
fifteen years on the throne there had been no distilled perfumes.
These, brought from Italy, must have been a great boon in days
when bathrooms were non-existent. At Cambridge University in
1571 the Vice-Chancellor decreed that the scholars and residents
were forbidden to bathe in any river, pool or pond, by day or
night. Undergraduates who offended were to be beaten with
rods, graduates were to be fined 10/- and placed in the stocks
for a day in the College Common Hall.

Turning here from the material to the spiritual part of the parish life, we are overdue for our visit to the Church. At the beginning of the century we should see a simple rectangular building, in which the Chancel was merely the east end of the Nave. At the west end of this church was a new tower, in which hung three bells. This tower must have been a source of pride to the parish, for we read that old John Gase, who died about 1494, had left in his will 6/8 each towards the building of the tower for the bells and the new chancel. Looking down the church, we shall see a screen dividing nave and chancel, the screen being surmounted by the Holy Rood, adjacent to which might be burning several candles to the Holy Cross, the Blessed Mary, St. Ann and St. Bartholomew, all of which were commemorated in the will of a parishioner. In the chancel at the beginning of the century, the stone altar would be in its proper place, but by mid-century reformers' zeal, with government backing, would almost certainly have ended in its removal and replacement by a wooden table in the middle of the church.

As the years go on more attention is given to the church. In 1553, when an inventory of church goods is made, there is a note to the effect that one chalice was sold by consent of the parishioners so that the roof of the church might be re-covered with Horsham stone. It confesses also that one chalice was stolen from the priest's house a year or two before. Under the will of Robert Chandler of Piperham, died 1560, the church received one shepe and he left 2d. to the poor man's box, which was probably kept over there by the font. This font was scooped out of a large octagonal stone supported on a smaller octagonal pillar, and appears to have had no ornamentation. It has been replaced since 1871. Twenty years later we should find a large and heavy oak chest, fitted with three padlocks, one for the curate's key and one for each of the churchwardens. In its safe keeping remained the holy vessels and parish registers. Engraved on the front panel were the initials of the two churchwardens, Henry Hopkins and John Ockley, with the date 1574, the year after the first date of the local parish registers.

For seating we shall probably find simple oak benches, with a few better carved, the property of the more wealthy parishioners. In a general description of 1577, a clergyman wrote that "In the churches, bells and times of morning and evening prayers remain as in time past, saving that all images, shrines, tabernacles, rood lofts, and monuments of idolatrie are removed and defaced; only the stories in glass windows excepted, which for want of sufficient new stuff and by reason of extreme charge that should grow by alteration of same into white glass throughout the realme, are not altogether abolished in most places at once, but little by little, suffered to decay that white glass may be set up in their room."

Under Elizabeth, churchwardens became almost ecclesiastical magistrates in their parishes, making rates for fabric maintenance, or providing books and equipment prescribed by Royal orders, and finally reporting offenders to the court of the Archdeacon. I have a note of five curates during the century, but unfortunately little personal detail. It is mentioned in the will of Quennell, of Lythe Hill, that the executor should continue to pay the curate's wages. William Meredith, curate in 1587, lost a daughter, Sarah, in that year and two years later took the lease of a recently built cottage near the church, which he held for four years. He then handed the lease to seven trustees, on behalf of the next parson. This cottage must have been an early parsonage house, for the lease was a repairing tenancy and forbade him to surrender it to other than the next incumbent. The known names of the curates in this century were Peter Bowley, 1521-1529; Robert Burton, 1538-58, who, I may add, received a legacy in 1539 from the Vicar of Witley of all his books; Richard Rompe, 1570-87; William Meredith, 1587-92; and a Robert Parson, curate, died in 1603.

A Rector of Chiddingfold, in which Haslemere was a curacy, the Rev. Lloyd, died in November, 1596, during a visit to Haslemere. He received burial in Haslemere.

We have heard something about the farmers of land, souls and stomachs, but one yeoman farmer at Lynchmere surpassed the rest in range of interest and ability. Roger Shotter, of Shulebrede Priory, some of whose relations lived in Haslemere, was born in 1553 and lived to the good old age, for those days, of 86 years. When he died, his vicar wrote in his parish register these words: "An expert chirurgeon and cured in his life multitudes of impotent poor pèople of foul and dangerous sorances, at his own charge, for God's cause—a lover of nature and a complete Christian.''

There are no records of doctors as such in Haslemere at the time, other than he, and it is obvious that no other doctor could have stood competition with his system. No midwife is mentioned, unless the entry "Mother Steere" in the Haslemere Church Register for deaths in 1587 might have referred to the parish midwife.

The greatest national import in 1559 was iron, to the amount of £19,559 10s. This high rate of import encouraged home production of iron for cannon, as well as for agriculture.

In 1543 Henry VIII had forbidden the clearing of common woods, either for fuel or for pasture; but unpopular laws are frequently found to be, shall we say, bypassed. Thus by 1570 there were very large numbers of iron furnaces in the home counties, each of which consumed 1,500 loads of wood per year. Viscount Montagu of Cowdray leased some land from the Quennells, in order to build the Imbhams Iron Works about 1570. Four years later this was taken over by the Quennells, and by a list of 1573 we hear of a double forge at Northchapel. The list does not mention the forge at Fernhurst, or at Lynch, or the foundry off what we now call King's Road, so that Haslemere was being ringed around with blast furnaces and hammers, if we include those at Thursley.

Such roads as there were, were fearfully cut up by the extra heavy traffic and laws were passed to try to place the cost of repair on the cause. There were, of course, to be found people who put purse before country, with connivance of high official-dom, for by 1589, laws had to be passed to forbid the export of cannon and the like, to countries with whòm England's relations were doubtful.

As for other occupations, many of the folk here played more than one part during their lives. We find Tanners, Clothworkers, Smiths, Tailors, Butchers, Bakers, Brewers, Coopers, Truggers, Bellow-makers, Weavers, and Shoemakers, and should we men-tion them, common Tipplers—these last were a hard-working section of persistent offenders, who contributed handsomely to the manorial purse by their fines. The Parish Clerk also was a man of many parts; in early days he had minor ecclesiastical duties to perform; he might keep the register entries, he removed stray or over-fond dogs from church. We hear, at this time, of one John Bridger, but there is no mention of such duties as were performed by the old Parish Clerk of a certain Suffolk parish. A visiting clergyman noticed that the clerk had a pistol in his pocket, and to an astonished query the old clerk replied: "Onless I fires it off afore your sermon, they burds will make such a racket as to drown your voice." Not infrequently the Parish Clerk was also Town Crier.

Our last character in the town is the Verminer, who was appointed by statute of Good Queen Bess. This man had the responsible task of destroying "Noyful fowles and vermyn," and to claim his salary had to produce mice heads, rats' heads and crows' heads. I understand that the modern name for such occupation is Rodent Operator, but how much better is the Elizabethan Verminer.

In their spare time the townsfolk of the sixteenth century found plenty of amusement. Apart from bull-baiting and archery, which were compulsory in earlier days, they could play cricket, football and bowls. In 1541, at a Godalming Court, two players, William Hayward and Thomas Court, with several others during a game of football at Haslemere, were charged with having struck a third party, John Blank. Was John Blank just an unpopular referee or a player who had missed a penalty in the last minute of a drawn game? We shall never know.

Indoor bowls were frowned on as leading to betting, and the Smithers family of Godalming had to appear at the Court for some infringement of the Act. Cards also were very popular and, though frowned on by law in 1538, the Government had to spend £2,837 10s. to import them in 1559. In the same year, tennis balls to the value of £1,669 were imported owing to increasing popularity of tennis in court circles.

Early in Elizabeth's reign there were muster parades of arms and armed men, and Haslemere may be said to have had a sort of Home Guard. Queen Elizabeth, like her father, Henry VIII, realised that a strong man armed is in a safe position in his own house, and in the first year of her reign she ordered wealthy landowners to keep 30 bows and 30 sheaves of arrows, and the middle class men one steel helmet, one long bow and one sheaf of arrows.

The Haslemere Muster Roll for 1569 contained 23 names, but in 1583 the number of names had grown to 40, and included one gunner, John Yaldwin.

We have no direct evidence of any royal visit to Haslemere, but in August, 1591 Queen Elizabeth was staying at Farnham Castle and having, I presume, eaten up with her retinue most of the countryside, she decided to visit Cowdray Castle. So, after mid-day dinner, she and her train left Farnham, and on her way to Cowdray must have passed very close to, if not actually through, Haslemere at about 4 p.m. on Saturday, August 15th.

It may have been the memory of Haslemere's charm on that hot August afternoon, or was it very good local beer, which persuaded her Majesty in 1596 to grant the petition of the towns-folk for a charter of a Market and two Fairs, with the associated court of Pie Powder.

Whatever the consideration, the petition was granted, and the charter of May 24th, 1596, was received by Haslemere, sealed by Queen Elizabeth, to the effect that "Whereas the Borough or Town of Haslemere is a very ancient borough and the Burgesses have returned at their own charges two bur-gesses to Parliament from a time when the memory of man runneth not the contrary, and whereas Richard II granted a charter of a market each week and one fair each year at Hasle-mere, to the then Lord of the Manor the Bishop of Salisbury, we deign afresh to grant for the relief of the Town and Borough and its poor inhabitants one market each week on Tuesday instead of Wednesday and two fairs yearly to be kept in the said Borough. Hoping thereby that the said inhabitants would then more strongly feel themselves bound to show and extend their service to our heirs and successors. We therefore grant to our dear subjects Walter Gase, bailiff, John Billinghurst, John Steede and Robert Boxall of Haslemere, that they shall have authority to hold the fairs and market and apply the profits of such, together with the taxes and profits of the Court of Pie Powder pertaining to them, without let or hindrance from any cause or matter past or present."

I do not think there would be any let or hindrance to the merriment and celebrations following the proclamation of the Queen, but on the morrow there would be a town of a colossal hangover. Walter Gase, who must have been aware of the forthcoming event, in the previous autumn had been an absentee at the Godalming court. But he developed as Charter Bailiff a considerably swollen head, for he again was absent from the Godalming court in Autumn 1596. His contempt of court was held to be an evil and dangerous example to all the inhabitants of Haslemere, and instead of the usual fine of 2d. he was fined the huge sum of £2. How the assessors must have loathed his manners and airs, but he learned his lesson the hard way as usual and we hear of his attendance at subsequent courts. We have now reached the end of the century and, as it happened, the end of Haslemere's close connection with the Crown as Lord of the Manor.

In 1601 Haslemere, with the Godalming Manor, was given by the ageing Queen to her old friend Sir George More of Losely. Sir George saw to it that his and Haslemere's interests were not forgotten, by returning his nephew, Francis Woolley, to Parliament in that year. We have now come a long way in the century; the small market town, isolated in acres of manorial waste and heathland, is developing into the busy centre of a countryside of smaller farmers of better agriculture, of iron foundries and enjoying the recognition of direct representation in Parliament.

Here I will ask, have we changed much? We had resident clergy then, who did their duty quietly for sometimes as long as twenty years. For health, natural selection and the survival of the fittest must have played a very considerable part, for I can only tell you otherwise of the kind and expert Lynchmere physician farmer referred to before. But the farmers, innkeepers, and tradesmen were all active as now, so where lies the difference, apart from speed in living, more general luxury and less general leisure?

First. In the material world for most of the century, news was, as it always had been, the result of proclamation or by gossip from one area to the next, and it was not till 1588 for hearsay. Travellers, pilgrims, pedlars all carried their tales and propaganda reasons, that Elizabeth and Lord Burleigh issued the first newspapers in the form of broadsheets to give official news of the Armada while it was in the Channel, and to counter lying rumours.

Second. I would suggest that in the 16th century most people had a livelier spiritual sense. They foregathered for corporate worship in the parish church, as well as for the miracle plays, and in some cases other parish assemblies. They still had a feeling of dependence on the parish priest, which was not always lessened by the discoveries each made for himself, in reading their newly translated Bible.

Sir Humphrey Gilbert, in his last voyage off to the Azores, spoke what was in the hearts of many of his countrymen: "Fear not, we are as near heaven, by sea, as on land," and though Haslemere probably knew little of the sea except by hearsay, the folk would have known the statement to be as true in reverse. A modern writer has spoken of the Elizabethans in this wise: "We may call these men what we will; they persuaded themselves of the righteousness of acts which shock an age, in some respects more sensitive, but they wrought mightily for England. A main source of their triumphs was their trust in God, whose cause they identified with their own; a faith which was a living impelling force." (Innes, England under Tudors.)

CHAPTER VI

The Seventeenth Century

PREVIEW OF 17TH CENTURY — THE LOCAL
SCENE — WAGE EARNERS AND THEIR HOUSES

As WE PEER BACK into the seventeenth century, i.e., the hundred years between 1600 and 1700, the picture of Haslemere that we are able to see is that of an increasingly busy and important little country town.

Secluded? Yes; Self contained? Yes, perhaps even a bit self important, but in spite of these qualifications, the centre of a busy semi-industrial countryside, prosperous, assured and spreading.

As we note this local prosperity, we wonder, particularly when we remember the upheavals of the previous century, when Catholic burned Protestant, and in turn Protestants burned Catholics—threat of invasion by the then Dictator of Europe, Philip of Spain, and finally the strong, but rather gangster-like, government of Elizabeth.

The year 1603 brought a Scotsman to be King of England, unable to understand English ways and methods of government, who was religious in his own way, but harried the puritan tendencies in English religious life, which had begun to give a sense of self-respect to the ordinary folk.

How could the common folk be prosperous, as we find here in Haslemere in the beginning of the century? The answer lies probably in the self-respect gained by the success of the English sailors and merchant adventurers, and government policies during the previous half-century; and by the translation of the Bible into English which, in that same half-century, had made it the chief book for reading. People had begun to apply in their own lives what they read for themselves.

But, however it happened, a more serious purpose in life was evident and was producing results in the material sense.

In 1605 the Gunpowder Plot to blow up the Houses of Parliament while in session was discovered and frustrated; but, though it failed, it hardened the opinion of waverers against the Catholic cause, and thus strengthened the hand of Parliament in any future contest with a dictatorial or non-Protestant king.

This feeling boiled to a frenzy under Charles I, and when his party had lost their battles, he lost his head.

Cromwell, after a period as Protector, in his turn began to treat Parliament and the people as nonentities, so paving the way at his death for the restoration of Monarchy under Charles II in 1660.

In 1685 James II began his reign with fair promises, but gradually infiltrated the Army with Catholic officers, encouraged Judge Jeffreys in the Bloody Assize and generally showed a ruthless tendency to co-operate with the French policy of exterminating Protestantism. In three years again the country was seething with rebellion, and when the Protestant William of Orange, whose wife had a claim to the English throne, landed by invitation at Torbay, the people, including General Churchill, flocked to make him king.

Hardly could the most farseeing of philosophers in 1600 have foreseen the see-saws of fortune and condition which awaited the children born in those first years of the century.

However, to our tale : it was only four years before the beginning of the century that Queen Elizabeth had been persuaded to grant a borough charter to Haslemere, and one year after the beginning of the century that Haslemere, as part of Godalming Manor, was granted by the old Queen to Sir George More of Losely. That Sir George More, the new Lord of the Manor, was, so to speak, a local man and had local interests in nominating the M.P.s for election may have had something to do with the later development of Haslemere.

A quick glance at the town shows a long main street sloping from either end towards a central causeway, flanked on the eastern side of the lowest point by the village pond, the overflow from which runs down through the fields to join the River Wey. There are about six or eight larger houses on either side of this street, with some smaller cottages between, and more are built as the century goes on. The majority are still timber and tile houses, but a few are of brick or the local stone.

Each end of the High Street is crossed by an east to west road, that on the south carrying similar houses, with few on the south side of the road except opposite the Market House, which is a timbered building, built and used as a Market House before the reign of James I, and lies more to the north of the present twentieth century site. A butcher's shambles occupies part of the centre of the open space north of the Market House, and nearer the pond is the pillory and ducking stool. In the country round about we could see some good farmhouses, a few not much altered today, as at Valewood, Clammer Hill, Imbhams, Lythe Hill. Away over the fields to the north of the town is the Church, sited just above another very large pond. Back again in the town we notice the many inns. Eating and drinking in those days was a serious business for serious men, and was a well catered-for undertaking.

Of the eighty odd houses in the borough at a little later date twelve seem to have been inns; a truly noble proportion, which showed a proper respect for vital needs.

Let us make a quick tour of these inns, but we had better limit our drinks to half-pints or we shall have to be taken home by wheelbarrow, or find ourselves in the pillory in the morning.

The Swan had been an inn, even before 1601, when we first hear of it in this century, and at this date was owned by Robert Sherlock of Kirdford. Some of the old inn was incorporated in the modern building, but it has been rebuilt more than once. In 1608 a house was built on a field called the Wyer Croft, so called because of lying near the Town or Wyer pond. This house, where now are the MacFisheries and Dewhursts, in 1631 was The Crown and later the White Hart Inn.

In 1626 you could get a drink at the Half Moon, and the present-day house is not much different externally, while before 1634 Thos. Chalcroft had open house under the sign of the George Inn, where Lloyds Bank now has its swing doors.

By 1634 the Bell was established in Lower Street, probably that old house opposite the Congregational Church, and served to catch the Shottermill contingent as they trudged into Haslemere.

At the corner of what is now West Street there was an Angel Inn where, until a few years ago, the old cottages into which it had been converted still stood.

Going along East Street by 1657 we shall see a White Horse Inn on the south side presided over by Thomas Overington, and by 1672 Thomas Chalcroft, son of the late owner of the George Inn, was the host of the Spread Eagle. Poor Thomas! I am sure he would have preferred the old George Inn opposite the Market House, but part of the George had been converted into shops, one of which was a tobacconist. The King's Arms in 1673 was, as we have recently seen it, prosperous with no White Horse yet beside it.

Reid's, the chemist, was in 1690 known as the Red Lion, even in those days it could supply a bottled tonic, and with an off licence; and at the same date the Grey Fox Inn dispensed alcoholic soothing syrups, etc., at what we know as Sawbridge, the chemist.

It was in 1613 that the moral lines now to be seen in Reid's shop were painted on one of the beams. It emphasises the need for the full employment of time, and that what is not learned in youth is later learned the hard way or not at all. Well, what, after all, did the people of those days do to earn their bread?

The Parson received his wages in the form of tithes, or some portion of them only, in the case of Haslemere, and was engaged and paid by the Rector of Chiddingfold, which was the mother parish, and for his services received £13 6s. 8d. per annum. As this salary could not, by any stretch of the imagination, be called taxable, even by present-day standards of taxation, he probably farmed his glebe land as well and in his spare time taught the children of the parish. For we hear in 1682 that a chimney was built and the Market House was repaired, out of Town funds, so that the curate might teach there. Even then he had to have a licence to teach from the Bishop.

The curate, in the earlier half of the century, was a local man, and had married in 1630 a local Shottermill farmer's daughter. Thomas Burges must have been a popular and hard working man, for we note that, by 1640, his congregation had largely increased, and as we shall find later, a petition with 54 signatures was made that there should be better provision for the curate, there being a strong case for making Haslemere a parish separate from Chiddingfold. That petition took 200 years to be granted, and that delay has quite a modern echo when we remember the present waiting time for new houses. The Rector of Chiddingfold had, however, increased his curate's salary to £15 per annum, and the Burges family seem to have had a little property at Houndless Water.

Money was raised about 1640 also for a considerable church extension, a north aisle being built, thereby making the church as big again as it was formerly.

Another class of worker was the doctor. Dr. Purchase seems to have been a local barber surgeon, as he was described, for the first eight years, at least, of the century, but he married in 1608 and no more is heard of him. Perhaps he was one of those fortunates who lived happy ever after, for there is no record of his death or that of his wife, at least in Haslemere.

There was also a Dr. George Clayton, also described as barber surgeon, who died in 1645. He, poor man, was probably worn out with work, for in 1636 there had been a serious epidemic of smallpox, when there were 23 deaths in one month of the summer. The total number of deaths for that year was 43, a number far beyond the usual average of 10-12 per annum. Apart from that and one or two other poor years, the health of Haslemere seems to have been good. There were five centenarians, also two over 90, and three over 84 years, in the first half-century. The older members of the community seem to have been stimulated rather than otherwise by the fretting world around them.

In the town itself, there were also a couple of blackmiths, several carpenters, a clothier and two mercers, a shoemaker, butchers, bakers, a tailor, a weaver, and a glazier, with several prosperous clothworkers and tanners, these last two occupations being important and apparently remunerative. At least one lawyer practised in Haslemere and probably influenced the choice of profession of young William Tanner, who grew up in the house now Town House.

A curious pastime—one can hardly call it occupation—was that of "Old Jones," who in the burial register is described as "cinder-picker." In the countryside round the town there were, of course, many farms of various sizes. Farms now mostly were subdivided by fences or hedges, the practice of commonland and farming in strips was dying out. In fact, in Haslemere, there is no certain evidence that there were ever any common-fields, and possibly the farms had been fenced and made into fields at a much earlier date.

Farmers were just realising the value of root crops as a means of employing the land which otherwise would have remained fallow, and farming may be said to have been on the up-grade. But the harvests were bad from 1643 to 1652.

As is usual, the exploitation of more valuable natural resources brought in its train a constant nuisance.

Iron ore, of varying quality, was found in the country around Haslemere, and consequently we hear of iron hammers and forges at Thursley, Pophole, Hammer and Shottermill, Fernhurst, Linchmere, Northchapel, Shillinglee, and Imbhams. The usual production from the forges was bar-metal for the smiths and farriers. At the beginning of the Civil War the Imbhams Iron Works, owned by the Quennell family of Lythe Hill Farm, made guns and shot for supply to King Charles' army and continued until stopped by force.

I suppose people got used to these iron works, as they appear to do in the North of England nowadays, but the countryside was described by some visitors of the time as full of the noises of hammers, and the sky with the furnace flames at night.

In connection with the iron-working, the parish registers note the death of a William Hayward in 1617, who had earlier lived near Shottermill. His occupation had been that of "bellowsmaker," which, with all the smiths' shops and iron foundries, had a contemporary importance.

On the top of Grayswood Hill, against the skyline, stood an old windmill which, with favourable winds, creaked noisily as it ground the local corn.

You will now want to know something more about where and how the people lived.

There were, apart from the inns, several big houses in the town and round about. Unlike many villages or small towns, there was no local manor house. Haslemere, as part of Godalming Manor, had been Royal property until 1601*, but the new Lord of the Manor lived at Losely, near Guildford—twelve miles

---

* Since Dissolution of Monasteries.

away. So that Haslemere, with its borough status, was able to pursue its life according to its own whims. It probably gained on the roundabouts of borough independence what it lost on the swings of manorial guidance.

One of the largest houses in the town was the Old Burgage House, on the site of the present Museum, which was occupied by the Shudd family, an old yeoman family which, towards the end of the century turned to Law. One of them, at King Charles's coronation, though a fairly wealthy man, refused a knighthood, and in addition refused to pay what was called a Composition Fee, in plain English, a fine for not accepting the knighthood.

Two other big householders at the time also refused the knighthood, and payment of the fine, to wit Mathew Cobden, a leading farmer who had just inherited the Town House property across the road, and John Steed, who, at that date, was living at Half Moon Farm and incidentally sold a good deal of ale. Town House, a brick house as now, though of two storeys only, was sold about the middle of the century to a Henry Watkinson, who was a man thrown up by Roundhead politics. He played some considerable part in local affairs and got into trouble over the employment of the town funds and died in 1669. After his widow's death six years later, her trustees sold the property to John Tanner, a lawyer and member of an old established Haslemere family.

The block of houses next below the Burgage House (or Museum), considerably altered since half a century ago, was owned by the Billinghurst family, but even in the seventeenth century was sub-divided into smaller sections, with a smithy at the north end.

The curate, Burges, lived at a then larger house called Goodwyns, not what we know now as such, but a little farther down the street. In essentials it remains as then, and he acquired it in 1636 from old Peter Gase (who lived across the road), probably with his wife's money. Here he lived for the next twenty-five years and raised his family. Close by the bottom of his garden was the town well, where he and his wife would have plenty of opportunity of gossip, or should we say exchanging private information.

It is not till after he left Haslemere that we read of an injunction in the local courts being made against a certain John Norman, that he should prevent his wife from washing bullock's entrails in this town well. So, at one spot in the parish, at least, the curate's influence was missed.

To go back to the Billinghurst family, at this time the head-quarters were at "Okes" in the High Street, with other members at Pilewell and Hazelhurst, Puckshott and Piperham, but the old Billinghurst living at "Okes" at the beginning of the century was a retired clothworker.

We know that the Tudor Tearooms* were once called the Sheepskin House, and that would be conveniently near for cloth making. Tanner's Lane at this time was known as Hall Lane, as it ran up to the Hall of Piperham, which lay near the Church. Old William Billinghurst was the farmer who leased Church Hill Farm, or the old Hall of Piperham, from the Boxall family. This old farmhouse survived till about 1850.

The old brick house to the south of the Church was, in 1615, owned by John Bradfold, but was soon afterwards bought by William Lusher, probably a gentleman farmer. Lusher's grand-daughter in 1673 married John Osborn, who was then farming at the Old Manor House in Three Gates Lane.

The house around which the present Georgian Hotel has grown belonged in 1624 to Richard West, a clothworker, who had recently bought it from Michael Gase, a weaver by trade. The Wests were a rising family and added to the house; and later, by marriage and inheritance, owned Roundhurst and Greenland farms, and also farmed Hazelhurst in Bunch Lane.

Right at the top of the town, and just outside the borough, was a large Elizabethan half-timbered house built in 1616 and was bought by Sir Poynings More, Lord of the Manor, in 1648. About 1640 Sir John Jacques, a local M.P., leased it, and after 1648 and until his death in 1688, James Gresham, a near relation of the Lord of the Manor, lived there. A Haslemere family called Fielder acquired the property in 1696, and the house, rather dilapidated by 1825, was pulled down and rebuilt as now, and is called Humewood.

What we know as the Manor House, Three Gates Lane, was, during a great part of the 17th century, known as Penycode's,

---

* Now (1956) an antique shop.

named after the family who had owned it since 1487. It had earlier been called Burghurst, after the family who then lived there, but with the lapse of time acquired the name of Penycode. It seems likely that much of the existing house was rebuilt about 1660, for about that date it was frequently called New House.

On the other side of Haslemere, Francis Jackman, a carpenter by trade, built Thursley End in 1639 on half-an-acre of land belonging to his cousin, John Steed, of the Half Moon.

There were other good farms at Whatmans, Valewood, Houndless Water, Sturt, Wakeners and Courts Hill, to say nothing of another inn, the "Flower de Luce," at Carpenter's Heath (Mann's timber yard).

We must pay a visit to the Church which, as we said earlier, acquired a new aisle in 1640.

CHAPTER VII

More Peaceful Days

AT THE BEGINNING of the century the Church was like a long room with a tower at the west end for the three bells. There was a carved oak pulpit, possibly given in 1623 by John Billinghurst, whose initials and that date were carved on one of the panels, also the initials of the churchwardens, Robert Lusher and Francis Teeling. In 1639, old John Steed, of Half Moon, died, leaving in his will £30 towards buying a new church bell. The size of the parish had grown with the extending iron works, and as a result of the impetus of the New Borough status, so that it was found necessary to increase the capacity of the Church by building a north aisle of the same size as the original body of the Church. Enthusiasm during the building must have outrun discretion, or the architect been slack in supervision, for in 1641 Richard West, of Georgian House*, in his will, thought it necessary to leave £3 towards a new ceiling for the new part of the Church.

Further repairs were needed in 1675, for a travelling diarist, John Aubrey, records that painted on the south wall of the Church, near the south door, was an inscription to the effect that the Church was ceiled and beautified at the charge of the parish, and the wall at the east end of the chancel was new built at the charge of the Rector, Mr. John Layfield, Anno Dom. 1675; Peter Hall, gent, and John Newland being church-wardens.

The curates during the seventeenth century were Robert Parson for the first three years, then Robert Billinghurst of local family 1603-27, then Thomas Burges 1627-1653. After this date the Church register was turned over for custody to a lay person and the entries to 1658 are missing. For the next thirty years there are mentioned various curates who were in Haslemere for short periods only, but in 1688 William Joynes came and took duties till 1700, when he was drowned one August night at Churt.

---

* Of course, its later name.

In 1678 an Act of Parliament was passed, with a penalty of
£5 for non-observance, that no corpse should be buried in any
other stuff than a garment of sheep's wool only. This Act was
passed to benefit farmers and to help home manufacturers and
was in force for about 100 years. A certificate of compliance by
the persons responsible for burial was demanded. There are
many references to this Act in the local parish registers.

Travelling in those days was a simple but strenuous matter,
unless you had a large family, in which case you either didn't
travel, or you hired a huge wagon. For yourself and wife you
proceeded on a nag sufficiently sturdy to carry yourself and the
wife on a pillion. As the century wore on, the nobility and
wealthier citizens might acquire coaches of a very cumbersome
type, as did Pepys, the diarist, to his great pride. A certain
number of stage coaches were also known to have been plying
for hire, on some of the more important main roads. Even in
these, sometimes advertised as "The Flying Coach," it was
unusual for an average rate of more than five miles per hour to
be maintained. Roads were literally nobody's business.
Theoretically they were the care of parishes, but there was no
sufficient authority to ensure regularity or sufficiency of repair.
A story is told of a rider approaching what looked a muddier
than usual stretch of road, who hailed a yokel on the hedge
bank as to the safety of the road. "Yaas, there's a good bottom
areet," says he. So, after proceeding and getting down to the
horse's saddle in the mud, the rider shouted back to the yokel
his disapproval. "Wull, goo on," says the yokel, "you ain't
reached the bottom yet."

Now after work, houses and roads, we must talk about play.

Life had become more serious, as we found earlier, for
until Elizabeth's reign half a century before, there had always
been innumerable church festivals and saints' days, which were,
in effect, public holidays. With the abolition of these at the
Reformation, people's tastes and habits did not suddenly change,
but this may have accounted in part for the merriment and light-
hearted and adventurous spirit so evident during the earlier part
of Elizabeth's reign. The Puritan spirit, however, was slowly
gaining and by 1623 even Sunday became a day of awe and
foreboding, rather than the spiritual and bodily refreshment
which might have been.

Games out of doors were hockey and, of course, bowls, with a new Bowling Green in 1660-1, which Thos. Mayne, butcher, had laid out and levelled at his own cost at the top of Shepherd's Hill. Cricket and football were also played, the latter in no organised way. Cricket had its ardent devotees even in 1622, when, in the Church Warden's presentments for Boxgrove, just north of Chichester, five men were presented at the Archdeacon's Court "Who with others in their company whose names I have no notice of, for playing at cricket in the churchyard on Sunday, the fifth of May, after sufficient warning to the contrary for three special reasons: first for that it is contrary to the 7th Article; secondly, for that they use to break the Church windowes with the ball; and thirdly, for that a little childe had like to have her brains beaten out with a cricket bat."

"Also I present Richard Martin senior and Thomas West the old Churchwarden for defending and maintaining them in it."

"We present Anthony Ward, servant to Mr. Earle, our minister, and Edward Hartley for playing at cricket in evening prayer time."

I wonder if the minister himself found himself sometimes saying "Well played, sir," instead of "Amen."

There was still sufficient common land where hunting on foot could be a general interest, though taking game was, in law, prohibited to those with less than 40/- a year in land. Bull and bear-baiting were prohibited by law, quite rightly, but Maypoles and dancing were also forbidden till Charles II as sinful practices.

After the Restoration in 1660 many of the sports were again permitted, but in 1670 an extension of the previous game law forbade the killing of game by anyone who had less than £100 per annum freehold or £150 per annum leasehold estate. But I am sure that Haslemere men were not too downcast by that law; poaching was always an attractive pastime, and there are later records of Haslemere men who were past masters in the craft.

By Queen Elizabeth's Charter two fairs annually were granted to Haslemere, on May 12th and September 25th, and these probably were held in the open space to the south of the old Market House.

There were always plenty of markets and fairs to visit, where in addition to the buying and selling, were Punch and Judy and freak side-shows, tumblers and acrobats, with all the gossip from far and wide.

During the earlier years of this century, the opposing forces of Royalist and Roundhead were slowly aligning themselves into two parties which threw the country into war from 1642-1649.

One local family which was climbing into prominence during the early part of the century was the Yaldwin family of Blackdown. In earlier days the surface of the land had been their care, but in the 17th century iron working helped to fill the family coffers. By 1640, the old house at Blackdown had been rebuilt, as the date on the door posts still bears witness, and as a strong supporter and friend of Cromwell, the William Yaldwin of the day became Lord Lieutenant of Sussex in the 1650's. Thirty-six years later on, a member of the family owned the old Manor House in Three Gates Lane.

As the House of Lords rejected the prospect of the trial of the King it was abolished, and after the King's execution on January 30th, 1649, there was a proclamation of The Commonwealth of England, without King or House of Lords.

In 1653 Cromwell himself dissolved Parliament and summoned a hand-picked, as he thought, Parliament in its place. He was moving too fast towards Dictatorship even for them, and he repeated his previous trick of dissolving a Parliament which did not serve his purpose. Thus, in 1655 was the beginning of what was called The New Tyranny, and England was divided into ten military districts, each controlled by a Major-General. Finally, he instituted censorship of the Press.

He died, perhaps fortunately, in 1658, and Charles II was crowned in 1660, in a wave of anti-puritan feeling in London and the bigger towns.

Any reaction from Puritanism would appear to have been slow in the countryside; and was produced mainly by the hypocrisy and overbearing ways of false Puritans. It has been said that the increasing purity of English literature and honesty of English politics was grounded in the true Puritanism and formed the inspiration of later religious revivals.

PIPERHAM FARM, now Church Hill, tower of St. Bartholomew's Church
beyond, from a painting about 1865.

OLD FARM AT CRITCHMERE, about 1880, now Royal Oak Inn.

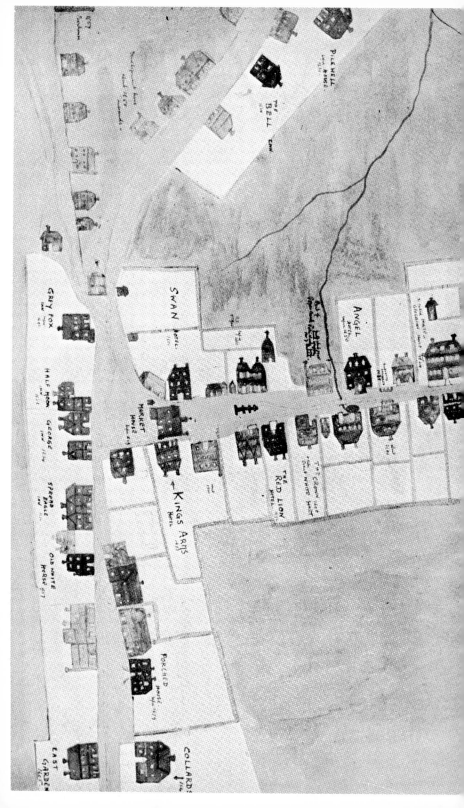

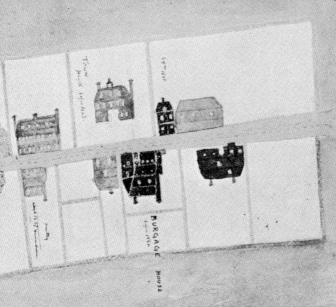

TOWN fire Losses

Town

BURGAGE House

HASLEMERE House

Spring

Haslemere

1600 — 1700

HASLEMERE HIGH STREET, looking south, from a painting about 1865. Note open gully under road marked by small posts.

VIEW UP HIGH STREET, from a painting made before conversion of Swan Inn, before 1800.

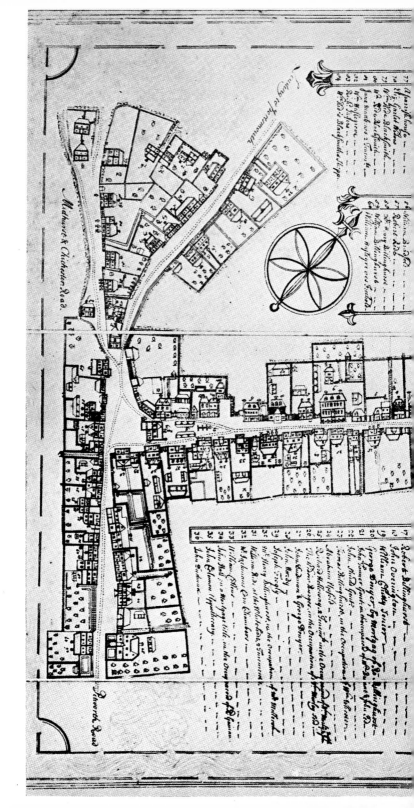

THURSLEY END about 1900, originally built about 1639.

HASLEMERE HOUSE — from a painting before 1820 — then largely
pulled down and rebuilt as Humewood.

LYTHE HILL FARM HOUSE. Main portion probably 14th century decorated portion about 1580.

IMBHAM'S FARM AND POND — the pond was once a Hammer pond.

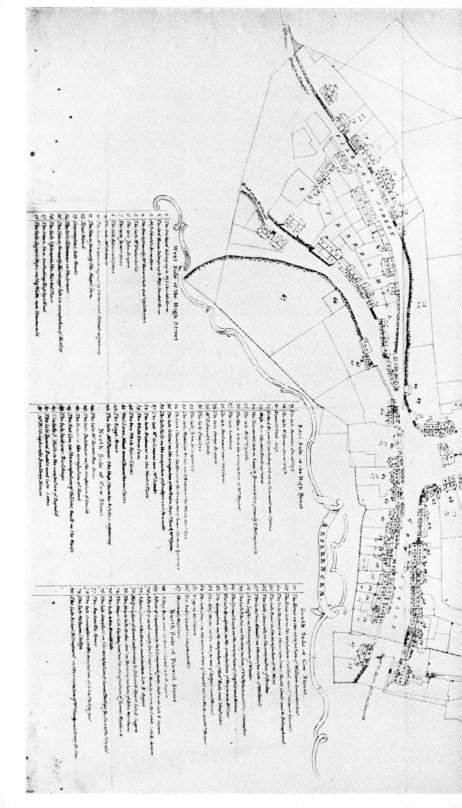

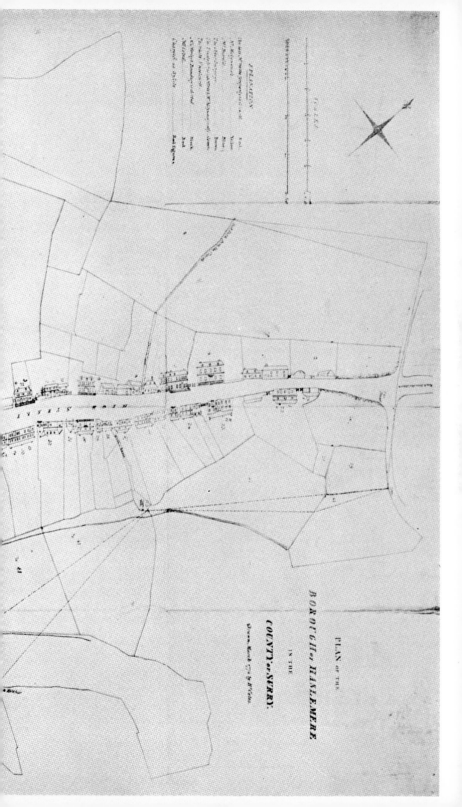

PLAN of the

BOROUGH of HASLEMERE

IN THE

COUNTY of SURRY.

"GOODWYNS," prior to 1880, now shops above Well Lane.

LANE END FARM, 1875, now demolished, at entrance to present Holy Cross Hospital.

VIEW FROM LAWN OF CHERRIMANS, SHOTTERMILL, 1857, looking down to the Mill. Anchor House is near left edge, Brookbank on the right. From a crayon and wash drawing.

VIEW FROM SHEPHERD'S HILL, about 1800. The Chichester Coach —
painting in Haslemere Museum.

HASLEMERE WINDMILL, before 1870

VIEW UP HASLEMERE HIGH STREET, about 1870. Buildings on extreme left now replaced by Comrades' Club and Midland Bank.

VIEW OVER HASLEMERE, about 1885, from foot of College Hill.

As to the Civil War, in the main Haslemere was by-passed. Farnham, however, was a strategic point and was occupied in 1643 by Sir William Waller. Early on the afternoon of December 12th, 1643, rumours began to spread through the little town of Haslemere that the Roundhead army was on the road to Haslemere. What a to-do in the little town. Would they stop in Haslemere, or were they marching through to Midhurst or Arundel, where were Royalist strongholds? Gradually the certainty of the news overshadowed all other Sunday distractions. Some made ready to receive the hungry and thirsty troops. Housewives made an extra baking to mollify any billeted man. Valuables were hurriedly stowed away under the floorboards or hidden in the garden, and to be sure the lasses of the town prinked up their hair and found the extra trinket for bewitchment. But it was twelve long and dirty miles from Farnham, and at least two-thirds of the march must have been in the dark. To give you a slight idea of the difficulty, Cobbett riding from the Farnham direction nearly 150 years later, even with the help of a local man, lost the way to Hindhead one night.

However, they piled into Haslemere town about midnight, and were probably too weary to do other than snatch a quick meal before getting a few hours' rest. Orders had gone out that the main body were to proceed at dawn to Arundel, and a smaller detachment to capture Cowdray, then belonging to a Catholic Royalist.

Cromwell himself is reported to have stayed at Blackdown House with his friend Yaldwin, presumably on a scouting visit.

Captain Quennell, of Lythe Hill Farm, had the year before raised a band of seventy-two troops for the King's army, but it had been quickly disbanded.

It is to be hoped that they were of better quality than described in a letter to the Deputy Lieutenant of the next county in 1625.

"I have seen your pressed men and have sent to the Lords to let them know how forward you are to put the King to charges to no purpose. You sent for your 200 men about 130 of the basest beggars and the poorest boys and lousy rascals that ever I did see for soldiers. I cannot blame you that you desired to rid your countie of them for 16 pence per man."

I wonder if any long memoried Roundhead remembered Quennell's name, as they marched by the next morning. If so, Quennell would probably have lost a pig or two and some chickens at least. The old father of Captain Quennell at Lythe Hill Farm, just mentioned, was staggered in 1649 by the news of the execution of his King. He sickened and died the same year, and so rapid was his illness that he called in the curate, Thomas Burges, for ghostly comfort and to make his will. This the curate wrote down at the dictation of the sick man, in the presence of Lucie Cheesewright. This is all we hear of Haslemere in the Civil War, but I feel sure that the parish clerk, at the Restoration, might well have copied what another parish clerk entered in his register : "This day, God be thanked, our true King rode thr' on his way to London, and a service of thanksgiving was held in our church, Master Macclesford whom God hath preserved to us, reading the service, and sermon on the text, 'Fear God and Honour the King.' So, God be praised come our troubles to an end."

But, poor man, he was wrong, for in 1688 there was a further revolution leading to the settling of a Dutchman on the English throne. But William of Orange was a Protestant, and that was what England wanted.

Haslemere was now well on its way to becoming a pocket borough : it certainly was in the pocket of the Lord of the Manor, and so continued with little intermission till about 1684, when other pockets talked louder, and acquired sufficient of the vote-carrying freeholds of the town. It was a simple arithmetical sum—possession of an ancient freehold, made one a burgess—being a burgess meant you had a vote. Control of the freeholds meant control of voting power. In later years, much misplaced ingenuity was spent in the concoction of faggot votes —by the splitting of the log of the single burgage into the faggot bundle of multiple freeholders.

Of local interest, more particularly, was a grant in 1606 by Sir Geo. More, thereby strengthening the charitable provisions of the Queen's charter of 1596 to the Bailiff and certain leading townsmen, of the profits of letting the wasteland of the town. The money so received was to be applied to poor relief or for the benefit of the townsfolk.

The poor, says the good Book, ye have always with you, and the seventeenth century town officials fully realised the truth of that quotation, and in the main Haslemere did its best to cure that evil.

But, while they considered looking after their own poor, and I am afraid sometimes an official enquiry found that charity had begun at home, they took extra good care not to look after anyone else's poor folk.

There was passed at the local Burgess court an order that—"None in this parish shall grant or let an house, room or part of a room, for the habitation within this borough of any foreigner, upon pain of a fine of £10 unless the Bailiff or overseer of the poor recognise fully that the person so applying for lodgement be fully able to maintain themselves and family. One or two responsible persons must stand bond if proof not available." There were also rules made for the transport back to his own parish of any temporary visitor who might otherwise have become a charge on parish funds.

After many adventures, death of original trustees, non-appointment of successors, abstraction or division of funds, this trust was recognised under James Gresham, and by 1675 enough money had accumulated to build the Toll Houses (now Almshouses) in Petworth Road.

It is interesting to note that by the beginning of the Civil War small change had become scarce, and in consequence permission was granted by Parliament for the issue by traders of private tokens worth $\frac{1}{4}$d. each. This continued till 1672, when $\frac{1}{4}$d. or $\frac{1}{2}$d. became in sufficient supply as coin of the realm. There are at least three known Haslemere tokens, issued by John Ede at the Swan, 1665, John Osborn, of Haslemere, 1666, and Henry Shotter, in Haslemere, 1667.

The plague of 1666 does not seem to have left any record in Haslemere, which rather bears out my previous suggestion as to its comparative seclusion.

In 1684 there was a muster of troops at Guildford for the company of Captain Covert, and soldiers were to be found by a long list of named people, Haslemere included. Balchin, Wakeford, Overington, Mount, Marks, Etherington, Breda, Fagent were the appointed men who were to appear at 8 a.m.

on 20th May, 1684, arms completely fixed and burnished, wearing red coats, for the purpose of mustering and exercising. Each soldier had to bring with him two days' pay and powder and ball proportionate.

The usual dress of village men would have been wide linen smocks over the shirt and breeches and heavy home-made shoes and stockings. Their womenfolk wore simple linen or woollen gowns with shawls or gaily coloured kerchiefs round their heads. The more well-to-do men of the neighbourhood wore a snuff brown coat, with plain linen collar, brown leather breeches and top boots, topped by a stiff-brimmed hat, having a tall tapering crown, the apex being cut off flat. The occasional court or county type wore a variously coloured coat, cut to knee length, lace ruffled at the cuffs, shoes with large rosettes over the insteps and silk stockings. His breeches may be of silk or black velvet. His long hair, carefully curled and perfumed, hangs to his shoulders, spilling over a wide lace-edged collar. A truly magnificent figure. His lady, tight bodiced, with long wide skirt of any lovely material, looks ornamental, if not practical. The wretched children of this pair will be dressed, even like their parents. Before condemning these last, let us remember Shakespeare, who probably dressed in his later years in this fashion, with others of repute like him.

To paraphrase Burns—the dress is but the guinea's stamp and a man's a man for a' that, and I may say, a woman, too.

CHAPTER VIII

The Georgian Age, I

BROADLY SPEAKING, the 18th century was, for England, a peaceful century. After the turmoils of the previous 100 years, with its conflicting religions, ideals and changes of government, England wanted time to settle down. Robert Walpole, as Prime Minister under a King who spoke no English, was in practical control of the country for twenty years to near the mid-century. He was a good debater, financier and administrator, and headed the great families of that time. He pursued peace in his foreign policy, and he encouraged material progress, liberty of the press and free justice and parliamentary rule. On his fall from power, and the declaration of war with France in 1742, England began under William Pitt a series of wars abroad, which extended the Empire enormously.

During the first half of the century religious indifference increased with the material prosperity. Pauperism increased, slowly at first, but more quickly following the Enclosure Acts, and towns enlarged greatly in population with new manufactures.

The Squires, as Justices of the Peace, exercised control of the countryside and were, as time went on, assisted by the clergy, who more and more tended to derive from the land-owning class. At the beginning of the century, enclosures and open fields were both to be found in most parishes. Improved methods of agriculture tended to the enclosure of more land, for these methods were unworkable on the small strips of the old common-fields.

In the Haslemere area there has been found no trace of the common-field system. The field at the North-west of the High Street was known as Town Field, but no evidence exists of common-field usage.

We may consider that there were some freeholders with others as larger or smaller copyholders; the small farmers adding to their income by weaving or spinning. Below these was a growing class of labourer, depending on wages, a little land of their own, with common rights for cows, sheep, pigs and chicken. Beneath these was a pauper class, which increased enormously in the second half-century. Haslemere Church registers show this increase very clearly. In the seventeenth century only three or four poor persons receive such mention; but two in 1741; one in 1775 and 1777; two in 1778 and 1780; and fourteen in 1785.

This was the last era when the village was the normal unit of society.

Transport in the early eighteenth century for ordinary folk would be on foot or horse-back. Covered wagons and stage-coaches of a heavy type provided transport with shelter from foul roads and weather for those who could pay.

Contrary to many authorities, there was undoubtedly, and in spite of the uncared-for condition of the roads, much wheeled traffic.

In 1732 coaches ran over Hindhead to Portsmouth, or through Chiddingfold to Midhurst and Chichester. The road from Godalming to Haslemere was not definitely a turnpike road until after 1758, and by 1769 this road was included on a list of new mail roads.

An undated advertisement in Haslemere Museum states that "Post Coaches, late Quennell's, run to Chichester, Midhurst and Haslemere, from the Bolt in Tun Inn, Fleet Street, and the Golden Cross Inn, Charing Cross, every morning except Sundays at 6.0 a.m. to the Swan Inn, Chichester." This notice has been dated as about 1790. As this is a coaching century, I propose to begin a tour of Haslemere in the mid-century by approaching from Hindhead, leaving the main road at the Gibbet. We shall turn down Hindhead Lane, as the Haslemere folk called it, passing Windygate, and then up over Infield (Inval) Common into Bunch Lane. Here we pass an old friend, Hazelhurst, now owned by a Mrs. Yalden, widow of Edmund Yalden, late rector of Newton Valence, near Alton. Just before entering Haslemere Parish we see Weydown Farm on the slope to our right hand, still flourishing in the Madgwick family. Later in the century it was sold to Thomas Martin, and finally to William Briant, a timber merchant. As we come down the slope of High Lane towards the Church we can see the panorama of the little town in the dip. We shall note the increase in buildings in the town since the earlier part of the previous century, and the newer houses, such as Church Hill House and Oaklands, are beginning to be weathered. Away to the south a line of houses now creeps up Shepherd's Hill and along the south side of Lower Street, which we should not have seen 100 years previously. The history of Haslemere in this century is to a great extent a reflection of political activities.

A few words here may be of interest about some of Haslemere's parliamentary history. For the first twenty years of the known representation, the nominations and elections appear to have been entirely in the hands of the More family of Losely, who in 1601 were granted the manor and hundred of Godalming by the Crown. The next sixty years followed the same pattern. In 1661 the Bailiff of Haslemere, probably Henry Watkinson, of Town House, was reported to have boasted that as returning officer he would return whom he pleased. This, on a petition, got to the ears of the Parliamentary Committee of Privilege, who ordered the Sergeant-at-Arms to bring the Bailiff of Haslemere in custody to the bar of the House.

On 21st May, 1661, the Bailiff was so brought, his return amended by substitution of the names of the previously defeated candidates! Mr. Speaker then reproved him for his offence and, after being duly threatened with lawful penalties, the Bailiff threw himself on the mercy of the House. After his case had been discussed he was again admitted, and on his knees begged the mercy of the House. He was then discharged from custody on payment of fees.

This was not an isolated instance of high-handedness, for in 1678 a stranger, a Mr. Dorrington, stood for election, together with the local candidates, who were Sir Wm. More and Mr. James Gresham. Haslemere did not at that date like strangers, and the Bailiff took prompt action. He, the Bailiff, received notice of the election on Thursday, February 6th, and went about 4 p.m. to the usual place by the Market, where the Town Crier announced the receipt of the Sheriff's order for an election, and that this would take place on the very next day. Early the following morning, accompanied by twenty-four of the local freeholders, he went into the upper chamber of the Market House and, after causing the Market bell to be rung, read the notice in Latin and then in English. Without delay, Sir William More and Mr. Gresham were elected and the Bailiff signed the indentures of return. Specious reasons were advanced to the unsuccessful candidate for the speed of election, and this time official anger was not roused.

In 1681 Mr. Onslow, a candidate whose victory in the new election was numerically correct, was unseated by the Bailiff. This return was later reversed by the House of Commons after the attendance of the Bailiff of the Borough of Haslemere.   Mr. Onslow took proceedings against the Bailiff at Kingston Assizes without recorded result.

In the same year, before the Justices of Peace at Guildford, an interesting case came up. John Smith, a chapman of Haslemere, gave evidence that he was at a Mr. Collins's house at Enton, where Thomas Hall, in the course of conversation, asked him why he did not vote for Onslow and Dorrington.   John Smith replied that he would not stand for them that voted for the Rump Parliament, because for anything he knew the Rump Parliament put the King to death.   Next witness, James Figg, a maltster of Haslemere, stated that a week before the election he met Thomas Hall in the chamber of a Mr. Cooke, who was a mealman there.   Thomas Hall urged him (Figg), as he had done divers times before, to stand for Onslow.   Figg replied that he would never stand for an Onslow, for he did not know but that one of their ancestors might have had a hand in the death of the King.   Whereupon Thomas Hall answered that he deserved it for running from his Parliament.

In 1698 the House of Commons, by a small majority, rejected as frivolous a petition against the two elected candidates for bribery.   It was alleged that Sir Theophilus Oglethorpe, one of the candidates, while soliciting the support of a certain Mrs. Carter, who was apparently scared of alienating her friends, was alleged to have said : "Mother, you shall never want."   He was also accused of giving two young women each a straw hat during a fair at Godalming.

Various minor complaints of irregularities occurred during the elections of the next twenty years, but in 1722 James Oglethorpe, a figure of some national note as well as intriguing interest, was elected top of the poll in Haslemere. This position he retained during the elections of the next thirty years. James Oglethorpe has often been confused with an older brother of the same name who died in infancy six years before the Haslemere M.P. was born. He had been in the Army for twelve years before the date of his election and had seen active service in several European campaigns. His martial spirit led to a duel in the High Street, Haslemere, two days after his election, in which he ran his opponent through the stomach, and wounded the hand of one who tried to stop the fight. He considerately bound up the cut hand, but history does not relate what happened to the more severely wounded opponent. A month later he killed a man in London who had robbed him of a guinea. But he took his seat in Parliament without further public comment.

After his next election in 1727 he interested himself in prison reform and, as a result, a Committee of the House of Commons made recommendations to remedy many of the previous abuses by those in charge of prisons. Samuel Wesley, jun., wrote of this work:

> Yet Britain cease thy captives woes to mourn
> To break their chains, see Oglethorpe was born.

In 1732 he obtained a Royal Charter for establishing a Colony in America called Georgia, in order to settle debtors from English prisons, and others. He arrived back in England after two years in the new colony, bringing with him a party of Indians, whom he housed at his house, Westbrook by Godalming, after one of their number had died in London from smallpox. He returned to Georgia in 1735 taking with him John and Charles Wesley, the former with another chaplain to convert the Indians and minister to the Protestant settlers; while the latter was to be secretary for Indian affairs.

In November, 1736, when Oglethorpe returned to England, the boat ran into a fearful storm off the Bristol Channel and Oglethorpe and a Mr. Tanner, jun. of Haslemere were obliged to jump out of bed in their shirts and with the Master of the ship and a woman who was on board, all gave help to the previously tired sailors in hauling on ropes. By their common effort the ship was safely docked at Ilfracombe.

Oglethorpe maintained his friendship with the Wesley family, perhaps remembering also his youthful indebtedness to Samuel Wesley, sen. He was made General in 1738 and took part with the Government forces against the Jacobite rebellion of 1745.

He failed to gain a seat in the election of 1754, which was also memorable for the use made of the Red Cow public-house in Petworth Road. Of this one burgage, which usually provided one vote for the owner, eight votes were manufactured by subdivision of the freehold, and six or seven more from the White Hart and White Horse Inns. A ballad, "The Cow of Haslemere," was composed by an Oxford don on the subject, which runs to forty-two stanzas. Archdeacon Cobden, half-brother of a noted local resident of the day also could not contain his indignation at the chicanery exhibited in the parliamentary elections, and similarly wrote a poem called "Haslemere Women and Men," of which there are 149 lines.

There exists also a Haslemere Election Song of 1761 of five verses only, among the Losely MSS. to the honour and glory of the old candidates.

At the elections more and more voting power was literally bought by certain candidates, by the means of buying up the local freehold property.

After the celebrated 1754 election there was a House of Commons enquiry at which the late Mr. Webb was accounted to own thirty votes, Mr. Molyneux ten votes, and Mr. Burrell nine votes. Mr. Webb's burgage holdings had cost £20,000 and produced a rental of £160 per annum, but could now be bought for £15,000.

There were in addition six to eight independent votes which might now be bought, belonging to

Mr. R. Billinghurst, attorney	3 votes
Miss Shudd	3 votes
Mr. Wm. Bristow, blacksmith	2 votes
Mrs. Cobden, widow	2 votes
Mr. Undershell, tanner, of Southwark ...	1 vote
Mr. Nicholls, oilskin maker	1 vote
Thomas Denyer, farmer	1 vote
General Oglethorpe	1 vote

Two other votes were in the hands of trustees to be disposed of by Mr. Webb's devisees and Mr. Molyneux jointly.

Here is an item from a post-election expense sheet:

> To stop Will Upfold's mouth, at not being made Election Bailiff and disappointing him of being made gamekeeper to please other people ... £7 7s. 0d.

and here is an invitation to a Party dance :

> "Sir Thomas Hardwick has ordered an entertainment and a Ball, for our gentlemen's friend and well wisher, at Luff's of the 'White Horse' on Monday Eve next, to which as such by the direction of Mr. Luff, I invite you Mrs. Heather and your daughter and brother and sons, with compliments to them.
>
> Sir, your most humble servant,
>
> RI. BILLINGHURST
>
> Mar. 4. 1768."

In 1776 Sir James Lowther bought the Haslemere Manor and a number of the burgage freeholds, the remainder being bought by the Burrell family, so that by 1791 there were no independent burgage holders, and till the end of the century Lowther and Burrell, or their nominees, were consistently returned.

Of local events, about 1715, the Town or Wyer pond in the High Street was filled up, at whose instance history does not state. Grumbling and discontent in the town followed, chiefly from the farmers of the waste land, and from the town Trustees, who, both, saw some of their profits vanishing.

By 1722 this Town Trust needed a re-organisation, owing to death, or removal to other areas of the Trustees. New Trustees were appointed:

> Richard Billinghurst, tanner, of Collards, East Street.
> William Bradford, blacksmith, High Street.
> Henry Billinghurst, maltster, High Street.
> William Billinghurst, tallow-chandler, High Street.
> William Cobden, tanner, White House, High Street.
> William Ride the younger, blacksmith, Shepherd's Hill.
> Edward Ride the elder, innkeeper at the White Horse.
> Thomas Denyer the elder, joiner, Lower Street.
> Thomas Denyer the younger, innholder (White Lion).

They however surrendered their trust deed in 1739, owing
to difficulties in operation.   In 1757 there was a civil disturbance, for twelve townsfolk met together in a riotous manner, as
it was later described at a Godalming Court, and broke the
windows of William Ride the elder and William Ride the
younger.   Furthermore, the crowd assaulted young William
Ride, when as constable he attempted to make some arrests.
At the same court, a local baker was fined heavily on account
of short weight bread; this was evidently considered a most
venal offence; an offending butcher received much lighter
penalties.   In 1754, at a Godalming Court, the Haslemere
constable, William Ride (blacksmith) was fined for allowing a
common beggar to beg publicly in the borough.   The constable
certainly had fallen from grace, for it was not long previously
that specific bye-laws had laid down stringent penalties against
any stranger who appeared without visible means of support
(apart from two legs).

In 1765, there was heard in the King's Bench an action of
Deer Stealing alleged to have taken place in Shillinglee Park on
the night of May 25th.   Two local Haslemere worthies were
charged, William Bristow, blacksmith, and Daniel Budd, husbandman, of Porched House, Haslemere, and the Tithingman
had orders to deliver their bodies to the County Gaol.   John
Bristow, of Wisborough Green, husbandman, and John Mitchell,
of Oaklands, Haslemere, tanner, were prepared to stand bail.
Evidence was given by James Peto to the effect that 3 men
were seen by a labourer between 1.0 and 2.0 a.m. after he had
noticed that some of the Shillinglee Park palings had been
broken down and deer had escaped.   The labourer had reported
to James Peto, a keeper, who followed on horseback the blood-
stained trail of the three men.   This led back past Lythe Hill
to a lower barn called Three Gates, where a saddled horse was
found.   While one of the trackers watched from behind a hedge,
a man came and took the horse away.   After searching the
barn, Peto and the High Constable, James Sadler, went to
Haslemere Town, arriving between 12.0 and 1.0 on Sunday
night.   By this time they had one or two others following
them, one of whom was drunk, and from remarks passed by him
search was made at the King's Arms Inn without success.   Then
Bristow's house was visited and searched, again unsuccessfully,
but a certain man, Puttick, gave information that Bristow had

a stable at the Sign of the Crown, but search there also revealed no venison. The wretched landlord of the Crown was, with his house, then searched, but again fruitlessly. But, in the garden was found a sack containing a hind-quarter of venison. This success was marked by the assembling of the search party and witnesses at the White Horse, probably for refreshment after their efforts, and the drunk citizen was committed to prison, and the innkeeper discharged.

Later a party of seven men confessed to the stealing and that Bristow had received some of the venison. This was not the only occasion when Bristow was a receiver, for a year previously H. Herrington (the drunk man above-mentioned) had brought back 3 poached pheasants to Bristow, and on another occasion a brace of hare, and of hen pheasants.

Bristow, in addition of being a blacksmith, apparently made some grandfather clocks, had been bailiff for the Town, and Constable at various times.

Among the records for the century are a number of lists giving names and occupations, also three maps of the Borough which show each house and householder in 1722, 1735 and 1775.

In 1710, there were 49 names of these who polled in the election for Knight of the Shire; this figure gives a probable freehold population of two hundred and fifty persons.

In 1739, a certificate of the names of all persons in the parish mentions 115 persons as liable to land tax, which makes a parish population of about 450-500. In 1761, 44 persons, again probably the freeholders, signed a congratulatory address to King George III on his accession.

By now making a tour of the Town at the mid-century, we shall more easily form a general idea of the town's development and life.

Below the church, the road to the town crosses by a causeway and bridge, a pond of some size and depth, for even in 1776 a boy of 16 years old, one Francis Bennett, was a " drown casualty " in Church Hill. You may notice in the present railway cutting sides some oak trees which, I am informed, antedate the cutting, and were probably seedlings at the edge of the pond, at the date of this accident.

To confirm the story of this pond, on Rocque's map of Surrey of 1762, a large pond, a stream running down to it and out of it, is shown. The stream proceeds south-west to the mid-point of Bridge Road, back of Pope's Mead, where it is joined by the stream from the High Street and so down across the meadows to near the bottom of Tanners Lane where was Pyle Marsh. Thence it flowed at the bottom of Oaklands garden to Fosters Bridge, by the north side of the present railway to the Railway Arch, where it is joined by the stream from Bunch Lane and Weydown, and so on between King's Road and the railway to Sicklemill. The old house here on the north of the road just across the pond is Bridge Hall.

Going up the rise ahead of us we note the Pathfields leading back to the middle of the town. This was a necessary short cut to the Church from the lower part of Haslemere, when the path across the fields, where now is Bridge Road, would have been flooded.

On the crest of the slope on the right is a small farmhouse with cellars. The hearthstone of one half of the cottage, if observed from the cellar, will be found to be the grave-stone of Elizabeth, wife of William Chitty, died 1726, and in the wall of the cellar is cut 1627, which we may take to be the date of building.

Proceeding on our way we pass a Borough bound stone, a few yards before we reach the waste ground at the top of the High Street. On the left there, well set back, is Haslemere House and the Parsonage, owned by a Mrs. Margaret Woods, widow of a tailor. She is living down in the town and it appears to me very likely that she has let this house to the Curate, the Rev. John Veneer, who has a fair-sized family. It has four sitting-rooms and four bedrooms, not forgetting a cellar and brewhouse, and was built about 1616.

Immediately on the waste land at the top of the High Street was an old cottage, a blacksmith's shop tenanted by John Combes, who stops his hammering just long enough to note our little party of strangers turn down into the High Street. We can imagine him turning to his mate again and saying, " Warn't be long afore they're coming in for shoein' if they travels much around here."

We also note that there is no continuing road to Grayswood as at the present day, and to reach Grayswood it is necessary to go round by Three Gates Lane and the Windmill on the edge of Grayswood Common.

Looking down the High Street we see on either side old-fashioned timbered and brick houses in the main, with two taller brick houses on the right. Fields are on either side of the road as we start down the street.

We will notice the houses on our right. First comes a farm with extensive outbuildings, nowadays "Heathedge," leased by Mr. Hack from John Shudd, the Attorney, who lives across the road.

Next we pass a red brick house of three storeys, now known as "Town House," early Georgian type, owned by John Tanner. He was a supporter of one of the local M.P.s, General Oglethorpe, and sold this property to him in 1747, three years before his own death. There is as yet no record that the General ever lived there.

General Oglethorpe, who founded the new colony of Georgia in what is now the United States of America, in his salad days was a fighter. In 1722, a few months before his actual election in Haslemere, he had a dispute with Thomas Sharpe in High Street. Thomas Sharpe drew his sword and the General as promptly drew his and wounded Mr. Sharpe in the stomach, and a Captain Onslow, who apparently intervened as peacemaker, in the thigh; Captain Onslow seized the blade of the General's sword and his hand was much disabled. The mob, which had quickly gathered, prevented further incident. The General, who was not wounded, bound up Captain Onslow's wounds and sent a surgeon to him. History does not relate what happened to Mr. Sharpe; I expect the Curate was sent for, surgery not being capable of coping at that date with abdominal wounds. If the General underwent a prison sentence it must have been short, for later the same year he took his seat in Parliament as Member for Haslemere.

Below this house are the two semi-detached houses of the Undershell family, a family of tanners, who were also the owners of the Fleur de Lis on Carpenter's Heath, an inn about this date, and some lands called "Skatehunts" under Lythe Hill.

Below them was a smaller house lived in by Jeremiah Cock and his wife, Elizabeth, and her father, James Gace; their house borders on Pathfields.

Beyond this path is the " Tudor Cottage," where Edmund Upton and his wife, Mary, lived.   He was a maltster.

William Cobden, the tanner, lived in the " White House," now the Georgian Hotel.   The next two cottages, at one time " Causewayside," now shops, were also owned by him.

At the lowest point of the road was a house, late the " Angel Inn," lived in by the widow of a Thomas Ride, who had died in 1720.   Since his death, it has been divided into two tenements. He would have missed, if he had still been alive in 1740, the old town pond called the Wyer Pond.   This was filled in between 1710 and 1722, and at the time created a stir in the town.   The pond was formed by the presence of a number of springs, in the east side of the town from Well Lane downwards, and emptied itself as a small stream in a gully under the main road, running down what is now West Street to join the stream from Church Hill Pond.   In 1642, new premises were built just north of the pond, and about 1727 the new White Hart Inn was built on the recently filled-in pond.   By this pond must undoubtedly have stood the ducking-stool which had been ordered to be built in 1658, for the treatment of witches, women scolds and short-weight bakers.

Considerable levelling-up of the road must have been done at this point, for about 1890 an old road surface paved with rough bricks was found about 4ft. below the present 20th century level.   A little south of the pond were the pillory and the shambles.

Continuing over the causeway, on our right lay a detached house* occupied by Mrs. Margaret Woods, widow of Peter Woods, who built the house in 1725 on a piece of Popes Mead, which he had bought from John Shudd.

A small house set back from the road was the property of William Coleman, who had married the daughter of James Osborn of Lythe Hill Farm.

We then come to the two cottages which contain shops, the first a butcher's shop run by John Dudman, who also rented part of Scotland Farm, and the second by William Upton, a mercer.

---

* Now converted into shops.

Next we find the Swan Inn; John Sayers is the innkeeper and his family had been the innkeepers there since at least 1688. Dying in 1738 he was followed by his son, Richard.

An inn had stood on this site from a very early date, for in 1601, an inn bearing the name of " The Swan " was built, or re-made out of an older building. No doubt but an excellent meal could be found there, for his brother Richard keeps a butcher's shop near the foot of Shepherd's Hill, and runs two farms including one at Clammer Hill.

To continue our survey, we bear round to the west along the Portsmouth Road or Lower Street for some way, by the gardens of the Swan and the hedge of some pasture land, and at about halfway along the present street, come to a small house set back from the road belonging to Mrs. Carter, the widow of a stone-mason.

Next is John Bradfold, a tanner, with his tanyard, adjoining the rear of the house. His father, also a tanner, who had died in 1711, had rented another part of Scotland Farm, and in his will had left to his grandson, John Neale, his largest fowling-piece.

He is followed by Richard Gamon, a glazier, who has his stores and showrooms up in the town.

A little farther on lives Robert Billinghurst, baker, whose father had been a weaver and town-crier, and next to him, John Overington, recently a farmer in the Witley end of the parish. Just beyond this lives William Chitty, an old carpenter, whose son, also a carpenter, lives on the opposite side of the road.

The end house on this side reaching to the boundary of the Borough, is Pilewell House, where lives George Denyer, whose house for more than 100 years was the property of the Billing-hurst family.

Just beyond is the so-called Pilewell, which was an excellent spring, supplying to part of the inhabitants a good water.

Returning along the south side of Lower Street, is the house of John Berry, a retired husbandman; next a shoemaker, James Costen, followed by a house of Edward Ride. Another John Berry, retired, a yeoman, lives in a detached house adjoining, and in the following semi-detached house the shoemaker John Dudman and Elizabeth Ride, widow.

Next come the gardens stretching down from Shepherd's Hill, and near the corner are the houses of John Chase and Richard Smith, a carpenter.

In the angle is the Old Malt House of John Chase, a brandy merchant, much later on a corn chandler shop and store.

Across the road as we ascend Shepherd's Hill is William Ride's blacksmith's shop, conveniently placed at an entry to the town. No building occurs owing to the high bank, till near the crest of the hill where, in the island formed by the old and new roads, are the cottages of John Grevatt, a labourer, and William Upton, a young farmer.

Returning down the hill by the new-made road on our left is the Parish House, for the poor and aged.

Widow Garlet lives below this adjoining the house of William Ride, junior, who, in 1751, was Town Constable and Bailiff the following year.

Below this, Jane Matthews, widow of a shoemaker, owns two cottages set back, next the house and garden with summer-house of William Haslegrove, shoemaker; and lastly, the house and shambles of Richard Sayers, the butcher; he was an oncoming man and we shall meet him again at a Manor Court.

At the east corner of Shepherd's Hill and south of the Market Place, is the Red Lion Inn, formerly known as "The Fox," and held by William Billinghurst. Next to him was Half Moon Farm; at about the date 1742 it came into the possession of William Cobden the tanner, and his brother, Edward Cobden, the celebrated Archdeacon, and was divided into two holdings comprising several shops. The next house is divided also into two portions, the first and westernmost being the George Inn kept by Robert Ride, and the second half again divided into two shops, of which one was a tobacconist kept by William Bradfold.

Lloyds Bank is the modern development of this, and at this point a little path led up over a stile to the fields and hill above. The next house is the Spread Eagle Inn, divided into two portions and owned by Thomas Denyer.

There are three small tenements next, belonging to William White, a bricklayer, later represented by the present White Lion.

Next comes the old White Horse Inn property, but its use as an inn had ceased by 1657; this is now Stafford's cafe and the adjoining house. Robert Clement owns both.

Richard Withall lives in the following house (opposite Green Frog Bookshop) and John Habens, an innkeeper, owns what is today an office.

Here is now a house at the end of the Borough, " Uptons," in two tenements, with a large garden and summerhouse, lived in by William Ride, blacksmith, and Barbara Courtness, widow of a Chiddingfold farmer. At the top of her garden, known as East or Bramble Garden, is still one of the old Borough boundary stones. Just beyond their garden, but in Thursley Parish, are the houses now known as Thursley End, built about 1639, but at present tenanted by Francis Jackman's widow.

Across the road is " Collards," built about 1540 by Thomas Billinghurst, and 200 years later lived in by a descendant, Richard Billinghurst, lawyer and steward of the Godalming Hundred.

The next house, Porched House, is in two portions, owned by Richard Billinghurst, and has R. Phillips, a bricklayer, as tenant in the east half, while Moorey Baxter occupied the west.

Following this are four cottages belonging to John Jackson, and we then come to the Red Cow Inn, famous a few years later, as a freehold providing eight votes. The innkeeper is William Ede. This inn is now the Green Frog Bookshop.

In what is today "The Old House," at the corner of the High Street, lives Moorey Baxter. Next to him lives John Fielder, and at the King's Arms, Noah Bromham is the innkeeper, soon to be succeeded at his death by Moorey Baxter.

At the White Horse Inn, built only in 1716, resides Edward Ride, whose wife had built the inn. He is the local postmaster, whose duties lay in providing horses and carriages for hire.

We will return later to the Inn for our mid-day meal and shall, no doubt, hear a good deal of local gossip.

At the corner of the block of houses farther up the street, first comes John Dudman, a shoemaker, and next to him, James Coleman, and John, his son, doctors.

In the old three-gabled house, now a chemist's shop, we find Richard Gaman, the glazier. His occupation here might well account for the presence of a window of ancient heraldic glass, of which unfortunately only one or two pieces survive, and may be seen in the Haslemere Museum.

William Collins, lives in the next house, " The Crown " or " Great White Hart Inn," where today is the butcher and the greengrocer; he is an innkeeper as well as soap-boiler, and the following house contained Mr. Jackman's corn chambers (now a garage), later occupied as a tallow-chandler's business by William Ride.

Beyond him was the new White Hart, tenanted by William Ride; this is now the block of new shops—Pinks—and it stood on or close by the site of the Wyer Pond referred to earlier.

Next comes Mr. Mellersh's house, the lower part of which had been occupied until his death recently, by old Dr. Middleton Miles. I should think this must have been his surgery and consulting room as he owned a little property called " Loves " under Lythe Hill. This was the house known to older Haslemere people as " Farncombe," now converted into Maison Henri.

Above him lives Joseph Frogley, the son-in-law of Richard Dudman, a butcher, who owned one of the shops on the other side of the High Street, opposite the Market House.

Just above this house, Frogley has built a barn, and two cottages were later built on the site of this barn, where now stands the Haslemere Garage (and Newcombes and the sweet shop).

Next again, John Hardy lives in an old house which was, a few years later, 1753, pulled down and rebuilt as the pleasant little house known as " Rosenhurst," which has now in turn been replaced by Harrods and the Dairy.

Above John Hardy, John Dudman and George Denyer own two small cottages, where now are Bicknells and the Boot Stores. These two names remind me of an old marriage settlement made by a Haslemere resident of this date on his son's marriage. He gave his son, on his marriage, various property round Haslemere, and included his own house where he and his wife lived, with certain reservations; that certain rooms should be for themselves, a horse provided by the son whenever his father and mother should wish to go out, and that they might return again when they themselves wished. I think, however, that the arrangement did not last long, for a house was built on one of the pieces of land soon after, and it is probable that the son and his wife were the occupants.

John Dudman and George Denyer may have lived in these two small houses on their retirement, after providing handsomely for their young people.

Next comes a small house belonging to the widow Burges, occupied by William Morley the Parish Clerk.

Here we come to Well Lane which leads south-east off the High Street to the Town Well.

Just above this lane live Will Morley, junior, land surveyor and maker of the Borough Maps, and John Buckle, in two little houses, now forming an estate agency.

We recall this had been called " Goodwyns," and 100 years before had been the home of Thomas Burges, the Curate.

In the next house lives Abraham Upfold, a tailor.

Above him is an old blacksmith's shop, where William Wheeler lives—this had been known as " Oakes " and had belonged to one of the numerous Billinghurst family—it, as many other houses at this date, was divided into two parts, and by 1740, William Bristow, constable at various times and a blacksmith, and his wife Mary, were living there. This was " The Small House " and upper part of the present " Goodwyns." William Bristow, like many blacksmiths, made grandfather clocks; one made by him was sold in 1939 in Godalming, with a brass dial and 30 hour movement.

The large house, which we next reach, is " The Burgage " house, where John Shudd, the attorney, lives. It stood on the site of the Museum and was rebuilt and enlarged before 1730.

Lastly is a double house lived in by William Briant, a wheelwright, and John Ede, now roughly the garden of Burgage House and No. 88, High Street; and adjoining this and to the road to Grayswood lay a field containing one or two barns known as " Pound Crofts."

On the waste ground here at this time stood the Town Pound.

CHAPTER IX

The Georgian Age, II

IT IS NOW time for dinner and we will retrace our steps to the White Horse to enjoy a good 18th century meal. As one writer has it—iris-tinted rounds of beef, marble-veined ribs, gelatinous veal pies, colossal hams, gallons of old ale, binns full of old port and burgundy, and the all-pervading feeling of omnipotence from the guests, who order what they please to the landlord, who can produce and execute everything they can desire. 'Tis a wondrous sight !

The inn was only built in 1716, and so the standard is good, the innkeeper, Edward Ride, having the official job of post-master. This refers to the keeping and hiring of horses or carriages for riding or driving from one posthouse to the next.

While we are feeding, there enters one, who we are informed is John Butler of Bramshott. He is a local ironmaster, and has just been visiting his ironworks at Fernhurst, one of the last to be started. He is delighted, so we overhear him say, to have received a further order for cannon for the American and Spanish wars.

Across the room, another pair are discussing the Will of old William Cobden, the tanner, on which a pamphlet had been published anonymously, by his brother Edward. This Edward Cobden was Rector of Acton, Chaplain to George II and Arch-deacon of London.

Nearby is James Simmons, who has a paper mill at Sickle-mill, and several farmers are in the midst of a group about William Ride, just in from his corn and tallow chandler's shop, and are having the usual arguments about the price of corn and wondering how much longer would be maintained the fixed price of corn and the bonus on exported surplus.

As they move off, we notice another couple discussing James Lucas, who has recently moved from Thursley Parish to Lythe Hill Farm. He will be a good farmer to do so well as James Osborn who died there a few months ago.

It was market day yesterday, a Tuesday, and the town was packed, we hear, owing to the fine weather. Men are still moving the sheep hurdles and cattle pens from above the Market House, which we notice is farther north than it stands in the 20th century. There was also grouped around the building a number of small shops, and a Butter Market house in the east side and Fish Market house on the west. Into the space under the centre of the house corn was brought.

The earlier Market House of the 18th century was of wood and stood almost opposite the King's Arms. Within the Market House, in the great loft or chamber, were held the Manor Courts every year where, for many years, to the middle of the 18th century, Richard Billinghurst, of Collards, presided as Steward.

Election of the local M.P.s took place in that chamber, and permission had been given by the Lord of the Manor to use this room by parties and others on Market and Fair days.

Having settled our lunch with a dram of good cognac, perhaps brought along the byways over Blackdown from France by smugglers, we will set off down the Portsmouth Road to Pilewell Marsh, noticing up the hill in front of us the old Courts Hill Farm and barns. They are in Thursley Parish and are owned by James Simmons in right of his wife, Frances Penfold, whose family have lived there from 1650. At the corner where we turn up Tanners Lane, formerly known as Hall Lane, is a little cottage on our left, probably that which William Shotter built as a dye house on the waste in 1589. As we go up the lane we cross the little stream again which runs down from the town and Church Hill through the Pilewell Marsh, and see on our left the house and sheds of John Mitchell, a tanner. We wind gradually up to the Church, first passing the old Church Hill House, perhaps in earlier days Hall of Piperham, recently tenanted by John Wakeford and owned by Peter Burrell, one of the local M.P.s.

We find the Church a simple room type of building with an equally long north aisle, and a low tower at the west end containing five bells. It is roofed with Horsham stone and has a

wooden sundial on the tower.   It is full of box pews with a great
seat in the north aisle next to the pulpit, which always passed
with the Half Moon property and was where William Cobden, the
tanner, used to sit in his life time.

There is a gallery at the west end, built in 1714, where the
singers and, in later days the musicians, sat.   The note for the
leading singer was given by a pitch pipe now in the Museum,
which appears to have been made in the 17th century.

A similar gallery at the west end of the north aisle provided
seats for some of the leading families.   We also notice the royal
arms set on the front of the main gallery.   The pillars which
support the painted arches, between the aisles, are of oak and
of large dimensions.   There is a simple type of rood screen, and
a plain octagonal font.

The Curate, the Rev. John Veneer, and William Morley, the
Parish Clerk, occupy positions under the easternmost arch during
the service.   By another door the Curate comes in and greets us,
and tells us that the church is a chapelry of Chiddingfold since
the year 1180 and that in 1363 a burial ground was consecrated
and dedicated for the use of the parishioners of the village of
Haslemere.   Some rebuilding had taken place about 1490 and
the north aisle would appear to have been added about 1640.
(By 1864 a report on the church states " The Church needs rebuilding, it is a disgrace to the parish "—this was actually done
in 1870).

We now return to the top of the High Street again, taking
leave of the Curate, at his gate, at Haslemere House, and walk
along the lower London Road, i.e. Three Gates Lane.

We soon pass another Borough boundary stone, and in a few
hundred yards reach the entrance to Meadfields and Witley Farm.
Meadfields is one of the oldest known properties in the district,
receiving mention in an old Deed of 1230.   It is now tenanted
by Jane, widow of Thomas Denyer.

Close by is Witley Farm, tenanted, I think, by William
Dudman.   Turning at the bend and at the road fork is the
triangular piece of land known as the Roundabouts, owned by
Mr. Yaldwin, junior.   This was near the Butts, which 200 years
earlier were ordered to be maintained for the practice of archery.

Keeping on over the common, we reach the Windmill, actually within Witley Parish. Haslemere Windmill was a smock mill with a fixed millhouse; the cap only revolved, and it was turned into the wind by chains.

By dropping down the lane now we should reach Grayswood and so on to Godalming, passing the remains of the Gate House of the old Stroud House which was in ruin. Francis Jackman, a timber merchant, had recently leased the Stroud property for the wood cutting.

By taking the right fork in Three Gates Lane we drop down to New House, the present home of William Yaldwin. Away on our left is Clammer Hill, owned by James Osborn, a bachelor and nephew of the late tenant of Lythe Hill, whose sister keeps house for him.

Turning right towards Holdfast, we pass now just in front of the New House, and join the present road down to Holdfast Farm, which is now owned by Peter Bennett. Here we cross a small bridge over the stream which runs down from the springs on the east side of Haslemere to Imbhams Farm, half a mile farther down, where was lately an iron furnace. This farmhouse was the Old Manor Farm of Imbhams, a small estate in Chiddingfold and Haslemere, and is tenanted by Robert Mitchell. We then walk up the lane to the main Chiddingfold highway. A half-mile farther east is Lythe Hill Farm, just hidden by a slope, at present tenanted by John Lucas. The house is half timbered, and was enlarged in Elizabethan days when it was the home of one of the Quennells, the Imbhams Ironmasters.

Turning again towards Haslemere, we reach the Almshouse Common, noting on our right a small farm called Skitredons, originally the cleared land of one Alice Skutte, alive in 1388, and now a flourishing little farm tenanted by Peter Bennett.

On our left is a little house called "Cockles," tenanted by Francis Sheldon, whose wife, a Madgwick, owned the property by inheritance, since 1628 at least, when Thomas Madgwick was reeve of Haslemere. (Her father also was reeve in 1691). Francis was reeve of the tithing of Haslemere in 1749.

We then pass the almshouses on our right, which carry a plaque to state that two were built in 1676 from the profits of letting the Town Waste.

On the opposite side of the road are three detached cottages
and at the top of the rise, on the left, the small farm of Lower
Courts. We meet nothing on returning to Haslemere except the
old barns of the Swan Farm on our right.

To round off our tour of Haslemere we will start again at
Pilewell and go down the Portsmouth Road, noting the stone
house on our right, now a shop[1], and continue over Foster's
Bridge, crossing another branch of the Wey where the stream
from Bunch Lane joins that from Haslemere town.

We mount Clay Hill, in 1748 much steeper than today, and
just over the crest was an old cottage. Next, bearing left, we
pass the old Hanger Hill Farm and soon reach Sicklemill where
are the flourishing paper mills of James Simmons.

To the north we see Lane End Farm in Thursley Parish,
which Robert Bennet farms, and a little farther west, through
the trees, the farmhouse of Thomas and Anne Cherriman, in
Frensham parish; and just beyond this, Shottermill, an iron
mill, in Lynchmere parish.

We must now turn east along Sturt Hanger and pass
by Sturt Farm, tenanted by John Coombs. The road here was
soon to be improved. Turnpike had begun and this was the
way from the Portsmouth Road at Hindhead to Chichester. A
short distance farther on we find an inn on our left, the Fleur-
de-Lis, built about 1550, owned by John Undershell. A few
hundred yards across Carpenters Heath, which is first mentioned
in 1503, is the Blue Bell Inn, so we shall not lack for refreshment.

We turn up the lane by the little stream which is another
head of the River Wey and we shall pass Houndless Water Farm,
occupied by John Peter, and at the end of the lane, Stedlands
Farm. We climb the steep little hill to Hook Lane[2] and if we
turn to the right we shall reach Whatmans Farm, owned by
John Billinghurst, and if we turn left we drop down to Scotlands
Farm, occupied by John Batchelor, who is also a carpenter.

We shall find a wide strip of waste here leading back to the
town, and at the top of Shepherds Hill, in front of the old house
occupied by Edmund Upton, we notice a group of local people
engaged in playing bowls on the green there between the two
roads. A keen match is in progress, the visiting side having
come in from Roundhurst, where there is also a good bowling
green on Blackdown.

---

1 See p. 49 footnote.   *2* Now Scotland Lane.

We shall now drop down Shepherds Hill to the town, returning to the White Horse for the evening meal.

After filling ourselves again, Edward Ride, the innkeeper, asks us into his own room for a chat and tells us that there is a flourishing weekly market which has been held since 1221, and that two fairs are held each year on May 12th and September 25th for three days each. On Guy Fawkes Day a large bonfire is lighted in the Market Square and is always an anxiety, with no fire brigade and the town pond now filled up.

The ducking stool was only a memory of the older inhabitants, for it was taken away when the Wyer Pond was filled in. [It is recorded that the base of a post was found on digging in front of the new White Hart Inn site in 1907, and it was suggested that it was the base of the sign of the inn, but I fancy it was the base of the ducking stool post.]

The pillory and stocks were not apparently much needed, (and I can find no record of their usage), although the town was fined in 1600 for not providing them.

A cricket match—Haslemere and Thursley—is recorded in 1753, and we saw a bowls match in progress on Shepherds Hill during our tour of the town. Bowls had been first noted in 1661, when a Thomas Mayne, butcher, undertook, on leasing the property, to keep the bowling green as it ought to be kept.

Card games of various kinds were played in the inns and at home, and a game called "Nineholes."

Fishing, also shooting, was a pastime for some of the population, but it was illegal for anyone with less than £100 per annum to shoot game.

Dr. Coleman was the senior medical man in Haslemere, since old Dr. Middleton Miles had died a few years previously in a house a little farther up the High Street. Young James Coleman was probably assisting him. John Veneer, son of the local Curate of Haslemere, was also in training for medicine.

There was also a Dr. Richard Glenviel living here; he had earlier been a soldier, and thus might be said to represent the R.A.M.C.

Dr. Coleman was fortunate in having had, for a time, two midwives in his area—Jane Collick, born 1702, died 1733; and

Hanna Bennett, died 1736—probably at the Frensham end of the parish.   Their work was very arduous and they did not live to a great age.

There were few hospitals in England.   At the beginning of the 18th century the only public hospitals in London were St. Bart's and St. Thomas's.   In mediæval England, under the Monks, there had been about 750 hospitals, of which about 200 were leper houses.   These all disappeared with the dissolution of the monasteries and were, in part only, replaced by almshouses of the 16th and 17th centuries.

Private charity, in the provinces, was the only alternative to parish relief.

In 1722 there was in Haslemere a parish house at the upper end of the west side of Shepherds Hill, and the almshouses, supported by market tolls, just above the common in the Chiddingfold (now Petworth) road.

Taking medicines seems to have been a pastime for some folk even in the 18th century.   John Shotter, of Godalming, one of the Shulebrede family, in his will of 1761, left his wife a handsome annuity of £40 per annum and sums up to £10 per annum in addition, while she is a widow, to expend for herself on doctors, surgeons, apothecarys, nurses and tenders.

The local post in 1748 was brought by mailbag on horse over Hindhead, and at a later date, 1801, is stated to have arrived in Haslemere at 3.0 a.m., and was picked up again at 10.0 p.m. for London.   A letter to London in 1801 cost 9d.   However, even in 1769, there was a daily postal service, except Sundays, to Haslemere.

The Borough of Haslemere was a manor within the Manor of Godalming, and as to local government a multiplicity of officers is found.

The Bailiff attended parliamentary elections in place of the Sheriff, who was usually barred from entry into the Godalming Hundred by the special privilege of the Hundred of Godalming as ancient Royal demesne.

The Steward and Bailiff were normally appointed by the Lord of the Manor.   In the middle of the 18th century the Steward happened to be a Haslemere lawyer, Mr. Richard Billinghurst, and Richard Smither, in 1739, was chosen Bailiff for the Borough

Manor of Haslemere, at a view of Frankpledge held with a jury of 17 men on Wednesday, April 25th, in Haslemere Market House, and Henry Billinghurst was chosen constable.

William Morley, junior, and George Denyer were chosen as ale conners and tasters, and Jas. Costen and Hardy were chosen as searchers and sealers of leathers.   John Dudman, Richard Sayer, William Dudman and William Read, four butchers, were presented for producing veal under age and fined 4d. each.

One of the duties of the Bailiff was to act as returning officer at the Borough Parliamentary elections.

For the civil district, a reeve and tithingman were annually chosen at the Godalming Manor Court. William Cobden was reeve in 1744, and in 1750 a woman, not an exceptional thing, Jane Denyer, widow, was reeve and held office by tenure of Meadfields.

For the parish, overseers were appointed, originally by the Justices of the Peace, to levy and enforce the payment of a poor rate, and were later elected at the Easter Vestry, each overseer representing a distinct tenement and to act in rotation.

Widows had also to undertake such service, and a little later Crabbe describes such a one :

    "No parish business in the place could stir,
      Without direction or assent from her.
      In turn she took each office as it fell,
      Knew all their duties, and discharged them well.
      The lazy vagrants in her presence shook,
      And pregnant damsels feared her stern rebuke."

Haslemere appears to have been reasonably tidy in such matters, but it is on record that in a not far distant parish, between 1810 and 1820, of the 72 marriages, no less than 69 have been unchaste before marriage.

There appear to have been some Borough regalia—two staves of office, one for the bailiff 7ft. 3ins. in length, undated, and a second for the constable 6ft. 3ins. in length, which has painted on it the letters C.R. 1672. Both staves show signs of gilding. A second pair has come into the possession of the Museum which may be a pair supplied to replace those (above described), which were retained by Mr. William Bristow, bailiff, in 1752, when there was a notable dispute over the apparently irregular election of his successor.

In 1755, at the Court Leet, Robert Phillips was bound over in a fine of 20/- to deliver up to the Bailiff within ten days the brass gallon corn measure which belonged to the Market.

In 1759 there is also mention of a Sword Bearer, one William Upfold, but his sword of office cannot now be found.

The houses of the people in the town were partly of the half-timbered sort, with a few later brick and tile.

Water supply was by well or springs. The latter would normally be the safest, sanitation being entirely primitive.

Furniture, according to an old writer of this date, was mainly of English oak, with long, round or triangular tables;

"......chests of drawers, also side cupboards with large doors at the bottom, and on the top short pillars with a kind of terrace, small doors within, much carved;

armchairs with wooden bottoms and backs, clothes chests, four-poster bedsteads with framed heads and testers, all of which were much carved with flowers, scrolls, images, etc......"

Wainscoting was of English oak framed with a flat moulding, the panels all cleft from a tree.

With the younger people it was now the fashion to have deal dressers with shelves over, for pewter, etc.   The tables and chairs were of Norway oak.   With the higher sort of people walnut veneer was most in vogue; mahogany was not yet in general use.

The best chairs were turned ash, dyed or stuffed with Turkey or other such cover.   Walnut tree chairs with French legs now began to be made by cabinet makers.

Bedsteads were made of beech owing to scarcity of English oak, without foot-posts, but having a raised bedboard and tester hung up to the ceiling, with much lace on the furniture.

Most households did their own spinning of linen, and made bread, and even prepared their own household physic.

The usual drink was a good ale, wine being available for those who could afford it.   Gin, referred to earlier, was in early 18th century both cheap and common with townsfolk at any rate, though brandy, we have seen, was sold at the foot of Shepherds Hill or perhaps brought in at the back door at night by a smuggling friend.

At the end of the century there were only 144 houses and 642 inhabitants recorded as living in the parish, but we still have many of the names persisting:

Bicknell	Coombs	Chitty	Denyer
Dudman	Frogley	Hack	Hardy
Madgwick	Morley	Smithers	Upfold etc.

These and others were all counters in the political game and were, husbands and wives, all severely pilloried by Archdeacon Cobden, brother of the Haslemere tanner, in a rhyming pamphlet on the state of the Haslemere electors :

> * " THE MEN : a company of knavish sots—faithless to all but trusted to their pots.
>
> THE WOMEN : the wretched candidates are curst to canvass for the female interest first."

The three maps of the century, 1722, 1735 and 1775, are helpful in showing changes of ownership, but show little or no development. Haslemere was now almost crystallised for 200 years, and it was not till later on in the following century that much development in housing occurred. Two further maps, both made in 1758, by William Morley, show the alteration of the road at the north end of the town. The first shows the High Street ending at Pound Corner and the second (in the same year) shows the New Turnpike continuation of the High Street to Grayswood in its present line.

---

* Two of the 149 lines of the rhyme.

CHAPTER X

Victorian Scene

CRICKETING SCHOOLMASTER, NONCONFORMITY,
FRIENDLY SOCIETY, BAND, NEW TOWN HALL
— RAILWAY — CHURCH — TENNYSON —
DEVELOPMENT

In the opening year of the new century, James Boxall, the schoolmaster, was looking up the High Street from the great upper room of the old Town Hall. He was listening with half an ear to the droned repetition of his class of children, and he could see against the Georgian House, farther up the street, the chestnut tree planted eight years before by his old friend, Clark, the Sexton. The young tree was growing well, but he was getting old and could not expect to see it in its lovely maturity. He turned to dismiss the class and then went to a cupboard from which he drew a number of half-finished cricket bats. Old Boxall loved cricket, and made these bats for some of his pupils after school hours and before walking home to Shottermill. A few years later, in 1807 to be exact, his wife inherited a house near the lower end of Shepherds Hill, into which they moved for the last five years of his life. An oil painting, now in the Haslemere Museum, of about this date, depicts a cricket match in progress on the old bowling green above Shepherds Hill. James Boxall, no doubt, spent many happy hours coaching the village boys as they slogged away with his bats.

No hint seems to have reached Haslemere of the anxieties in the world beyond. By comparison, in a small village in High Suffolk we may read : We, the undermentioned persons did on Saturday, the 28th day of April, 1798, voluntarily subscribe (1) to assist, in case of an invasion, with our horses, wagons, carts; likewise in marking and driving our own stock for refuge from the hands of the enemy (11 names); (2) in clearing the roads and lanes and assisting in removing the stock. Then follow 26 names, including a fiddler.

Possibly Haslemere felt safe in the pocket of Lord Lowther, for, by 1806, Lord Lowther's agents were able to report to him that: "Since his Lordship had acquired two-thirds of the freehold property in the town, there had been considerable improvement of late therein." This improvement may refer to the buildings which, as stated before, were much renovated by imported labourers who would, of course, add to the votes in favour of their employer at any election.

During these rather unquiet times a nonconformist colony was steadily spreading in the town and, though in 1777 there was record of no nonconformist, by 1804 a small congregational chapel was built on the south side of Lower Street, which is now used as a Sunday School.

At a later date, during some extensions to the building, the coffin of the founder, Christopher Lee, of Shottermill, was found in the ground beneath the floor of the chapel.

Some further steps in the development of corporate responsibility were taken in June, 1806, when a meeting was held to discuss the formation of a Friendly Society. It was decided to hold an annual meeting on the first Wednesday in June at the Kings Arms Hotel. Candidates for election should be between the ages of 16 and 20 years. Each man must come annually to the Kings Arms on the appointed day at 9.0 a.m., decently clothed—or forfeit 2/6. Each man must wear a clean favour, in his hat, of 1½ yards of blue riband. A procession was then formed to march to church for a service and sermon, after which, headed by the local band and carrying beautifully painted flags, the party made visits to nearby large houses and returned for dinner at the Kings Arms. A hearty dinner was provided and all charges were paid for out of the club box. A further rule stipulated that no one should leave the club room till after 5.0 p.m. under forfeit of 6d.

In the evening the band turned out again in procession, returning with a masquerade consisting of men dressed as soldiers, sailors, and grotesque women, ending up with dancing in the High Street. The club was a Local Mutual Benefit Society and merged ultimately into the greater national clubs.

Lord Middleton, to whom the club rules had been submitted, generously gave his approval.

It is not known who organised this early band, but in 1837 there was a band known as Berry's Band, run by Edward Berry and William Berry, brickmakers. In that year a division of opinion as to whether or not to play for the Coronation of Queen Victoria caused dispersion of the band. But from its wreckage Wm. Bridger organised a new band, which continued under the name of Bridger's Band right through the remainder of the century.

In 1813 a meeting of inhabitants was held at the White Horse Inn to consider establishing a school for the education of infant poor, on the principles recommended by Dr. Bell. This school was later known as the National School.

The Parliamentary representatives may have intended a compliment to their pocket borough when they replaced the old timbered Town Hall by a brick edifice. The new Town Hall or Market House was built in 1814 on the south side of the old site, and originally comprised an upper room for elections, local courts and manorial business, surmounting a large central and two lateral archways. In one archway was a small lock-up for prisoners, and in the other a stairway leading to the room above.

No picture survives of the earlier building, but the old Market House at Godalming (which had been replaced at the same date) must have closely resembled that at Haslemere. Away back in 1752 complaint had been made to the Lord of the Manor that he should keep the Market House in repair, so that, much as we deplore the loss of a picturesque antique building, there was probably justification for the new brick one.

The weekly market had dwindled away to nothing, according to a writer in the Gentleman's Magazine of 1802, and the tolls and profits which earlier on had been worth £50 per annum, now contributed nothing to the upkeep of the Almshouses.

The outstanding piece of local news in 1815 was of numerous complaints at the Manor Courts of straying hogs. These complaints continued to be made at intervals until 1827, when a pound for stray hogs was provided, and one, Abraham Welland, was appointed as Pound Keeper. He doubled that office with that of Town Crier, and it is not without humour to recall that while the pigs raised their protesting voices inside the pound, their keeper also raised his to announce their detention and the

cost of custody. Welland served these two offices till his death
in 1837, and his successor, elected at a court leet, continued in
office till the courts ceased in 1839.

A little picture of child life in 1826 has escaped loss by the
record which has been preserved among the Penfold papers with
reference to a dispute of ownership of a certain small freehold
property on Shepherds Hill. This little property belonged to an
old man called Robert Briant, and because it carried a voting
privilege in the elections was a sort of Naboth's vineyard to the
eye of the local Lord of the Manor. Evidence was given by a
Mr. Penfold, a blacksmith, 39 years of age, who said that he
went to school at Mr. Boxall's for 3-4 years, and said further
that the boys, when they went to the house of office in his
master's garden, used to steal along the lower part of it. They
would then jump over the fence and steal the apples which grew
upon a tree which then stood there, where there is now one standing. He said that the boys were not allowed to play in their
master's garden, but went out on to Shepherds Hill in front
of Boxall's house, though they sometimes stole down through
the garden and went into the old tenement in order to play at
marbles. He remembered that the ground behind the old tenement was overrun with wild raspberries and weeds.

Then came a second witness, James Upfold, who said he
went to school at Boxall's. He recollected that the master used
to tell the boys not to go into the tenement or steal the apples
behind the tenement as it was Webb's property. But he said the
boys were frequently flogged for going there. Briant succeeded
in his claim at first, against the evidence, it seems; though later
he lost his case.

In 1828 there was a proposal to bring a railway through
Haslemere, but the proposal was received with disfavour, and
no train arrived for just over thirty years. But four years later,
in 1832, the Burgesses of Haslemere received a staggering blow.
The little town was disfranchised by the provision of the Parliamentary Act and lost its status as a borough. No longer could
boast be made of two Parliamentary representatives, and there
is little of local interest to record in the next quarter century.

A few gleams of facts have escaped the mists of that era and
we hear of a notable firework display during the celebrations at
Queen Victoria's accession in 1837. An old Haslemere worthy

remembered the rockets and Roman candles, and a Catherine wheel twelve inches across, which illuminated the gardens of the Curate, the Rev. John Chapman, at the top of the town.

At about the same date, the Church suffered from the hand of the improver. The old arches with heavy oak pillars, between nave and aisle, were swept away, to be replaced by elegant iron standards, and a new pulpit and reading desk substituted in place of the old three-decker pulpit.

A band of local musicians had led the church music from the early part of the century, to the accompaniment of a clarinet and bass viol. In 1839 a grinding organ with a number of tunes was installed in the gallery, but it ceased to be used in 1842. At about this date we learn from an old commercial directory that the Market was only thinly attended and that the population was 849 and had decreased by 38 in the ten years previous. There were also two schools, one being the National School.

Stage Coaches, which had thronged the Portsmouth Road to the number of 24 a day, began to lessen in number about 1841 on account of the new railway line to Southampton via Alton. There were, it is true, still two Chichester coaches which travelled along the turnpike road through Grayswood to Haslemere for Midhurst, and beyond. These coaches were labelled " Duke of Richmond " and called at the White Horse every day, except Sundays, at 11.30 a.m. and 2 p.m. The post arrived and departed each day at 7.0 a.m. in 1839, and during the next twenty years the postman walked with the postbag to and from Liphook, remaining there overnight in order to bring back the early morning mail to the post office, which was kept by Sarah Upton at a cottage in the High Street (since demolished and replaced by a multiple store).

After 1841, there being a railway line at Woking, the coaches for London were there run on to trucks, the passengers taking seats in the carriages, and so were carried on to Nine Elms, the then terminus. On arrival at Nine Elms the coaches drove off the trucks and took their passengers to their haven at Hatchetts Hotel, Piccadilly. This pleasant variety in travel came to an end in 1859, when the new London to Portsmouth line signalled its first passenger train through Haslemere. As a small side issue we note that the railway cutting below Haslemere Church brought about the loss of the old ponds, of which mention was

made earlier.   The presence of a number of railway navvies in
the area had not been without exciting incident. In 1852 the
first policeman was appointed and in the newness of his office
made objection to, and forbade, the holding of the usual
November 5th bonfire in the High Street.   In revenge some
local lads burnt the barn and workshop, at the top of the town,
of a local congregationalist, Stephen Pannell.   Later on, this
policeman rashly arrested a Jack of Lent.   This Jack of Lent
custom was an old event and served as public rebuke for any
locally unpopular person.   Such a person was placed in effigy
on a horse, which was then driven through and across the town,
the effigy being finally hanged or burnt.   This custom had
gradually been dying out, but the action of the constable on
this occasion was followed a day or two later by a hundred or
more navvies making a march through the town with another
effigy.   The constable wisely refrained from further action.   Soon
after, a witty placard was printed and posted up throughout the
town, the headlines being "Brutal Murder — £100 Reward."

Further trouble with the navvies arose, two years later, over
the arrest of one of their number who was confined in the cell
under the Town Hall.   A large gang got a plough coulter from
a field below Collards in order to force open the door of the cell.
An inspector and constable who attempted to prevent their action
were attacked.   The inspector, who was struck by the coulter,
died as the result of the blow.   After this a new police station
was built about 1855 along the Petworth Road beyond Thursley
End.

The last years of the previous century had seen certain other
lawless happenings.   The Rev. James Fielding was in 1786
appointed Curate of Haslemere, where at first he lived at Town
House in the High Street.   Three daughters and a son were
there born to his wife, but he apparently found that the ordinary
round of home and parish duties did not offer enough outlet for
his energy.   From an old memoir we read: " When the coach
was robbed on the Portsmouth Road by Parson Fielding and
others, he is said to have brought the mailbags and money to
his house in the High Street called Town House.   The bags were
hidden in the cellar, where later on they were found; it is also
known that in a house called Chase Farm, later owned by him,
the brass plate of a mailbag was found."

The two brothers, Drewett, who were hanged for a mail robbery at North Heath, Midhurst, in 1799, were stated by a near contemporary of Parson Fielding to have been men in his employment.

It was also said that a Lady in Pink was wont to appear in Town House, but whether she came after the money bags or was connected with other of the Parson's ill-doings, I never heard. This is the man, whose daughter being dead, built a large family vault in the churchyard. While it was being prepared for his daughter's burial he went down into it, and danced, saying it would make an excellent ballroom.

He bought also Whatman's Farm and part of Stedland and Owlden in 1792 and, about 1803, Church Hill House. He then built Denbigh House (so called after a distant relative, Lord Denbigh) on Whatman's Farm. This property came, after his death, to a son, James, and later was demolished for the building now called Lythe Hill.

In 1856, just prior to the coming of the railway, there were extensive enclosures of the neighbouring common lands. Until the mid-century all the country from Shottermill to Farnham was heathy common land and much of it was contained in the old Woolmer Forest. This was not, of course, all forest as we understand the word nowadays, but open heath country with tracts of primeval oak, beech and alder trees. The Government of the early century had, however, planted much of the area with fir trees, thereby rousing the ire of Cobbett. Cobbett, we may remember, made very slighting comment about Hindhead, and Haslemere was "that sink hole of a borough."

The roads to Farnham over this waste were said to be so bad that any who valued his carriage springs drove via Milford and Elstead. By the enclosures, some seven to eight thousand acres of common land were lost to the public, and a great number of the houses in Hindhead and Grayshott stand on old common land. Much of the money received in payment of these lands was allotted to the making of new roads.

Three things now contributed to the revival of Haslemere. In 1864 a Mr. Stewart Hodgson came to live at Denbigh House, which he soon rebuilt as the Lythe Hill House of today. He bought annually more property in the neighbourhood, including the Manor of Godalming, so that Haslemere had for some 15-20 years a resident Lord of the Manor. Stewart Hodgson was instrumental in encouraging much of the development which later occurred. He was spurred on in his wishes by the ideals of the first Rector of the new Haslemere parish, for Haslemere became an independent parish in 1868 by separation from Chiddingfold, whose dependent daughter she had been for at least seven hundred years.

This first Rector, the Revd. Sanders Etheridge, was a good leader and had progressive ideas. He may well have noted a Diocesan report of 1864 which stated, "Haslemere Church needs rebuilding; it is a disgrace to the parish." Two years was time enough for him to organise the parish for rebuilding the Church, which was carried out in the year July, 1870-1, material from the old church being re-used. Mr. Hodgson gave freely to this rebuilding; a cricket ground in his own park at Lythe Hill to the town; and a workmen's club to the townsfolk in 1886.

It may here be said that, from about 1825-1850, cricket was played in a field just north of Pound Corner, known for long as Cricketing Field. Before this time that field had been known as Rackfield, a name which commemorated the cloth racks for stretching lengths of cloth which had occupied the field until that industry had died out locally with the development of powered machinery.

In 1850 a piece of ground on the Manorial waste at Haste Hill was levelled by the co-operation of local farmers, who gave the labour and transport for the work. Here cricket was played until 1868, when the new Lythe Hill ground provided a good pitch and larger outfield surrounded by magnificent scenery, where many well-known people, such as Conan Doyle, Tennyson*, E. W. Hornung, came to hit or chase the leather until 1900.

The third event was the decision of Dr. Jonathan Hutchinson to make his summer home in this area. Dr. Hutchinson, a member of the Society of Friends, a Yorkshireman, and later Knight, F.R.S., bought Inval in 1866. He later added to the house more accommodation for his family and began, in 1888, his Museum. This Museum was catholic in its interest and scope, accepting the dead or fossil specimens, but strongly stressing an educational purpose by emphasising continuity and exhibiting living specimens of animal or plant life wherever possible. He later gave fortnightly lectures, and the subsequent growth of the Museum has only been paralleled by the interest aroused and imitation in other centres.

* Son of the poet.

In dealing with fires, no improved methods had been used, beyond the hand squirt and the rake, until, in 1877, Charles Bridger succeeded in organising a Volunteer Haslemere Fire Brigade. Its first call was not until 1878, a year later, to a brewery, but the engine was not needed. This Brigade acquired a hand pump engine, and turned out in relatively good time for local fires until 1907.

By 1875 Haslemere was making an appeal to the world of culture as a rest and health resort. Professor Tyndall, Sir Jonathan Hutchinson, Allen Chandler, Lord Tennyson, Sir Robert Hunter and many others, writers, painters, sculptors, philosophers, all came to settle in and round Haslemere. These were the notable forerunners of many who have, not infrequently, spent leisure, ability and means for the further development of Haslemere.

A Horticultural Show had been an annual highlight in the summer of each year from 1870, and proved an excellent means of outdoor social exchange.

Haslemere was becoming neighbourly, and held what were called Neighbourhood Parties, but even then neighbours recognised that there were some who must not be smacked on the shoulder, with a " Hullo, old boy !" No, the catechism was still taught with its insistence on respect where due, and most earnestly practised.

Wells had, until the late eighties, been the only source of water supply, apart from rain-water, since the Weysprings had been cut off or piped away. But about 1890, Mr. Hodgson granted leases to take water from the Pyle Well in Lower Street to two standpipes, and that system was multiplied and saw the century out.

The old Windmill which stood on Grayswood Hill, and had worked regularly until at least 1864, had been allowed by disuse to fall into a precarious condition. The owner of the Mill had, furthermore, transferred various portions to his watermill at Shottermill. No society for the preservation of Haslemere then existed, and the old Mill was pulled down as a ruin by 1888. The house now known as Higher Coombe was built soon after, close to the site of the old Mill.

Haslemere had reason to be grateful to another local family—the Penfolds—for the valuable gift in 1898 of a site and building designed as a Hospital, on Shepherds Hill.

The Penfolds were an old Haslemere family who, since the middle of the 17th century, had owned property on the adjacent Courts Hill. This Cottage Hospital served the needs of the district until 1923, when a larger building was erected by public subscription.

A few words may now be of interest about the local government. Haslemere had continued as a Borough until 1832, when the loss of Parliamentary representation occurred, and courts leet were still held in respect of manorial affairs until 1839; after which, by common consent of Lord and suitors, the courts were discontinued. There is no record of a court Baron since 1694, so we can realise that more control was being exercised increasingly by the magistrates' courts. From 1839-68 parish control rested with Hambledon District Council acting through local overseers and the Chiddingfold Vestry. From 1863, when Haslemere was constituted a parish, the Parish Vestry, which consisted of two parish overseers, one guardian and one way warden, exercised control in the Haslemere Parish, together with the Rector and any nearby magistrate ex-officio.

In 1894, the new Local Government Act resulted in the formation of a Parish Council for Haslemere, in which so many councillors were elected per 100 of the population. The new Council were to do the work previously divided between the Board of Guardians and the Highway Board. Breaches of the peace were the responsibility of the local constabulary under the magistracy. The first Parish Council were a representative selection :

> Stewart Hodgson, gentleman,
> Turner Bridger, auctioneer and estate agent,
> Allen Chandler, barrister,
> James Sturt Edgeler, saddler,
> Peter Aylwin, chemist,
> John Moorey, bricklayer,
> John Wornham Penfold, architect and surveyor,
> R. W. Winstanley, surgeon,
> W. S. A. Ardagh, surgeon and physician.

Sir Robert Hunter was elected by the Council as first Chairman.

Two years later the " Surrey Times " printed the following : " No parish council in the county has done better work than the Haslemere council. Sanitation, allotments, charities, lighting, roads, footpaths and waste lands have all been thoroughly but prudently looked after, and the burden thrown upon the ratepayer in the shape of a rate for Parish Council purposes has been limited to ½d. in the pound. A better combination of efficiency with economy could not be wished for, or hoped for. The result is due to the spirit in which the members of a thoroughly representative council have worked together and, above all, to the invaluable help accorded by Sir Robert Hunter as Chairman."

A notable cultural experiment was the work done locally by Sir Jonathan Hutchinson, first in his Museum and secondly in the popular lectures which he gave Sunday by Sunday on many subjects. To illustrate his talks, he began, as previously stated, a collection of specimens of the structure and activities of living things and of the world in general. This collection grew so largely that he provided more suitable housing in 1895 and engaged a curator in 1897, Mr. E. W. Swanton, who continued in office till 1947. The growth of this Museum and of the idea at its root has still further enlarged, as will be noted in the next chapter.

Alfred Lord Tennyson lived at Aldworth, which he had built, for some years until his death in 1892. He received visits from friends and notabilities and members of the Royal Family, but made few local contacts. The house here was an escape from the relative publicity of Farringford. He not infrequently visited the annual Horticultural Show in the Lythe Hill grounds, and might be seen on occasional walks over Blackdown, or at Haslemere Station.

It is related in " Field Paths and Green Lanes " that a local rustic, on being asked where was Mr. Tennyson's house, replied, " Tennyson ?" and again, " Tennyson ? I never heer'd tell of that name." The last journey, at dusk, on a farm cart flanked by torch-bearers, which took him through the streets of Haslemere en route for Westminster Abbey, must have brought home to the least intelligent onlooker some insight of the greatness of the Lion who had chosen a retreat near their little town.

By the Jubilee year of 1897 the population of Haslemere had reached the 2,000 mark. The Jubilee itself was celebrated with a carnival procession, fireworks and a bonfire on Haste Hill, and an enormous beacon fire on Hindhead composed of 14,000 faggots.

In the next year, the Pound for stray cattle, which had been closed for about twenty years, was re-opened for the reception of stray horses. The hogs, of which we heard much at the beginning of the century, seem all to have been eaten, or their descendants educated to less wandering habits. In this year also the Haslemere Town Hall, as it now was more often called, was given by Mr. Hodgson to the Parish Council.

Through these closing years of the century a revival of Peasant Arts and Crafts had been occurring. Joseph King had started in 1894 a weaving industry, his work-place being in the meadow below Foundry Cottage, to which at that date access was only by a blind country lane. In 1898, Godfrey Blount founded a Peasant Art Society in Derby Road, which taught and made a wide range of products. Early in the new century two further industries, Weaving and Woodworking, were begun in the Foundry Meadow, a Pottery at Hammer in 1901, and another Weaving Works in College Hill for altar cloths in 1903.

CHAPTER XI

To These Present Times

The new century was ushered in by the South African War and the death of Queen Victoria. Haslemere took passing notice by suitable celebrations, but in more orderly fashion than of old. The annual fairs were no longer cattle affairs, but purely pleasure events. Until 1876 a considerable number of cattle had been brought for sale and there was little or no merrymaking. But now sideshows, swings and roundabouts filled the High Street, made holes in the roads, needed the drafting of special police, and in September there were about 2,000 people merrymaking in the High Street at 8.30 p.m.

The following year the fair was moved to a field off Tanners Lane, and a little later, back nearer the town, till September, 1906, when another move was made and the first fair on Clay Hill was held, where it has since been. The weekly markets are stated to have been well attended about 1885, but had gradually lapsed with the fairs.

Still waters are alleged to run deep, and one glimpse of the deep occurred in 1892 when, at Shottermill, police had to be called in to disperse people who were playing what is called Rough Music, an old method of public disapproval of wife beating. A second glimpse is given in March, 1900, when a case against several Haslemere Hotels was heard at the magistrates' courts. Evidence was given that Shovehalfpenny and Tip-it had been played for money stakes at the White Horse, the Swan and the Good Intent Inns, and Tip-it or Coddam at the White Lion.

Cricket continued with enthusiasm on the so-called Recreation Ground to the north-west of Pound Corner till 1923, when the Haslemere Hospital was built on that site and cricket and other games were transferred to the field on the hill south of Haslemere (opposite the entrance to Redcourt) which was acquired as a War Memorial.

By 1903 the population of Haslemere Parish had risen to 2,650, and the appointment of a new Town Crier was canvassed. In due course a Mr. Chrisopher Elliott applied for the post and was duly appointed.

A further consequence of the increase of population was the need for a new church. As a result of generous subscriptions St. Christopher's was built.

Now came the era of interminable discussions over the water supply, more adequate drainage, and the dangerous and narrow strait of Penfolds Corner*.

A Gas Undertaking had flourished in Haslemere since 1869, and in 1880 the Church was so lighted. This company named a new terrace in what is now King's Road as Gashouse Terrace, but, with the new century, had to meet competition from an Electricity Company, which by 1905 could number 66 customers who had bravely exchanged gas or lamp for the new and, perhaps one might say, match-less light, but electricity was only available in Haslemere from 1910.

Cesspool or bucket sanitation until 1905 was the high-water mark of local sanitary efficiency; in fact, one hotel had a cesspool in the cellar, but the local death rate from typhoid and diphtheria threw considerable doubt on some of the methods. A story related during a parish council meeting recounted that a resident, showing a friend over his house, came to the cesspool and pointed with pride at it. He remarked that its great advantage lay in the fact that it never wanted cleaning out, for the well was close by.

Of some local interest were the deaths, within a week of each other in 1905, of two old Haslemere worthies, aged 99 years, William Upfold and William Oakford, who were both born on July 23rd, 1806, and were actively associated with the old Fair when in the High Street, and in their old age were in proud possession of health and faculties.

With all the development in and around Haslemere more transport was needed, and new types of transport were tested. In 1906, between Haslemere and Farnham, a bus of 24 h.p. to carry 17 passengers was given trial. It attained a speed of 15 m.p.h., on the level and the tyres were solid. It was reported

---

* At that date a narrow lane.

to be not powerful enough for the hilly country. An electric tramway was proposed to do the same journey, but did not reach practical test.

About the same date a great democratic venture was started and, as is not unusual, was a little premature. Close to the station a certain Mr. Williamson opened a fried fish shop, but, after a few weeks, his hopes of easy money were dashed by the publishing of letter after letter in the local press of complaint against the nuisance. Arrivals by the 6.19 train, evidently then the chief patronised evening train, were greeted, not by the normal refreshing clarity of the Haslemere upland air, but by blasts of Whitechapel, etc. Letters also were printed from solicitors near and far, so that in the end Williamson, after a spell of Saturdays-only frying, gave up the struggle and the business of fried fish.

There followed a furious protesting letter from an evidently interested but unlearned person, which here follows in part : "That is Haslemere all over, they are like a schoolboy if one tries to get on better than the other they are down on him. So I think if Haslemere was packed up in a tin box and sent to the Room of Horrors and take some of the people with it, they would not be missed or wanted, but I hope they will not take the fried fish shop with it for that is what is wanted."

As a writer in the local handbook here said : "The 1735 plan of Haslemere is interesting in showing the locality of the old Town Hall and Pillory, both of them long since vanished, etc." But the plan is interesting also for another reason, for it showed conclusively how comparatively small had been the growth of Haslemere during the past two centuries. "While Grayshott has sprung up on the spur of Hindhead, whilst the slopes above Shottermill have become dotted with red brick villas, Haslemere itself has managed to retain much of its old-world aspect." These words were written about 1914 and by that date Haslemere had passed another stage in its life. Its distance from London and position in a so far unspoilt countryside, retaining a sufficiency of traditional charm and yet furnished with many modern amenities, had made Haslemere a paradise for the mélange of culture, achievement and wealth, who attended church parade week by week, in carriage or gig, at the Parish Church and made the unending round of social calls during the busy weeks. The first World War broke this crust, compelling all to work together for the security of home and country. The post-war Haslemere began slowly to stretch building tentacles into the surrounding lanes and fields, between a number of larger estates which still maintained their integrity.

In 1913, Haslemere was promoted from Parish Council status to that of Urban District Council; and the more usual accompaniments of urban life were soon in evidence.

The electrification of the London-Portsmouth railway in 1937 had helped to popularise the district with a new class of people. Commuters, as they are called, or in more common speech, daily breaders, of whatever rank, found the distance from London, now only one hour by numerous trains, was no hindrance to working in fug or fog, and returning to sleep in fresh air.

The inter-war years were full years in local life; cricket improved and regained popularity with the infusion of new blood, the provision of better pitches, and the enthusiastic presidency of Mr. F. A. Oldaker.

Football clubs sprang up in several parts of the Haslemere district, which benefited from the competitive stimulus of local leagues. The Bowls Club came to new life on the Recreation Ground; still on the same hill as in the 17th century, but more to the east of the old green.

Youth clubs of all sorts, church, scout, sea-scouts, air training and the rifle club, all have lined up with the old forces in the greystone Church on the hill, to promote discipline, loyalty and citizenship.

The Haslemere Pantomime continued its remarkable annual successes, with eight crowded performances by enthusiastic producers, players and audiences. A highly successful operatic society, under the leadership of Mr. William Muir, carried on the work of the Choral Society which had given its first production in 1874, and gratified hundreds more people with an annual production of Gilbert and Sullivan.

The Musical Society played an important part in raising the local standard of musical appreciation, by offering concerts of graded music, together with chamber music concerts.

Various plays were staged in the Haslemere Hall, more often than not with the help of Mr. Allen Chandler, jnr., as producer.

During and since the second world war, there have been several additional companies of local players who have given of their best to counter war fatigue and post-war disillusion.

The development of the work at the Haslemere Museum has shown a quiet but striking growth. From its small beginnings at Inval in a private garden, the Museum was transferred to, and housed in, at the founder's expense, a range of one-storied timbered rooms, on a site above East Street. In 1926, thirteen years after the death of Sir J. Hutchinson, the Museum Trustees raised sufficient funds to buy "The Lodge" in High Street.

To this building, which incorporated remnants of the old "Burgage House," were transferred the contents of the Museum. Since that date the new Museum has benefited from many valuable and interesting gifts. From 1897-1947, as previously stated, the Curator was E. W. Swanton, A.L.S., who was privileged to work closely with the founder for his first seventeen years of office. In 1913 Swanton collaborated with P. Woods, C.B., in the preparation of an authoritative record of Haslemere, now out of print, called "Bygone Haslemere."

Through all the years, the Museum has maintained the aim of its founder as an Educational Museum, by stressing the experimental and comparative approach to Museum collections and specimens.

Exhibits of local plants, which are growing at any given season will be found in the Hall. Many working models for various crafts are on show, together with an observation beehive. Local Crafts, peasant and otherwise, archæology and geology are well displayed, as also many bird and insect specimens.

For many years past, children from local schools have visited for demonstrations and talks, handling objects and small animals. Now children come from fifty-six schools in Surrey, twenty-seven schools in L.C.C. areas and many other counties for conducted demonstrations and instruction by the present curator, Mr. J. Clegg, and his assistant staff.

The gift by an anonymous donor of an extension to the grounds including two large and several small ponds, adjoining the Museum, has added notably to the study of fresh water biology.

This gift was rendered more valuable by the inclusion of a building, which has been converted into a field-laboratory for the use of teachers and students.

In 1933 there had been a threat to the Urban status of Haslemere. Envious eyes had sought its inclusion within another district. However, the case for the retention of its Urban power was ably presented by the Haslemere representatives, and Haslemere was allowed to continue its steady expansion with the subsequent inclusion of parts of the surrounding areas. But it had a narrow escape from a return to being a Rural District.

The war years 1939-45 resulted in Haslemere being scheduled as a safe area and therefore suitable for the reception of evacuees. Women and children from South London districts were billeted on usually welcoming hostesses, while hotels were filled to the last bed. Two departments of the Admiralty were transferred from the vulnerable Portsmouth area to the then empty Lythe Hill House and estate, which soon extended its borders to include Whitwell Hatch. Many of the Admiralty staff have accepted the convenience of accommodation in this area and have made their contribution to the education and entertainment of the town of their adoption.

A war memorial of the first World War stands in the centre of the town, now surrounded by a grass plot; the cars which once almost submerged it are banished to a vast new car park behind the High Street.

What the future holds in store behind the various curtains, Iron, Oil or Atomic, none can foresee; and as another writer put it, " The curtain of the future is always drawn."

The next stage for Haslemere must surely be to work for a re-grant of its ancient Borough status, which it lost in 1832 owing to internal decay.

If encouragement be needed in local or even in national life, we may call to memory the lines written by Bunyan on Mansoul : " For here lay the excellent wisdom of him that built Mansoul, that the walls could never be broken down, nor hurt by the most adverse potentate, unless the townsmen gave consent thereto."

And so, after reading the story of this little town, we look to the future with justified confidence, remembering also Mr. Churchill's words in 1940.

Come then, let us go forward together with our united strength.

POPULATION OF HASLEMERE PARISH

About 1800	642	
1842	840	
1897	2,000	
1903	2,650	
1921	3,865	
1931	4,340	
1933	10,000	including some new areas
1954	11,740	present U.D.C. area

LISTS OF NAMES

These lists of names are placed together as an appendix, in order to avoid breaking the continuity of the history.

The lists are those, chiefly, of local inhabitants who were taxable. It should be remembered that there were a number of inhabitants, at all dates, who could not be taxed on account of poverty.

These persons, therefore, should be taken into account in trying to form any estimate of population.

However, it will be of interest to many, to note the names appearing as generation succeeded generation.

EXCHEQUER LAY SUBSIDY 184/4
6 EDWARD III. 1331-2

A tax of 1/10th in the case, as this, of Ancient Demesne; the tax being levied upon movables.

Robert de Stotele

Roger Haselhore

Alice de Pokshudde

Richarde le Stede

Matilda Watman

Richard Piperham

John le Tornour

Richard, son of
    Alice Piperham

Richard Wateman

Richard atte Rodgate

William le Taillour

Richard Poghelye

Agnes Poghelye

Richard Hondeleys

EXCHEQUER LAY SUBSIDY 184/29
4 RICHARD II. 1380-1

A Poll Tax at 12d. per head of population over 15 years of age.

Agnes Arwesmith

Thomas Bocher

Cristina, his wife

Richard Boxfold

Sybil, his wife

Thomas Breningfold

Isabel, his wife

Alice, his daughter

Robert, the son of
    John Scoter

Richard Burghurst

Alice, his wife

Alan Carpenter
Joane, his wife

Thomas Chesar
Agnes, his wife

Robert Chonnesone
Matilda, his wife

Richard Comsifold
Matilda, his wife

William Comsifold
Isabel, his wife

John Gace
Isabel, his wife

Henry Goudegrom
Eleanor, his wife

John Goudewyn Senr.
Julia, his wife

John Goudewyn
Alice, his wife

Richard atte Hall
Margery, his wife
Matilda, his daughter

Richard Haselour
Matilda, his wife
Isabel, the mother

Thomas Hertes
Alice, his wife

John Mapelderwell
Isabel, his wife

John Marion
Isabel, his wife

Walter Piperham
Joane, his wife

John Prinz
Agnes, his wife

Henry Sadeler
Isabel, his wife

John Smith
Joane, his wife

John Stottele
Gunhilda, his wife

William Tanner
Margery, his wife

John   ⎱ Servants
Richard ⎰ 4d.

WOODS MSS. LOSELEY DEEDS. RENTAL

2 Hy VII 1486

Borgage of Hasylmere		12¼d.
John Alyn	la Boteys ante portam	2d.
	Gardino voc le Pyle	4d.
John Bocher	Clammerhyl	7d.
	le Ball	6d.
	Crowchredon	6d.
Henry Boxfold	Old Haselmere	4d.
	Dunceodd	1d.
William Boxfold	Colleges	12d.
William Covert	Imbham	9/4d.

John Faryndon	Whitwelle	5/6d.
	Stedland	3/4d.
John Faryndon	Old Hasylmere	12d.
John atte Felde de Petworth	Medefeld	2/2d.
John Gase	Berfeld	5/4d.
	Halland	2/0d.
	Chounsons	2/2d.
	Old Hasylmere	8d.
William Kilby	Berkhurst	8d.
Henry Mapeldurwell	Sopers	8d.
John Osbern	Osbern's More	4d.
Richard Person	Boxfold's More	15d.
	Skatehunts	8d.
	Pylemede	2d.
William Penycod	Skitreadon	3/0d.
Stephen Penycod	Gate at Kilby	1d.
John Piperham	For his	5/0d.
Thomas Pope	Skitreadon	3/0d.
	Smythes	2/4d.
John Prynce	Shepehawys	8d.
Peter Quennell	Hatchers	4/5d.
	Steres	6/0d.
	Somersbury	4d.
John Stede	Whatmans	5/8d.
	Clammerhyll	16d.
John Wakeford	for his land	2/0d.
Thomas Wakeford	late of Wm. Neal	11d.
Richard Wassheford	Curfold	22d.
	Bunkers	8d.
John Westbroke	Imbhams	2/4d.

EXCHEQUER LAY SUBSIDY 184/138
16 HENRY VIII. 1524-5

	Value	Subsidy	Goods
Robert Aleyn	20/0d.	4d.	
William Aleyn	£6 13s. 4d.	3/4d.	,,
Thomas Billinghurst	£5	2/6d.	,,
William Byllinghurst	26/8d.	4d.	,,
John Boxfold	£5	2/6d.	,,
Thomas Boxfold	20/0d.	4d.	,,
William Boxfold	40/0d.	12d.	,,
Edward Brether	20/0d.	4d.	,,
John Burges	26/8d.	4d.	,,
Robert Chaundeler	£13 6s. 8d.	6/8d.	,,
Robert Chaundeler in next subsidy	20/0d.	4d.	,,
John Couper	60/0d.	8d.	,,
Richard Couper	60/0d.	8d.	"
Thomas Couper	20/0d.	4d.	Wages
Thomas Edsawe	£4	2/0d.	
George Farndell	40/0d.	12d.	Goods
Roger Foxe in next subsidy	20/0d.	4d.	Goods
Richard Lawborne	20/0d.	4d.	,,
Robert Marten	40/0d.	12d.	,,
William Payne	£6 13s. 4d.	3/4d.	,,
Henry Penycode	26/8d.	4d.	,,
Stephen Penycode	£16 6s. 8d.	8/2d.	,,
Thomas Penycode	33/4d.	4d.	,,
Richard Person	60/0d.	18d.	
Richard Pope	20/0d.	4d.	,,
Thomas Pope	£4	2/0d.	
John Raynold	40/0d.	12/0d.	,,
Thomas Stede	£4	2/0d.	,,
John Taylour	20/0d.	12d.	Lands
Thomas Turner	20/0d.	4d.	Wages
John Weler	40/0d.	12d.	Goods

ELIZABETHAN MUSTER ROLL.

II ELIZABETH 1569

against the Catholic rising in the North of England

Persons to supply arms since 10th May. II Elizabeth

Robert Chaundeler for £10 in goods	bowes	1
	sheaf of arrows	1
	scull	1
	blackbyll	1
Stephen Penycode for £10 in goods	bowes	1
	sheaf of arrows	1
	scull	1
	blackbyll	1
The common Armourer there	Almainer	1
	bowes	1
	sheaf of arrows	1
	scull	1
	blackbyll	1

Haslemere
Billmen of ye best sort —

Richard a Pulford	John Ocklie
John Bridger	Steven Bridger
Ryc. Boxehold	Henry Hopkin
Walter Gase	James Begley
John Corte	

Billmen of the second sort —

Thomas Mower	Ryc. Osborne
George Bright	Willm. Fachen
Wm. Denier	Peter Kempe
Henry Baker	John Ffarnden
Tho. Talbot	

Bowmen of ye best sort —

John Bradfold
John Haselgrove
Wilm. Hulat
George Wakeford
Tho. Penicod

Henry Allen	goods	£3
George Baker	goods	£3
John Billinghurst at Townsend		£4 lands
Paul Clifton	goods	£3
John Cobden gent.		£4 lands
Robert Collins	goods	£3
Anne Fielder widow		£3
Michael Gase	goods	£3
John Hughes	goods	£3
Richard Leonard	goods	£3
Robert Lusher gent.	goods	£5
George Owton	goods	£3
John Steede		£4 lands
Francis Teeling		£3 lands
Thomas Welland	goods	£3
Richard West	goods	£4

HEARTH TAX

Exchequer Lay Subsidy 188/481 — 1663

HASELMORE BOROUGH

William Alberry	3	William Lander	4
William Baxter	4	William Lander	4
Robert Billinghurst	2	John Lake	2
Widow Boxall	4	Nicholas Levett	1
Richard Bradfold	2	William Markes	4
Robert Bradfold	1	George Osborne, gent.	4
Nicholas Bridger	5	Thomas Overington	1
John Carter	2	Thomas Philips	1
Thomas Chalcroft	2	William Rapley	3
John Dudman	3	William Ryde	4
Thomas Dudman	7	Widow Shipsoe	1
William Durrant	5	John Shudd	3
John Eade	3	Henry Snelling	3
John Gase	1	Laurence Sturt	3
Michael Gase	2	Edward Underhill	3
Oliver Gase	2	Edward Upton	2
Richard Gase	6	Nicolas Valler	1
Richard Harryson	3	Henry Watkinson, gent.	6
John Hart	2	Henry Watkinson, gent.	5
Joane Haselgrove	4	Henry Welland	2
Peter Hull, gent.	3	Robert Wilkins	2
Roger Jackson	2	Richard Yalden	5
Harry Keene	1	Thomas Yalden	2

HASELMORE BOROUGH — Not Chargeable

Matthew Bidwell	2		Thomas Foorde	2
William Bridda	1		Joan Friben	1
Robert Bridger	1		Thomas Hardy	2
ger	2		Alice Heath widdow	2
John Bridger	2		Richard Mant	1
Agnis Bridger	1		John Matticks	2
Elizabeth Browne	1		Thomas Mayne	3
Thomas Clarke	2		Elizabeth Mirrion	1
Andrew Clarke	2		John Norman	1
John Clarke	1		E. Norman	1
Thomas Combes	1		James Quennell	1
John Day	1		Thomas Quennell	2
William Denyer	2		William Summers	1
Anne Downe	1		Stephen Swetman	2
John Ede	1		Abraham Upfold	2
Widow Fagin	2		Peter West	1
William Fagin	1		James Wilson	2
Robert Fagin	1			
Thomas Fagin	1		John Hart — Constable	

HASELMORE TYTHING
i.e., parish outside the borough

Persons chargeable

John Billinghurst	1		Henry Holte	2
Robert Billinghurst	!		John Kent	4
John Boxall	3		Jane Lines	2
Robert Broadfold	5		Richard Lushur	4
William Broadfold	3		John Lunne	1
John Carter	1		James Osburne	4
William Collen	3		Thomas Penycod	3
James Courte	3		Thomas Phillips	3
John Edsall	4		William Upton	1
John Farneden	3		Augustine Wakeford	2
Charles Fauchin	2		Richard West	5
James Gresham Esq.	7		Henry White	!
William Haselgrove	1		Richard Yalden	1

Not chargeable

a	Buse widow	1		Miles	1
	Chalcroft	1		Pannell	1
	Courtes	1	Ch.	Parry	1
	Downes	1		widow	1
A	Fuller	1		Augustine Wakeford	1
Abigail	Gammon	1		lyning	1
	widow			alen	1
	Jenner	1			1
	Jenner widow	1			1
	Miles	1			1

A certificate of the names of all known persons
dwelling within the Parish of Haslemere 16th August, 1739
An aid of a land tax

Mr. Yalden
Mr. Wakeford for his house
      him for his meadow
Peter Bennett for Skitreadons
      him for Mr. Tanner's
      him for Holdfast
William Dudman for Mr. Tanners
      him for his house
      him for Witley Farm
James Osborne for the tithes
      him for lands late Lushers
      him for his other lands
John Lucas for Mr. Smith's
Thomas Glasier
George Snelling
      him for Southlands
Thomas Bicknell
Mr. Simmons
      him and Thomas Wakeford
Mr. Sparkes and John Maunt
Joan Upton, widow
John Courts for Sturt
George Chandler
John Coombs senr.
Mr. Undershell for his three houses
      his lands called Skatehunts
      him and John Marshal
Edmund Berry
William Miles and Thomas Stedman
Mr. Veneer and Doctor Coleman
John Habens for Henry Courts
      him for Sopers
      him for his two houses
      him for "Ye Red Cow"
Edmund Upton for his house and land
Mr. Cobden for his house and land
      him and J. Varndell
      him and James Glasier

Mr. Cobden for Chickhams and Somersbury
Richard Sayers for his two farms
      him for The Swan
      him for his other tenements
William Upton for his house
      him for his stock
Doctor Coleman
Widow Mitchell
Mr. Billinghurst for Whatmans and Balaams
      him for Collards
John Billinghurst for his house
      him for his malt house
      him for old Haslemere
Jane Ride and William Bradfold
      her for Pilewell Mead
William Ride for the White Hart
Mr. Yalden junr. for Roundabouts
William White
Mr. Tanner for his house
      him for Steadland
      him for Whitwell
Mrs. Mellish and Thomas Martin
Doctor Miles for Loves
William Hack for Balls
Noah Bromham for Osborn's Moor
William Briant and William Ride
Robert Mills
William Bradfold
William Ride junr. Innholder, and Mr. Woods
Moorey Baxter and John Fielder
      him for William Morley
      him for his house
      him for his stock
Noah Brumham and Richard Chittey
Jean Dudman and Joseph Frogley
John Billinghurst for Scotlands
James Marshal for Mr. Luffs
Elizabeth Ride for Ye Deane
      her for Ye George
John Dudman for his house
      him for Meadfields
Thomas Denyer and John Witcher
George Denyer
      him for Money
Joan Carter
John Grevatt

William Bradfold and William Read
Mr. Woodger
William Ride — blacksmith
     him for his other tenements
William Read for his house
Richard Smither
     him for his house
William Upfold
George Denyer and Robert Billinghurst
Richard Maidman and Thomas Sayers
William Wheeler
John Fielder and William Ride
William Morley and John Valler
Moorey Baxter and Jane Hull
Richard Valler and ye
  Widow Phillips
John Overington
William Bristow
William Haselgrove
John Jackson
John Chase
William Chitty
William Burt and John Buckle
John Shudd
John Hardy
Mr. Randall
Mr. Brooks for his salary
Robert Philips and Doctor Coleman
William Ride for his shop
Jane Ride for Pilewell House
William Coleman for his house and meadow
The Lessors of Ye Shambles and other profits of the
  Town
Margaret Woods
Jeremiah Cox
Henry Court
James Costen
Mr. Douglas and William Mills
Doctor Myles and William Ride
Jane Ride for her house and field
John Hunt

INDEX

L

Lane End Farm, 80.
Launder, John, 30.
Layfield, John, 51.
Lee, Christopher, 87.
Lilley's Garden (Fleur de Lis), 30.
Lloyd, 36.
Lonecock, Thomas, 14, 15.
Longhurst, 7.
    William de, 6.
Loves, 74.
Lower Courts Farm, 80.
Lower Street, 61.
Lowther, Sir James, 65, 86
Lucas, John, 79.
    James, 77.
Luff, 65.
Luke, the Clerk, 6.
Lurgashall, 4.
Lusher, George, 29.
    Robert, 29, 51.
    William, 49.
Lynch, 37.
Lyte, John, 15.
Lythe Hill, 74.
    Farm, 21, 32, 44, 56, 66, 70,
       77, 79.
    House, 92.

M

Madgwick, 15, 60.
    Thomas, 79.
Malt House, 72.
Manor House (Three Gates Lane),
    49, 50, 54.
Marchant, 9.
Market, 5, 20 and 21, 25, 39.
Market House, 21, 23, 44, 45, 62,
    72, 74, 77, 88.
Marley, 2.
Marks, 57.
Martin, Thomas, 60.
Matthews, Jane, 72.
Mayne, Thomas, 53.
Meadfields, 7, 13, 21, 31, **78**.
Meadfield, Jocelyn de, 6.
    Nicholas de, 6.
Mellersh, 27, 31, 74.
Meredith, Sarah, 36.
    William, 36.
Midhurst, 55.
Middleton, Lord, 87.
Mill, 15.
Miles, 21, 30.
    Dr. Middleton, 74, 81.
Milland, 3.

Mitchell, 28.
    John, 66, 77.
    Robert, 79.
Molyneux, Mr., 64, 65.
Moorey, John, 95.
More, Sir G., 40, 43, 61.
Morley, William, 74, 78.
Mount, 57.
Muir, William, 101.
Museum, 93, 96, 102.
Musters, Elizabethan, 39
Mutt, John, 62.

N

Neale, John, 71.
Newland, John, 51.
New House, 50, 79.
Newspapers, 41.
Nicholls, Mr., 64.
Norman, John, 49
Normans, 5.
Northdown, 6.
Northlands, 15.

O

Oakford, William, 99.
Oaklands, 28, 61, 66.
Ockley, John, 35.
Okes, 26, 49, 75.
Oglethorpe, Genl. James, 62, 63,
    64, 69.
    Theophilus, 62.
Old Jones, 46.
Onslow, 62, 69.
Osborn, James, 70, 77, 79.
    John, 49, 57.
Overington, 45, 57.
    John, 71.
Owlden, 92.

P

Page, 9.
Pannell, Stephen, 91.
Parish, end of 18th Century, **85**.
Parish House, 72, 82.
Parliamentary News, 61-64, 65.
Parson, Robert, 36, 37.
Passfield Common, 3.
Paupers, Rules for, 57.
Penfold, Frances, 77.
    M., 89.
    J. William, 95.
Penycode, 15, 21, 29, 31.
Penycode's, 49, 50.

HASLEMERE
1850-1950

G. R. ROLSTON

Dedication

TO THE SEVERAL FAMILIES
WHO HAVE LED HASLEMERE
THROUGH THE PAST CENTURY,
MANY OF WHOM FIND MENTION
AND NOT LEAST TO
A. J. DIGGLE, M.B.E.
CHAIRMAN, HASLEMERE URBAN DISTRICT COUNCIL
WHO HAS STEERED THE GOOD
SHIP HASLEMERE FOR THE PAST
THIRTEEN YEARS, 1951-1963.

CONTENTS

Illustrations

PREFACE

Since the very pleasant reception of my first book "Haslemere in History," I was encouraged (I might fairly say commanded) by the late Miss Agnes Hutchinson not to overlook details of the past century. "You have not said much about the years which I have lived through, and which have been such years of development." This was fair comment, though in a book which attempted to scan eight hundred years of history even in a small place, I had earlier felt that each succeeding century should, if possible, have a fair share of interest. This book is an attempt to remedy the lack of which Agnes Hutchinson (forthright member of a talented local family) spoke.

I have tried to show the development during the years from 1850 to the present time of our small town from sleepy village to busy commuter area. I have tried to give a picture of the lives of the people during that time and of how they lived and sometimes worked.

Not much can be said in this book of houses. Such must be reserved with notes of their occupants to perhaps a future book.

Memories of many inhabitants dead and still living, in addition to written or printed records, have helped me to build my story.

The method of telling the tale is by approximate decades, wherein there will be references to people and events, forwards and backwards as the tale unfolds.

This method I prefer to the water-tight compartment system, where church, town, business, council have their independent sections. The meal by such a method may be bulky and filling, but does not commend itself to me for a realisation of communal progress.

Such as it is, please take my book with my good wishes for a better understanding and love of our town, and leave it at the end with some regret.

G. R. ROLSTON.

Bambers, Haslemere.
November 1964.

The first decade opens with a glimpse of the first of a series of characters whom I hope to conjure up. This old man's life had covered most of the reign of George III, George IV, William IV and the early quarter of Victoria.

Acknowledgments

Acknowledgments are due to:

> Haslemere Museum, for facilities for consulting
>
> Annual Volumes of St. Bartholomew's Church.
>
> Parish Magazines.
>
> Newspaper Cuttings.
>
> Newspaper Cuttings of the late W. A. Sillick.
>
> Diary of late Miss Harrison.
>
> Past records of Haslemere Urban District Council.
>
> I am grateful for the memories of many people whom I have
> met during my past forty years in Haslemere.

The illustrations are from photographs from Haslemere Museum,
and a few of my own collection, and were made by Colin G.
Futcher, Haslemere. Mr. F. O. Meddows Taylor of Farnham has, as
with my previous books, been of constant assistance in production.

CHAPTER I

Setting the Stage

LOCAL CUSTOMS — RIOTS AND MURDER — RAILWAY
NEW POET LAUREATE — ENCLOSURES — EARLY POST

HE WAS GROWING OLD and he knew it at last that there was no
escape. For many years he had happily deluded himself, as he
divested himself of some of the heavier part of his work, that he
was as young as ever. Certainly he retained an alert, keen, outlook, and his looks did not pity him, but the keen relish with
which he had for so long tackled each new day's recurring problems, that almost impish zest, was now gone. It was a dull cold
morning, one of those with a grey sky and bitter wind, and he
hoped as he stood at his door looking up and down the High
Street of Haslemere, that old Mr. Fauntleroy at Churt would not
require a visit today. It was a bleak and unsheltered journey to
cross the open heaths of Hindhead on a day like this and, after
all, he was eighty years of age. He turned back again into the
house as his daughter Emma came down the stairs and took him
in to breakfast. Dr. Gordon was still hale and upright in spite
of his age and enjoyed, when the weather was fine, the journeys
he made to his remaining patients. He had lived at the White
House* for a great many years, over forty in fact, since the death
of his wife, with his only daughter, Emma, as his housekeeper.

Just as breakfast was finished, a maid came in with the
letters and an apology from Miss Sara Upton, the old Postmistress
who lived across the High Street. She said the mail had been late
arriving at Liphook, and George Timms, the postman, had only
just come in, after walking over as usual with the mail.

After a few minutes silence, broken only by the sound of
knives opening a fresh letter, the old Doctor gave an exclamation
of surprise as he read to his daughter. His correspondent said that
the vacancy caused by the death of William Wordsworth as Poet
Laureate had been offered to, and accepted by a young man, Alfred
Tennyson, who had come into public favour by a poem, "The
Princess" and, still more recently, by "In Memoriam." Emma, however, though agreeing that the author of "The Princess" must be
a most worthy successor to the Lakeland poet, had other news. A

*Georgian Hotel

friend of hers writing from the village of Kensington, wrote that in Hyde Park near them, a vast area of the parkland was being covered with great iron scaffoldings. This was to be the skeleton of enormous glass houses for a great exhibition of industry and crafts in 1851. Then, as her father left the table, she went off to her boudoir to peruse a new novel dealing with social problems, by C. L. Kingsley, called "Alton Locke."

A little later, Dr. Gordon left his house, and went down the High Street past the Angel Inn cottages to the next large stone-faced house* where his friend Dr. Bishop lived. Not finding him at home, he walked on past several little shops and the Swan Inn till he came to the foot of Shepherds Hill, where he had a few words with the blacksmith. He then turned along Pylewell Road past the Swan orchards, and paid a visit to Thomas Penfold, a young man whose health had not been satisfactory for some time. After the consultation, and having given reassuring and, he hoped, helpful advice, he made his way across the road to Shottermill and, as he entered Tanners Lane, noticed as usual the smell from the now disused tanpits behind Sheepskin House. At the end of the lane, passing Mr. Mitchell's house, he came to Church Hill Farm, a fine old half timbered farmhouse just past the church. It looked across the church green at its red brick neighbour, whose relative youth seemed starkly fresh against the mellowed timbering of the old farm house. He had a tiresome call here: the lady of the house was at a difficult age and had little outlet for her undoubted energy. Having no family of her own, her interest was focussed on the lives of others. Her husband, in addition to occasional parochial duties when his brother-in-law, the local curate, was otherwise engaged, also farmed the Peperham and Church Hill estate. As an old friend, Dr. Gordon had often been able to resolve small tensions which could have been alarming both within and without the household.

As he left the house again and turned down the hill to the little bridge, he stopped for a moment to absorb the pleasant view. Away beyond the Church Hill ponds, the slopes of Wiggins Farm were just showing a little green, as the corn was beginning to spread a carpet towards the houses flanking the High Street. Beyond the Town and upon Shepherds Hill were the fields, some green with old pastures, some newly ploughed, as those of the Half Moon Farm stretching over the top of the hill to the south. He felt rested by the familiar sight and, after leaving the little bridge, turned off along the Pathfields.

After lunch the old man retired to his study to read The Times and perhaps enjoy a short nap. He could not concentrate much

_____

*Now shops.

to-day and, as he listened to the wind now howling round the house, another picture came before him. Away back in 1807, he and his wife had had a ball on New Year's Eve and among the guests was the charming wife of Capt. Charles Lydiard, R.N., then away in the Channel fleet. About midnight a fierce tattoo was heard on the front door and a messenger, mud-bespattered from hard riding through the wild night, brought terrible news. Speaking first to Dr. Gordon, he told how in a most tremendous gale in the Channel two days before, Capt. Lydiard's ship had been wrecked off South Cornwall. The Captain with many others had been drowned. So the Doctor had the unhappy task of breaking the news to Mrs. Lydiard, and presumably assisting her to her home at Meadfields. It gave him a wildly sardonic pleasure to recall the last line of the magnificent marble memorial which now stood in the church, "To the best of husbands"; but she had remarried and survived her second even now, twenty years later. Here a very slight snore punctuated his reminiscences. The kaleidoscope went on as he remembered the hurry and grief on the day when, in the garden behind the tall pillared house further up the street, a small boy was drowned. The eldest son of a clergyman who had bought the Great House* he was drowned in an ornamental pond in the garden overlooking the valley, in the year that the young Queen had come to the throne. It was quite true, too, that he didn't like those unsuitable little iron pillars that young Chapman, the curate, had managed to get put in place of the good old oak arches and pillars at the church. There was a fellow if you like, who was always pushing into things and altering them, but to his credit he certainly had made a wonderful display of all sorts of fireworks for the village children in his garden at the top of the town at the Coronation. Now they had the Rector living at the Great House, and no doubt he had been proud to look out of his windows and see old Wm. Tidey and Martha Gibson marching at the head of the schoolchildren, when the National School was transferred from the Town Hall to the new School up by the Church—proud because he had been largely responsible for building the new school out of a barn. The thought of the Town Hall reminded him of the days when the elections for Parliamentary candidates were held there, and he had often been bailiff of the Town, and wasn't it in '25 that he had been called away from a Parish Meeting for a surgical operation? Now they had the two pest houses for infectious cases, on the Grayswood and Midhurst roads, though it had been difficult at times to get a nurse to go there with a patient. At this point he lost the threads of the argument in front of the meeting, as someone interrupted his remarks.

*Haslemere Museum.

He began tapping on the table with his gavel to bring the meeting to an end, and, as he opened his eyes, he saw his daughter Emma smiling at him. She had been tapping at the door and, receiving no reply, had come in to tell him that tea was ready. As he went down the passage he remembered the old words—"and your old men shall dream dreams."

Two years later, one early October morning, he woke as he thought, to the sound of a well-remembered voice. "It's all right, Martha, I'm coming," he said, and fell back on the bed unconscious. It was his last call, from which he did not return.

HASLEMERE IN THE mid-nineteenth century was a sleepy little town, so sleepy in the hollow of the gorse and heather covered heathlands of Hindhead and Blackdown that it had almost forgotten the proud days when it was a Borough.

The Borough, which had elected two members of Parliament for three hundred years, included the High Street and small portions of East Street, Shepherds Hill and Lower Street. Its total area had been only about forty acres, but it had been honoured with a Bailiff, a Constable and, at one time, a Swordbearer; the bailiff being privileged to hold a manor court and the parliamentary elections in the upper room of the old Town or Market Hall. The Manorial privileges were, of course, dependents of the great Manor of Godalming. Now all glory was gone, and the little town slept, perhaps dreaming at times of a greater future. Some lines written within a few years by a settler from a hardier part of England, after a visit to the parish church, may serve to make a picture:—

> "Long had stood the old Church building,
> Old and dreary, dark and mouldy,
> And an old man droned within it,
> And the old Clerk droned responses,
> And a droning people followed."

May day was apparently no longer celebrated with maypole dancing, as at several of the surrounding villages. Children visited local houses with garlands early on May Day before school, singing

> "This first day of May is Garland Day,
> So please you remember my garland, my
> garland,
> So please you remember my garland."

Bonfire night, the feast of Guy Fawkes, was marked by the lighting of a huge bonfire on Shepherds Hill above the Market House, when there was a plentiful banging of home-made squibs.

Other notable days were the festival of the Patron Saint, St. Bartholomew on August 25th, and the two annual fairs which then still attracted farm produce. A little old woman from Northchapel would bring home-made ginger bread which had a ready sale. The annual Club day in early June was the occasion for a procession through the town from the place of assembly, led by Bridger's Band. Members wore a bunch of pink and blue ribbons in their hats and proceeded to the church from which, after a service, they returned to the King's Arms Hotel for a gigantic lunch. Such a feast for one hundred and fifty members is noted as costing £29.15.11d., a sum which included beer, music and tobacco. In procession again sometime after the meal, headed by the band and bearing a number of beautifully painted flags, visits were made to the houses of nearby gentry. At this time many of the Club members would be dressed as soldiers, sailors or grotesque women. Dancing among the booths in the Town Square helped to round off later proceedings and promote digestion of the great luncheon. These processions faded out with the formation of branches of national clubs such as Foresters, etc. The two ancient fairs still attracted cattle and farm produce in May and September, and side shows, swings, roundabouts and hucksters provided fun for the considerable crowds which still gathered. During the summer, a few cricket matches were played, at this date, of course, on Haste Hill Common.

A Harvest Supper receives mention at this date, probably on a parish basis, for the local priest might have been called a squarson, in that he combined the attributes of local Parson with that of Squire of a fair amount of farm land. This parson, Hesse, who at that time was Rector of Chiddingfold (with Haslemere as a curacy) had been instituted in 1838. He had been infected, as had many thoughtful people then, with the need for direction and help in the daily lives of much of the population. Away in 1834, Poor Laws which had remained with few major changes since 1601, were reorganised, and groups of parishes were amalgamated into Unions with a Board of Guardians to administer Poor Relief. Haslemere, having lost Borough status in 1832, was directed into the Hambledon Union.

The chief part of Parish organisation was the Parish, or Vestry, meeting, which now represented the old tithing assembly of freemen, and administered so much of the business as had for a time been the duty of local Courts Leet, etc., but had now reverted to the Parish Meeting.

The Vestry proper still managed church affairs, property and charities, but the parish meeting, or the assembly of freemen, and now ratepayers, selected a Chairman, Waywarden, Overseers and Guardians from those who were liable for poor rate.

After 1868, however, when compulsory church rating came to an end, local government was drifting away from the old parish officers. The Rector, Parish Clerk and Sexton still had freeholds in their office and, with the Churchwardens, controlled church affairs. But for Haslemere, parish affairs were managed within the Hambledon District Union of Parishes by multifarious committees, together with the Vestry and Parish overseers, such committees as school boards, highway boards, sanitary authorities, police authorities, and beyond them all, the Justices of the Peace. By the mid-century, the parish constables were just giving way to the Peelers, as the members of the new force initiated by Sir Robert Peel were nicknamed.

This period was notable in the town of Haslemere for the stationing of its first Peeler, or policeman. This new man tried too hard to assert his new authority by forbidding the building of a bonfire on the 5th November night on Market Hill where for generations it had been held. Some of the teddy boys of the day in revenge made a bonfire of F. Briant's workshop at the top of the High Street just below the Pound. However, the cage by the Town Hall remained empty, for the culprits were not traced.

The last four parish constables in Haslemere had been James Teesdale, Thomas Gibbs, James Benham and James Steptoe. These had, as usual, been selected at the annual parish meeting which succeeded the annual Courts Leet, or Vestry Meeting.

James Benham was the proprietor of the Red Cow Inn, which is now Blackdown Bookshop in Petworth Road, and in his off times did a lot of cartage work. From one of his business trips to Windsor, he brought back the figure, or head, which is fixed in the wall at the back of No. 22 Petworth Road.

The town was gradually growing more boisterous with the influx of outside workers concerned with the building of the new railway from Godalming to Portsmouth, but years before, in 1828, there had been a proposal to make a Railway through Haslemere.

This increase in population helped to keep active the old customs and, as Christmas came round, so on December 25th the Mummers, or Tipteerers, as they were often called, visited the large houses and farms, sure of a hearty welcome. They went all dressed up in the proper garments, giving the old plays and singing:

"Here come I, old Father Christmas—Welcome or Welcome not—old Father Christmas never will be forgot."

The following year was free of incident apart from a strong recrudescence of an old Easter Monday custom. It had been usual to ride a "Jack of Lent"—a placarded dummy of an unpopular local person—on a horse or donkey, which was either ridden or driven about the Town. The ringleader of the "Jack of Lent" was a parish constable of the town who was fined £5—rapidly settled by his friends. The custom did not fall into disuse till at least the first Jubilee.

The landing of British troops in 1854 on the Crimea and its subsequent two years of misery and gallantry seems to have left no record in Haslemere, though in 1855 the town was shocked by a brutal murder. Owing to certain grievances over the arrest of one of their number, many of the navvies employed in cutting the new railway line had marched down to the town to rescue one of their friends who had been arrested and put in the prison cage by the Town Hall. A police inspector stood forth to harangue the men to try to get them to disperse. But he was hit violently by a navvy armed with a plough coulter, and died from the wounds.

A year later on old Dr. Geo. Smith died; he had been a notable character in his day and been associated, willy nilly, with a notorious character. He had married Sophia Fielding, the daughter of the then curate of Haslemere, who was reputed to have instigated, even if he did not participate in, several highway robberies. Young Dr. Smith had also been a bit of a showman, for in those days when there was no other private conveyance in Haslemere, he drove about in a spanking gig. At the time of his death, his nephew, still a minor, had recently inherited his great uncle's Denbigh House* property. This was a three-storied house, with a porticoed entrance, flanked by two windows, the two floors above having six windows each. Two gables ran north to south. It was in 1850 also that the local farmers banded together and with their labour and teams, cleared a piece of ground on Haste Hill Common for a cricket ground, which was used for the next fifteen years or thereabouts.

Other annoyances, though, were in store, for in 1855 the Government began a series of Enclosures of commonland. These commons had extended pretty continuously from Guildford as far as Petersfield, and an amount of this common land was sold and brought into cultivation, or developed as plantations or building land. Many of the villages and hamlets around were islands in a sea of common land. With these enclosures came squatters and broom squires, people who settled, built and in some cases, cultivated small sections of recent common land, or made heather brooms as an occupation, while living off the still abundant wild life. So a new set of names creeps into the registers and notes of this date, and the beginning of a settlement roots in the nearby area of Grayshott. To the east of Haslemere at Grayswood hamlet, there were in addition to The Stroud and Grayswood House, a number of

*Lythe Hill.

cottages and also the Wheatsheaf Inn which, however, had not then crossed the road to its present site. Ebenezer's Cottage and World's End have interesting sounds, but they are not easily found today, having assumed more up to date names. But although these houses were then all in Witley they naturally turned to Haslemere for their churchings and shoppings, and they were proud to lie under the shadow of the so called Haslemere Mill, which however, was still in their own parish. At this date their mill was doing yeoman service to the ever increasing population, some, as the navvies, only temporary, but with permanently large appetites. The owner at this time was Geo. Oliver, who also owned Shotter-mill, but lived in a small house which he had built at the top of Haslemere High Street, and which he called Olivers, just opposite the site of the old house of Fred Briant, burnt in the Guy Fawkes riot a year or two before. The Mill was a bit creaky in strong winds, but folk said it would last another generation.

Shottermill was another slowly growing area. It had recently been cut out of the parish of Frensham, and a church had been built just above the old farm of Cherrimans, where the Simmons's lived. Mr. Simmons also owned the Mill at Sicklemill, and a good deal of farmland as well, though George Oliver ground corn at the old Shotter Mill below the big pond. Critchmere was a little hamlet by itself with a small inn called The Royal Oak.

Down in the hollow where Frensham Hall then lay, one of the Baker family had kept house and hunted. At the sale of his effects his hounds were on the point of bargain when a friend sounded a View Halloo nearby. The bargain had to be cancelled, for hounds vanished.

Camelsdale was still only a few small farmhouses, cottages and a field named Camels Dene. But now the new railway was being built along part of its border with Shottermill and soon a few new houses appeared along the road to Fernhurst. As the neighbour-hood watched the clearing and making of a hard way for the rails, single line at first, and the foundation for a station being laid, deep creakings and crackings must have been noticeable in the peaceful facade of an ancient country town.

George Timms still took the post to Liphook, then the mail-coach post office, overnight, returning the following morning with the mail for Haslemere. Ever since 1852 it had been compulsory for each letter to have a stamp with the young Queen's head affixed to the container. Prior to 1852 postal letters had been charged one penny, but payment was made and the letter stamped at the sending off with a boxwood seal carrying a number. George Timms remembered how a man called Abraham Upfold had been his predecessor. Before Upfold, Timms had been told that Richard Deadman used to pick up letters left at Timms' grandfather's house and the accompanying pennies. He would then take off his tall hat, put the letters in his hat, cover them with a pocket handkerchief, and so proceed to Liphook. Timms himself had a small mailbag, but he had been told by old Sarah Upton that back in the 20's the Bag for Haslemere was considered heavy if it had a dozen letters.

The next year saw the end of the Indian Mutiny, and the assumption of government by Great Britain from the East India Company. In this year, also, the head of a family, Allen Chandler, first came to live in Haslemere—a family which was to have intimate connection with everyday life in Haslemere during the next hundred years. As a barrister and the heir of the Witley Park estate, his earlier life was spent in London. He retired from the life in London and from his profession, in 1858, and speedily was made J.P. and was Justice of the Peace on the Guildford Bench and Chairman of Guildford Petty Sessions. He also served on the Godalming Highway Board and Hambledon Board of Guardians which, at this time, had the parish of Haslemere under its wing. He was also active in the Liberal interest, and enjoyed a rag as much as any young-minded man should. His sense of humour was transmitted to his son, as will later be seen. About this time in Grayshott there were living at Purchase Farm in Whitmore Vale a family called Moore. One of the daughters became a Mrs. Robinson, and many years later she was able to recount how she had gone down to Haslemere on January 1st, 1858 and had seen one of the first goods trains from Godalming arrive and pass through the station on the newly·finished railway line.

In 1866 there were five up and five down trains from and to Haslemere which did the 40 odd miles to London in one and a half hours. On Sunday the station was closed from 11 a.m. to 4 p.m. with only three trains each way.

It may be of interest here to add a few notes on the construction of this railway line which was one of the early factors placing Haslemere on the map. Travel to and from Haslemere during the first half of the 19th century was by foot, horseback or coach.

An old local resident well remembered twenty four coaches passing along the Hindhead road (A3) every day, in addition to two of the Chichester coaches which came via Midhurst through Haslemere to London. He recorded that when the South Western Railway came down to Woking in 1840, the coach from Haslemere went so far by road and was then placed on a truck, passengers into carriages, and were all then drawn to Nine Elms, the then terminus. Arriving at the station, fresh horses were harnessed to the coach which then carried its passengers triumphantly to the White Horse in Piccadilly. The railway brought its lines to Guildford by 1845, and to Godalming by 1849, at which town was the southern terminus for the next nine years till 1858. During this decade a scheme for a railway passing through Haslemere to the coast on the atmospheric principle of traction was proposed. Although an Enabling Act was passed in 1846, it was here abandoned owing to non-success in other areas of trial.

As a private speculation Thomas Brassey, then a famous contractor, began in 1853 to build a direct railway line from Godalming to Havant passing through Haslemere. These thirty-five miles were completed in a little over four years and after some very tedious negotiations during the year of 1858 the South Western Railway leased the new direct line. This was a direct challenge to the London, Brighton and South Coast Railway which had a service to Portsmouth via Brighton. Following the announcement that a daily goods train would service the line from December 28th 1858 plans were laid by both parties for an expected battle. The train from London picked up Geo. Lythgoe, the local contractor and John Feast of Shottermill who was later promoted Railway inspector, arriving in Havant three hours earlier than advertised loaded with navvies and police well armed with truncheons, and found the Brighton contingent already in defended positions. Rails had been lifted and other obstructions erected. Two hours of battle followed, with the temporarily defeated S.W. army being forced to retire to Godalming. Legal processes followed and on January 24th a South Western train arrived from Godalming at Havant unmolested.

Haslemere no longer was a lost borough decaying in the Surrey Hills, but became increasingly a focal point for many who valued beautiful and quiet country and the pleasures of small town life at no great distance from the Metropolis. The station was small at first, and there was only a single line between stations for traffic. When a train was expected, a bell, rather like a huge dinner bell, was rung loudly by a porter who attempted at the same time to announce the destination of the oncoming train. It is also on record (private) that several young sparks on one of these early journeys down from London, hopped out station by station on the way down, and collected the bells one after the other. History, however, does not relate what the station staff at Portsmouth thought or said when they found a carriage full of large hand bells! Plus ça change, plus c'est la même chose.

An impressive disaster shook the town a little later in the year when, in some way not entirely devoid of suspicious circumstances, the two houses called Undershells just below Town House, were burned down. Clearing was promptly undertaken, and in the course of the year following new houses arose. It was in this year also that J. S. Whymper, the engraver and painter, came to live in Town House. When his family went there first, they found many old skins and other remnants of the tannery trade, and the mail bags which had been hidden there after the robbery on Hindhead. (This had been one of the houses owned and lived in by the Rev. Fielding).

The Rector of Chiddingfold who lived at The Great House across the road, now cleared away old Fred Briant's house just below Pound Corner, and turned it into an orchard and stables. This had been a freehold of the Briant family for several generations, and as a burgess, or voting property in private hands, it had always been a thorn in the side of the Lord of the Manor who mainly controlled the voting in the days when Haslemere sent two members to Parliament. Briant's vote given or withheld was worth a good deal of money, besides giving satisfaction to a family which had stood for personal freedom. Later this year, the old Farm at Church Hill, of which only a distant painting persists, was pulled down. After the death of his widowed mother, the Rev. Richard Parson had bought the property, and he now built a small mansion where had been a large half-timbered farm. His initials and the date (1860) were placed over the entrance door.

Early Stirrings

At the end of 1860 the population stood at 952. It was about this date that Miss M. Parson, sister of the owner of Church Hill, bought the old Admiralty semaphore house which stood at the top of Haste Hill, on land known as Whitwell Field and Whitwell Hatch Field. This semaphore house had fallen into disuse in 1847 with the development of telegraphy. This system, known as the Electric Telegraph, was developed just in time to replace the old manual signals. It had served to transmit messages for the Admiralty between London and Portsmouth since 1822, when it had superceded the first of its kind, originally worked on the shutter system. These buildings were now enlarged, while parts of the walls of the original semaphore House were incorporated in the walls of the dining room and hall, and it became known by the name of Highfield. Still later, in 1894, it was acquired by the Hon Ulick Browne, who greatly added to it, and it is now known from the name of the field in which it stood, as Whitwell Hatch Hotel.

Down in Cow Street earlier in the New Year, the Rector Hesse bought the old Porched House Farmhouse from Miss Gordon, daughter of the old Doctor. An early drawing of this interesting old house has survived the demolition which followed Hesse's acquisition. In its place he built two small stone houses on the site of the old farmhouse, which, as with many other houses in Haslemere had lost its primary use, and for many years had been occupied by two tenants.

Photography had come into use at this time, about 1862, and a photograph taken of the Market House shows a building consisting of one large room supported by a large central and two small lateral arches. On the large central gable was a clock, and surmounting the roof a bell in a small bell tower. In the east lateral supporting alcove was a locked cage for delinquents. In the west lateral support alcove a rather rickety staircase led to the upper room. In that room was held since 1843 the Vestry and Parish Meetings, the Infants' School, a Sunday School for children, various entertainments, penny readings, concerts and lectures. Down in Pylewell Street, a Baptist place of worship was built to accommodate the growing numbers of a sect* which neither attended the Established Church nor could find a home at the Congregational Church which stood a little further west on the opposite side of that street opposite the old Anchor Inn.

This was the second year of the American Civil War when the Southern States attempted to secede, and the sad struggle lasted for another two years. In 1863 Poland revolted, and in 1864 France attacked Mexico, while Austria and Prussia attacked Denmark. All these disturbances had a bad effect on some of the older residents. Old William Tidey who had been at one time parish schoolmaster, and later Parish Clerk, died. He had handed over his teaching post to Luke Woods.

Next door to the Swan, John Gibbs had a small barber's shop; and he too, died, but he was old. He had for some years been host at the Swan Inn where, however, his son Frank Gibbs now presided.

At the top end of the town near the Pound a small house was built which obviously was christened Pound Cottage. The pound for stray animals had been rebuilt in 1827, but fell into disuse about 1866, and so continued for twenty years.

This year was chiefly marked for the district by the settling in Haslemere of a Mr. and Mrs. Stewart Hodgson. A partner of the merchant house of Baring, he leased Denbigh House, and soon bought the Lythe Hill Estate. In 1868 he acquired Denbigh House, and after demolishing it, rebuilt it from a design by his friend, Fred Cockerell, R.A., and made his home there for the next twenty years. He gradually extended his ownership of land, eventually becoming Lord of the Manor of Haslemere and Godalming, and grew into a great public benefactor. This will appear as the story unfolds.

Two years after Hodgson's arrival, in 1864, a very different type of man arrived, firstly on a family holiday in the country, then of choice for the satisfactory upbringing of his family—Jonathan Hutchinson, of a Yorkshire Quaker family. Surgeon at the London Hospital and elsewhere, whose thirst for knowledge did not confine itself selfishly or to one small objective. He had a gift for teaching, and after a small start at his own house at Inval, an old farm which he later added to, he thought out plans which grew in time to a notable educational project. His Quaker upbringing also helped in the accumulation of a sufficient means to finance his projects for humanity. He realised the very healthy and desirable nature of the country round Haslemere, and by judicious buying acquired a large landed estate, which he farmed and later developed for housing.

---

*Baptist.

Over in Grayshott at this date, one or two families, among them the I'Ansons, had settled, in spite of the reputation for roughness which that hamlet then bore. There had been much pauperism and some victims from the enclosures, so that desperate characters hid themselves in the deep valleys, off the commons, such as Grayshott. There were several gangs of these men locally; a Blackdown gang from West Sussex, and a Hindhead gang based in the recesses of Hindhead and Grayshott. These men roamed the countryside in marauding parties, robbing and terrorising travellers and stealing sheep and other stock from isolated farms. Not always was their raiding successful. It has been recorded that two men paid a visit to a farm where was housed a notable boar pig. The first man went over the barrier in the dark to catch and kill his prey. There followed a great outcry mixed with the squealing of the offended animal. The man outside urgently called for information. "Have you got 'im, Dick?"—"No damn it" said Dick, "He've a got me." The boar had savaged his attacker.

At that time there were no good roads over the vast surrounding spaces, then unsullied by afforestation. A small guide then wrote, "Hindhead is approached from Haslemere at a point where there are a few small cottages and a public house called the Royal Huts, where coaches pick up goods and passengers." To reach Farnham directly, it was necessary to go up Woolmer or Glenlea Hill, cross the Hindhead road, descend to Waggoners Wells, rise to Grayshott where the Church now stands. The traveller then went down Whitmore Vale to Churt via Barford Mill, and so to Frensham Pond and thence to Farnham. The more adventurous traveller could climb to Hindhead as before stated, circle the Punchbowl and walk down Road Lane to Thursley and then over the common again to Frensham Pond, and so to Farnham. Road surfaces were intolerable, especially off the main coaching roads, and it was twenty years before the writer of "Green Lanes" could give high praise to the Thursley-Hindhead road as a wonderful surface which carried little or no traffic. He did not comment that the railway service from London to Portsmouth was then only just coming of age and its novelty and convenience still had a great attraction to business and private interest. Lastly, of course, the Pandora's box of the Internal Combustion Engine had not yet burst open upon the world.

But to that area during the summer of 1866, Alfred Tennyson came with his family to stay at Grayshott Farm, and fell in love with the wild and lonely heaths. It was not his first visit to Haslemere, for he had had a short stay at the Stoatley Farm in Bunch Lane during the summer of 1864. However, in 1868, Tennyson found a site on the south-east slopes of Blackdown, and laid the foundations there on St. George's Day. The architect was a young man called Knowles, whose acquaintance he made while waiting on Haslemere Station. Originally intended for a country cottage to alternate with his home at Farringford, Isle of Wight, the new building finally developed into a Victorian Gothic country house.

In 1867 also, Gladstone's Reform Bill had given the franchise to all rate-payers or lodgers who occupied premises to the value of £10 per annum, or within a county to £12 per annum. This, of course, gave many more Haslemere residents a vote and added to their stature in a personal and psychological way. The previously inarticulate multitude was gaining the use of a tongue and, in the next generation, a national platform.

In 1868, Mr. S. Hodgson, realising the value of sport as a training and means of pleasure, levelled a satisfactory piece of the Denbigh Park ground to form a good cricket ground. This ground was made available to the town cricket team, and it was used for twenty-one years, and was one of the most charming grounds in the county, both for local setting and the distant views afforded.

A Dr. Whiting moved into the town to replace old Dr. Hammond a surgeon who had recently died. Dr. Whiting settled in the High Street at No. 29, then called "Rosenhurst." In September, the Rector of Chiddingfold and acting curate of Haslemere, James Hesse, died. Although Rector of Chiddingfold, he had preferred living in Haslemere, to which he had moved in 1848, and had since then lived at The Great House. At his death, Haslemere was separated from Chiddingfold Parish for all ecclesiastical purposes. A new incumbent for Haslemere was appointed, the Rev. Sanders Etheridge, who became the first Rector of Haslemere. He lived at first in the High Street, but a new Rectory (now Sadlers) was built on the land just above Pound corner, opposite the Laurels* and there in January 1869 the new Rector went to live for the rest of his time in Haslemere—twenty-nine years.

Just a short story is appropriate here of the leisurely life of those days. This tale was told me ninety years after its occurrence by Arthur Whitcher, first Clerk to Haslemere Urban District Council. When Whitcher arrived in the Haslemere of 1894 as a young schoolmaster, the then Rector told him this story to show how different had been the Haslemere of 1868. When the Rectory (now Sadlers) was built, a number of Haslemere residents were invited to a house warming, and the time was fixed at 8 p.m. Mr. and Mrs. Etheridge went upstairs to dress about 7 p.m., but about ten minutes later a maid knocked at the door of Mr. Etheridge's bedroom to announce the arrival of Miss Parson from Church Hill. Said he: "Why is she so early? But show her into the drawing room."

*Humewood

Hurriedly completing his dressing, Mr. Etheridge came downstairs and in the drawing room greeted his early visitor. Full of apologies, the lady rose and explained to the Rector, "I am so sorry to be so early, but six of us ladies had engaged the cab to bring us here, and as my house was nearest, I had to be the first."

It took the new Rector just eighteen months to realise that he had put the cart before the horse. Away back in 1864 a diocesan report had stated about Haslemere that the Church needed rebuilding, and was a disgrace to the parish. But at that time, the Rev. Hesse was ageing and infirm, and much of his work had been done for some years by his eldest son, the Rev. George Hesse, acting as his curate. James Hesse was in no state to undertake the problem of rebuilding the old church. But his successor was a comparatively young man of thirty-three years of age, and during the year of his own rectory building, must have read the adverse report on the church. How quickly then must he have tackled the task of rousing the parish to a sense of great impending duty! At any rate, the last service in the old church was held on July 24th 1870. Just a year later, on July 28th 1871 the church, rebuilt to the same design, but on a larger scale, was reopened. The church had not altered in design since 1640 when the north aisle was added to enlarge the church "in bigness as much as it was formerly builded." Now a new chancel was built and the lower part of the tower, formerly the vestry, was included in the nave. The north aisle was also lengthened at both ends. Some drawings still exist showing the interior of the old church with great box pews for warmth, two galleries at the west end, the one for choir and children, and the other for certain important residents. Unfortunately the old font was made away with, and its place more than taken by an ornate marble bath.

During that year Mr. and Mrs. Gladstone were staying with the Tennysons in their new house at Aldworth on Blackdown. The Gladstones escorted Mrs. Tennyson to a morning service at Haslemere on one occasion—Alfred Tennyson himself never came. On one visit Gladstone himself came to the parish church escorted by the Tennyson boys. During prayers it was noted that he did not kneel, but merely held his top hat in front of his face.

A point for comment was that the Royal Coat of Arms which had occupied a proud place on the front of the West Gallery of the old church over the door which led from the vestry under the tower, was not replaced in the new church. Whose perquisite did it become, or was it merely cast out for firewood? Queer things happened then according to taste or caprice of those temporarily in charge of public possessions—the 16th century chalice of a neighbouring parish turned up in an auction sale half a century later without causing many ripples of curiosity or anger, and was happily restored to its rightful home.

Gas lighting of the town had been started in 1869, and the old Congregational Church showed its progressive outlook by installing this new convenience. It probably helped to keep the congregation awake on some occasions, for early gas jets flared, bubbled, and at times went out in a completely irresponsible way.

This was a time of much new building besides the church, for at Hindhead, near the Old Huts Hotel, Professor and Mrs. Tyndall bought some of the then available common land and began to build a country house. They lived at first in a log hut, and later when they were living in the new house, Professor Tyndall built a vast screen to keep out the sight of other new buildings of a less desirable character. His recommendation of the healthfulness of the air, and other amenities, was a great factor in introducing Haslemere and Hindhead to many cultured and well-to-do celebrities who began to settle here—at first slowly, but later in a faster stream.

Two local inhabitants met for a gossip in the High Street, and the one, a Mr. John Clark suggested the holding of a Horticultural Show to a Mr. G. Harrison. They worked out preliminary details, and in due course approached Mr. Stewart Hodgson of Lythe Hill, as he now called the rebuilt Denbigh House. A successful first show was held on August Bank Holiday, and was followed annually for many years by other exhibitions, later including children's races and exhibitions of handicrafts. The local band gave sweet music during the afternoon, and proved worthily that they could do more than lead the Mayday Club procession to and from Church.

In this same year School Boards were set up in every district and had to be supported by local rates. The next two to three years must have been very trying for Luke Woods, who had been master at the school by the Church for the past thirty years. He was too old to fit in to the new regulations easily, and he resigned in 1873 to be succeeded by Mr. Barkshire, who combined the office of Headmaster of the National Schools with that of Organist and Choirmaster. Luke Woods only survived two years in his retirement.

The Infants' School still continued to be held in the upper room of the Town Hall under the supervision of Mrs. Woods, and Albert Berry in his old age remembered starting his school days in her class. The playtime consisted in marching round and round the room, no doubt raising much dust as well as warming the feet.

Some development had begun along Pylewell Street with the two tall houses, Fern and Hazel Cottages just opposite Mr. Hale's old Cornstore. Within a few years a row of small cottages known as Western Terrace closed the view over the gardens and fields at the back of the High Street. Little shops were made from the cottages on the High Pavement, and it was in one of these that old Dame Puttick had had a Dames School.

In 1874 two interesting events occurred. The Haslemere Choral Society was started and continued for many years to give pleasure to participants on and off the stage. In the second place a nursing association was formed for the parish under the superintendence of the Rector's wife, Mrs. Etheridge. A Nurse Roberts was selected and continued in office for the next five to six years. Her duties were clearly set out as:

> To attend sickness and accidents among the poor as a prime duty and only, if free, to accept paid work.
> To follow implicitly medical instructions and, except by medical order, to administer no wine or spirits.
> To receive £1 a week salary.
> To keep a time sheet of work done.
> To keep a record of loans of nursing necessities.
> Patients to contribute 1/- a week to Nursing Fund.

Mrs. Etheridge continued to act as Superintendent until her death in 1893.

In 1875 it was found convenient to hold Divine Service every Sunday evening in the Town Hall; and this continued for several months.

About this time Dr. Jonathan Hutchinson decided to occupy his house at Inval more continuously, and then found that it was insufficiently capacious to accommodate his family and friends, so that enlargements were put in train. He, at this time, was interested in farming and the usual country pursuits of shooting and fishing. His sons remembered shooting game over the land now occupied by Farnham and Bunch Lane housing developments. But the acquisitive side of his nature was not satisfied with these pasttimes, and from time to time the Railway staff had frightening surprises in the crates addressed to him. On one occasion a large brown bear was seen half out of its crate when the luggage van was opened at Haslemere.

At that date there was only a small footway from the Railway bridge in Tanners Lane towards the Town. This footway crossed the small stream (which now passes under Bridge Road) by a little wooden bridge, and wound round towards the Town, emerging into the High Street at the field gate between Angel Cottage and

Dr. Clothier's house. The latter portion of this path lay beside the stream which emerged under the causewayed road from the springs further up on the east side of High Street.

In this year of 1876 was the last time when a bonfire was built and fired on Shepherds Hill Fields for Guy Fawkes celebrations. Many people in the town had been worried by the holding of the bonfire so close to the numerous old timbered houses, and the next year 1877 saw the formation under Mr. Ch. Bridger of the first Haslemere Fire Brigade. Prior to this date, curative measures when fire occurred were limited to buckets of water from a nearby cistern or well, and pulling away burning masses of building by huge grapples or rakes, such as may be seen in the Museum. In a few towns might be found a sort of large hand squirt for propelling a jet of water, one of which was used by a Mr. Fulk to extinguish a fire at the White Horse Hotel. The newly formed Fire Brigade was equipped with a horse drawn fire pump, and for the next thirty years, till 1907, they raced to fires, heath, house or rick, as needed.

The old established Bell Vale brewery (now a private house) changed hands. In Lower Street, while on the subject of drinks, the thirsty traveller had had to change sides. The old Anchor Ale House had lapsed from the provision of liquid refreshment to the status of private residence, and was soon to offer antiques for sale. But owing to the earlier influx of railwaymen into the town over the construction of the railway in and before 1859, and its subsequent widening in 1875 to double track, the then owner of No. 33 Lower Street, had leased his property to a Godalming brewer in 1867. This brewer found his lease so profitable that about this date he displayed a sign "The Good Intent," and eventually in 1875 he bought the property. It is to be hoped that his good intent was not followed by the fate of those in the proverb—good intentions pave the road to (another place).

During these years, a man called Aplin, who lived at Thursley End, used to be the postman for Lord Tennyson, and although his journey would be a pleasant walk in fine weather, the postbag to Aldworth could, at times, be a load. At that date, the lane from Haste Hill ran through open country to the county boundary, and thenceforward over open heath. But that lane was traversed by many very famous people as they came to pay homage to or to talk with the great poet. After about 1885 the Tennyson post was taken out by a girl, Miss Enticknap, one of the Aldworth staff. In his later years Tennyson was at times driven out to collect his own post from the Post Office in East Street, remaining in his carriage while a footman collected the letters.

The Tyndale boys, sons of the painter Walter Tyndale, who then lived at "Crofts," Petworth Road, would see the old man being driven past in his pony trap. On one occasion, so I was told by one boy, now over eighty years of age, the old man stopped the trap, looked across at them and said, "What handsome boys." Augustus Hare writing from Milford Cottage in 1877 says, "I have been with Mrs. Greville to Mr. Tennyson at Haslemere. It is a wild high brown heath with ragged edges of birch, and an almost limitless view of the Sussex distances. Jammed into a hollow is the house, a gothic house built by Mr. Knowles, that young brick-layer fellow (as Mr. Carlyle calls him) that Alfred (T) is so fond of. Though the place is in such a bleak wind-stricken height where the flowers in the garden can never sit still, the house is pleasant inside, well and amply furnished. Tennyson is looking older than I expected, so that his unkempt appearance signifies less."

Those were the days, we have heard people say of bygone times and occasions, but were they in cold fact so memorable? Perhaps not memorable, but some were at least worthy of recall.

An aged parish councillor of a nearby village told me the story of Naboth's vineyard set in Victorian days. A certain Sir Learned Lawgiver who lived on the outskirts of the village at the time of the enclosures acquired much of the waste and common land adjacent to his estate. He was resisted in one small area by a local smallholder who held title deeds to his own little property. The small farmer could in no wise or for no money be per-suaded to part with his little freehold. To him the learned law-giver is alleged to have said, "I shall best you yet, my man, my money will talk louder than your deeds." This is in fact what happened, and the small farmer was dispossessed. The victor, how-ever, later settled the defeated farmer on to a small property three or four miles away in the valley. "Sic transit gloria."

Not far away at the time, at a hamlet hidden in the hills, known then as Tatemer Town* there lived several families of squatters, broom squires and farmhands. These people all lived to a great age, and produced families of twelve to fourteen children apiece, who all enjoyed remarkably good health. The occupants of a nearby farm, were less fortunate. Illness stalked them. What moral can be drawn from that does not now appear. Was the farm well too near the dung heap, or the dairy fly-infested from the same source, or possibly a tubercle infected herd of cows. We may guess, but learn nothing, but my informant's father who lived at the hamlet was in conversation with two itinerant salesmen who expressed great surprise that anyone should live in such an out of the world place with nothing but gorse and heather for miles. The old man replied that they lived on because no-one could die there. He then called to witness another old man

*(Near Griggs Green).

working nearby and introduced him as his elder brother. "Yes,"
said the older man, "I'm ninety-seven years old and still good for
a day's work." When he was told what the salesman had said
about the countryside, he turned to his brother with the remark,
"D'you remember old Blucher White [dating him thus from the
Battle of Waterloo]? He was over ninety and got so tired of living-
on that, one night, he went down to the pond, cut his throat and
threw himself in. But even then he got better, and went on living.
No, we never dies here."

Another old Sussex countryman needed a tooth extraction.
He apologised profusely for causing such trouble, and explained
that he had been cracking cobnuts with his own teeth at the age
of eighty-five, and he had broken a piece from a molar.

In later conversation he said, that as a young man a similar
accident had occurred, and after the extraction he had walked the
four miles back to his cottage. On his way home he was joined by
a gipsy who noticed he was spitting blood, and enquired if he
had consumption. "No," said the farm labourer, "I've just had
a tooth out." "Ho," said the gipsy, "You needn't worry about
toothache ever again if you will only grow a small beard round
your chin." This the farmhand did, and was still so decorated when
he came for his second extraction seventy years later. In those
intervening years he had had no dental troubles and had, apart
from the two extractions, a complete set of healthy teeth, somewhat worn down, but eminently useful. The modern answer to
that would probably be the question "Was there fluoride in his
well water?"

Further along the same pretty Sussex lane lived an old woman
who had an unusual cure for warts. Such cures are legion and if
applied in some of the better known West End mansions will cost
the sufferer from £5 to £25. However this was simple and not
costly. First get a piece of clean laid straw—chew it gently to
soften the fibres and then wind it round the affected finger. This
wrapping should be left on for twenty-four hours, and after
removal buried in the garden. Cure was said to be certain and
probably happened in about 60 per cent of cases as in most other
cures, which was enough to keep the reputation of the white witch
or practitioner unsullied.

CHAPTER III

Perambulations

Away back in 1871 a Local Government Board set up by the Government brought the beginnings of sanity into local government with a centralisation of committees, and in 1878 the parish of Haslemere, together with the adjoining parish of Thursley was constituted a special drainage area. In pursuance of this act a Parochial Committee was set up. Haslemere thus began to emerge from the welter of parishes which had formed the Hambledon Union.

It was not, however, until 1894 that the first parish council was selected, and sat under the chairmanship of Sir Robert Hunter, the Solicitor to the General Post Office. Sir Robert, who fortunately for Haslemere had had the wisdom to settle in Haslemere in 1882 at Meadfields, was undoubtedly a man of vision in his ardent championship of the preservation of commons, footpaths and open spaces. It was more fortunate in that he was able to concentrate his attention on the pleasant country surrounding his home, and not merely on a long distant view. His ability in the presentation of his lawsuits re common footpath rights, and his practical ability and tact in organisation led later to the formation of the National Trust in conjunction with Miss Octavia Hill and Canon Rawnsley.

In the local scene, for some years, he later ensured in his chairmanship of the young parish council a high standard of local government and progressive improvements. He was supported by local professional and trade representatives as well as by local residents such as A. Chandler. It was due to his skill and foresight that Shepherds Hill Common was acquired by the Parish Council, from the two Manors which had earlier owned that land.

In 1880 the cottage once called Altamont Cottage was rebuilt by Mrs. Stewart Hodgson for use as a Children's Home, and was placed in charge of a Mrs. Goldthorpe as Matron. It is interesting to find this charity on the same hillslope as the old Almshouses of 1676. It was only a few years later, in 1886, that Mr. Stewart Hodgson as Lord of the Manor of Haslemere (and Godalming) repaired these two old almshouses and added a second pair to the south-east of the original two. A flash-back in history also reminds us that as far back as 1757 a small house was acquired on Haste Hill as a poorhouse—this was what later was rebuilt as Altamont Cottage.

At this date and for years previous, there had been two pest houses for Haslemere, one just below Dean House, Midhurst Road, but demolished before 1911, and a second, the cottage lying back from the road behind the milestone in Grayswood Road (once known as Rokers). To these houses were taken such people, suffering from severe infections, as could not be nursed at home.

There had been one or two midwives in the eighteenth century whose names have come down to us, but there is no record of any regular parish nursing service prior to that begun by Mrs. Etheridge, the wife of the new Rector, though there had been a small nurses' home started in Shottermill to send nurses out to individual cases.

This period was one of experiment and origins, and early next year some alterations and additions were made to Collards, one of the oldest houses in East Street. In the roof and elsewhere were found two rapiers and a spur, while a tile was found with the letters R.P. and date 1721 heavily incised upon it. It may now be seen over the door light. The letters R.P. stood in all probability for Robert Philp, a local tiler and churchwarden who lived a few doors further away in the eighteenth century.

At this time the old Haslemere pound at the top of the High Street where stray animals were held by authority till claimed, was closed for the next twenty years. Evidently the more pressing needs of housing the new influx of population had excluded the keeping of pigs, sheep and cattle from the town and its immediate vicinity.

By now the new houses at Western Terrace in Lower Street which had been built by E.W.T. in 1876 were losing the shine of their newness. It was at this date that Louis Jennings, author of "Field Paths and Green Lanes in Surrey" came into Haslemere from Midhurst, and these were some of the buildings which made him give anguished utterance of distaste. His plaints, however, fell on deaf ears, at least so far as the builder was concerned, for in 1882 a second block of four was added, creeping towards the town.

Gas lighting which had been in use in the town and at the Congregational Church for about ten years, was now installed in the Parish Church. It may, of course, have been the very cold winter which increased the popularity of gas, for the months around Christmas were the coldest on record since 1838.

With the influx of new residents there arose a demand for blacksmiths. Away back in the eighteenth century we may recall there had been a smithy on the site of the present Pound Corner crossroads, another at Heath Edge, later transferred to Lower Street, and one on the road to Shottermill. However, in the eighteen-eighties, Upfold had a smithy in a cottage, now absorbed into Goodwyns in the High Street. This and the adjoining cottage, both creeper covered, formed favourite subjects for artists of the day such as the Whympers who were then living at Town House, Mrs. Allingham and others.

The stone water trough for thirsty horses or for quenching red hot iron, is still standing on the pavement against the wall of the modern bank building.

A second smithy was in action on premises now occupied by Pannells Boot shop opposite the Town Hall.   Two more smithies could be found in East Street on the south side about Nos. 17/19. One of these later removed to premises on the north side of Lower Street, where the approach created some mild interest, being below street level, so that horse or rider had to get down a step. Later these premises were occupied by a smith called Maides, who in addition to farriery showed a talent for other iron working. The gates which stood for many years at the entrance to Manor House, Three Gates Lane, were hammered into shape in Lower Street, as also were the gates of the new school in Chestnut Avenue.

The surplus energy of some of the newer residents found expression on 9th August 1881 in the organisation and showing of an Industrial and Art Exhibition. Perhaps today such an Exhibition might be called a Hobbies' Exhibition, but the aims of the organisers went further than the mere occupation of odd bits of spare time. Here were exhibited serious undertakings of leisure occupations or of such crafts as might be said to be motivated by an aim to excel and satisfy.

During the four days of the Exhibition, 1,500 visitors were admitted to view the six hundred exhibits. Enthusiasm remained at high level, for five hundred and twenty persons came in the last day, although it rained heavily.

The Annual Flower Show took place on May 30th, and seems to have attracted four to five hundred entries. It was now beginning to be a fixture in the year, to which competitors and visitors looked forward with keen interest.

At Christmas the chief thing on record is of the very heavy snowstorm, and it proved to be the first of an irregular series of hard winters, culminating in the Great Blizzard of 1895.

During the year 1881, the Congregational body had built a new church adjoining their old premises in Lower Street. This old building had been erected in 1804, and was in future used as a lecture room and Sunday school. In digging the foundations of the new building, the grave of the first Congregational Minister in this area was revealed, the date of burial having been 1792.

A note in the parish magazine mentioned that Jane Bridger, Mary Ann Snelling and Emily Nash were awarded prizes for good darning. It is probable that most modern readers of this page may say "What is darning?" They have heard perhaps of "Darn it!" as a moderate expletive, but if they are still at a loss, let them ask grannie, who probably spent a lot of her leisure doing tedious darning—what she said under her breath at the same time is not our business.

There are some folk who still consider themselves underpaid, and the same issue of that Parish Magazine can give them food for thought, or fodder for their cannon, as follows:

The Parish Nurse was related to be a widow with two children, and had found it necessary to resign her responsible position. The reason she gave was that she found it impossible to manage on her salary of £40 per year. Her rules precluded her from giving wine or spirits to her poor patients except with medical advice. She had to provide her own food and not be paid by the poor. She had to take charge of and keep an orderly account of things lent out. Now, of course, a salary ten times as large would be recognised as barely adequate.

Miss Hunter remembers the years around 1885, which were soon after her family had decided to live in Haslemere, and had seen working the old Pug Mill on Clay Hill. This mill, of which a painting still exisits, stood on the ground by the railway on the site of the present Co-operative food stores. Miss Hunter and her sisters often watched the old horse making his circular amble.

At that date there were two doctors in the town—Dr. Winstanley and a younger man called Ardagh. When the latter first came to the town in 1886 he used to ride out to his patients on horseback, on a tall, gaunt bay, the doctor being dressed in black and wearing a tall hat cocked a little on one side. Within a few years he changed to a two-wheeled dogcart, perhaps in distant emulation of his senior, Dr. Winstanley, who graced a four-wheeled dogcart in the summer and a brougham in the winter.

It had been an earlier doctor—Whiting—who had lived in the High Street some years before, at a house opposite the Georgian, now alas swept away. His little house, double-fronted and welcoming in appearance, was approached by a few steps,

and survived till about 1930. Old Whiting, so a very old man told
me, who had been Tiger to the old doctor, set forth one day to
visit a distant patient in the Liphook direction. For this visit,
evidently a red-letter occasion, the lad had been provided by his
master with a high hat also. The dogcart sped along over the road
by Lynchmere Common, but a gust of wind or flick of the whip
precipitated the hat of the boy under the wheel of the vehicle. As
the boy recoiled aghast from the expected rebuke, old Dr. Whiting
drove on with scarcely a glance back at the mangled hat, and
simply said, "Never mind, never mind, two guinea fee to-day."

It will be of interest here to include two extracts from pub-
lications of the year 1885. The first is from the Century Illustrated
Magazine, and is the commentary of a visitor from America:

"All life and business centres in the High Street, in which,
dividing the commercial from the exclusive ends, the White Horse
Hotel stands. Trim and prim and English looking, but most
picturesque, it lies between a grocer's shop on the one side and
a Doctor's house on the other. Most admirable is a road* on the
outskirts of the town which runs down a steep hill, taking the
quaint little red tiled houses with it. These dwellings were of the
humblest kind, but sweet and clean with dimity curtains hung at
every window. Their small gardens in front were filled with sun-
flowers, marigolds and sweet williams. At Shottermill the general
store of the postmaster is lined with shelves which are adorned
with a stately frieze of Florentine oil flasks. There is also a dado
full of three feet high biscuit or cracker boxes ... "

References are made to the family parade to church, with the
Gaffer duly garbed in a spotless smock.

As with other foreign visitors in mediaeval times, the writer
remarks on bells, and says the English air is always resonant with
sound on a Sunday morning.

Our American visitor stressed the slow growth of Haslemere
during the past hundred years, but that recently if a newcomer
came, he was recognised as such at once, and everybody called in
the then hospitable fashion.

At the back of East Street there was not a house standing
beyond the gardens either north or south, and Half Moon Farm
really was a farm in the quiet occupation of Mr. Welland's cows.
If you had then asked for Museum Hill you would have been
stared at, and Mrs. Clothier's worst dreams never pictured the
conversion of her picturesque old-fashioned residence into the
Broadway.

---

*Shepherds Hill.

Old F. Jones who died in 1958 left a memory of a bank holiday in 1886. He remembered how he and his brothers were asked to go to the old Windmill on Grayswood Hill to assist in pulling it down. It was a great day for some of the people, with a barrel of beer provided by Mr. Oliver, the miller, to encourage good work. At the end of the day he and his brothers brought home some of the rough wood. Some of the wood and some of the mill equipment went to Shottermill, and some to Cooks Bridge Mill, Fernhurst. For the past eighty years it had been the property of the Oliver family and till the late 70's had been in good order.

The last class of little girls at the Town Hall Infants' School took place in 1885.

The years 1890/91 are given as the date of marked change in the town.

In 1887 the appearance of the town was little changed since 1735. The last house at the top of High Street, Oliver's, had recently been acquired by Miss Hesse, daughter of the late Rector of Chiddingfold and Haslemere, and Mr. Stewart Hodgson (of Lythe Hill) had only just built the Workmen's Institute, his gift to the town.

With these two exceptions, the High Street, as well as East Street and Shepherds Hill were much as they had been for many years. On the East side of High Street at the top was Priors shop* almost touching "The Lodge" (Museum), then came the Smithy and close to that the fishmonger's shop so dear to Mrs. Allingham and other artists. Next below came a chemist (Three Limes now) then two clusters of weatherbeaten cottages in perfect keeping with the village street, where rich and poor should meet together.

Now where is the grocer's, the smithy and the fishmonger's with its glorious colouring of Virginian creeper? Gone, all gone! Mr. Cecil Lawson has turned Prior's shop into a pretty enough cottage, and Mr. Penfold who loves the village, has in Mr. White's new house done all that was possible to preserve the old world look of the three buildings he was converting. Even Mr. Peter Aylwin has closed his door except to his intimate friends, and in place of one of those clusters of weather beaten cottages, we have now these brand new, very red and white, but doubtless very commodious shops with a smart pavement in front, instead of those ill-bred cobbles. An advertisement in black and white on the side of one of them, which stares at you all the way down the village, tells where Mr. Aylwyn's successor may be found. Thanks to Mr. Mozley, the old doctor's house remains as it was. From there

*The Small House.

to where High Street narrows into East Street there is little
change except a second and enlarged addition to old Clark's News
Shop. The White Horse Inn has been smartened up in front and
looks better for it. The increased accommodation there lies most
to the back, while the quaint old gables above Tanner's shop*
delight the eye as much as ever.

Now for a continuation of the tour. Starting from Hale's
corner there is a narrow thoroughfare as always, amid a jumble
of buildings. The old Swan Inn with the adjoining houses was
once a favourite subject for artists, but in a few years they will
turn their back upon Frank Gibbs' new shop* and work the other
way. Going by the Institute, which till late was the post office
and a china shop, we reach Mrs. Clothier's house with its railings
in front and coach house at the side. Her death soon afterwards
spared her the frightful transformation which took the place of
her pleasant home.

In 1887 occurred the great Jubilee of Queen Victoria. Haslemere was determined to underline this great anniversary of the
Queen whom all respected and loved. Three committees sat to
organise the day's programme. Monday, June 20th was spent
largely in decorating the town. No half-hearted measures were
offered or tolerated. Triumphal arches grew at every corner—
three were specially commended for their excellence. Streamers
of banners and pennons floated over the streets, flags flew from
all windows, various Jubilee devices and coloured draperies hung
from the walls of the houses.

On June 21st, to the early ringing of church bells, finishing
touches were put to decorations, and a brilliant sunny day greeted
all the awakening town. By 10.30 a.m., Tanners Lane, Pathfields
and Church Lane were thick with people making their way on
foot or by carriage to church. At 11 a.m. a service of Thanksgiving began, the Rector gave a short address and after the
National Anthem had been sung, all dispersed, to return to the
town for a public dinner. For this six rooms were used con-
currently—the Assembly Room, White Horse Club Room, Lecture
Hall, Working Men's Club Room and the Library and Infants'
School Room. In all 523 people sat down to feast, and the Loyal
Toast to the Queen was given in each room by a Chairman.

After a due time of relaxation, a vast crowd of people led by
the local brass band, walked up to the lovely cricket ground at
Lythe Hill, where a full programme of athletic sports had been
arranged. Special arrangements for transport to the ground of old

---

*Reid chemist.   *International Stores

and infirm people was made by means of a brake and pair of horses.

A massive tea of bread and butter and cake was attacked by 324 children in three of the town halls. By 8.30 p.m. large crowds had made their way up to Gibbet Hill, Hindhead, where a huge bonfire was lighted. At dark sixty more beacon fires were counted over the countryside around, and Mrs. Simmons (of Cherrimans) offered tea on the hill-top to all and sundry—a notable "At Home" —between 10 p.m. and 12 midnight.

Later the same year in August, a year of superlative weather— Queen's Weather as it was called—a very successful flower show was held. Bees were shown and demonstrated, also pottery, besides the usual fruit, flower and vegetable entries. Wild flower collecttions by children and table decorations have a modern sound. A flower arrangement in brown and gold, and a tall glass filled with bulrushes wreathed by bryony raised ecstatic comment. Lord Tennyson himself "our distinguished neighbour" was noted as a visitor to the Flower Show. This was an exceptional and gracious act by the famous poet, near eighty years old.

The poet's routine at Aldworth was breakfast in his own room, after which he would smoke a clay pipe of shag and birds eye for about two hours. This was to him one of his best periods for inspiration. He would descend at 11 a.m. and take a three to four mile walk with all the dogs, and his grandchildren if on holiday. Dressed in a black Spanish cloak with velvet collar, sleeveless, which covered a kind of poacher's knee-length coat with enormous pockets, and crowned by a large black sombrero, he would present an impressive figure. His physical presence was described by one observer as being like a great natural phenomenon. He had no care for appearance. He was seen by Mrs. G. Trevelyan on Haslemere Station sitting on one of the seats. She ran up to greet him, and noted that his hat was fastened under his chin with black elastic. He avoided, where possible, personal publicity, and it could be fairly said only a few years after his death that "there are comparatively few now who can remember the tall figure, with the long cloak and slouch hat, now lying back in his carriage waiting for his letters at the old Post Office in East Street, now wandering over Blackdown with the deerhound at his heels!" Yet he had lived close to Haslemere for nearly a quarter of a century. According to his biographer he went up to London, less frequently as he aged, and met friends there, old and new. He was also for a long period each year at his other home in the Isle of Wight—Farringford.

The house at Aldworth had been chosen particularly for its beautiful and retired situation, as well as for its convenience to

London or the coast. This example has been followed by many
fortunate people ever since. His desire for retirement was that the
great love for his art and the concentration which he devoted to
it, excluded any desire for regular participation in the social
round, though at times of relaxation and in his own home he
could be, and was, an ideal host. As host, it may be recalled that
various members of the Royal Family—Princess (Queen) Mary,
Duchess of Teck and the Duchess of Albany have walked up and
down the long Aldworth Terrace. W. E. Gladstone, the Duke of
Argyll, Lord Wolseley, Lord Napier of Dufferin, Lord and Lady
Dufferin, Boyd Carpenter, Jowett, Aubrey de Vere, Palgrave, and
Allingham all visited the Laureate on his Sussex hilltop. An old
inhabitant also remembered that he not infrequently walked into
Haslemere, smoking short clay pipes.

It has been possible to gather a few more crumbs of reminis-
cence from several old residents in Haslemere. One, Miss Margaret
Bridger, who was born in 1870 recalled with great pleasure an
incident in her girlhood. She was taken by a friend of the family,
Mr. Peter Aylwin, to Aldworth one fine day. Mr. Aylwin, then a
chemist in the High Street, was also interested in woodwork and
in the collection and sale of antiques. He was a close acquaintance
of Lord Tennyson who frequently visited his shop, both for goods
on display and for local news. On this morning, on arrival at Aldworth after driving up Tennysons Lane, Mr. Aylwin took the little
girl into the hall of Aldworth and bade her sit still on a chair
while he did his business with Lord Tennyson. A few minutes
later Lord Tennyson himself came down the stairs, saw the little
girl and, on hearing how she had been condemned to sit there,
invited her to come to his room where she could sit in the window
and admire the wonderful garden and view over the Weald. This
memory has been treasured over the eighty year gap, not merely
for the pleasure of that morning, but in gratitude for the kindness
to a child.

Tennyson was, as is known to many, short-sighted, and this
at times may have accounted for his apparent discourtesy to
some people, occasionally even acquaintances, until he was near
enough to realise the approaching person. There is no doubt that
this disability, allied to his constant absorption in his poetical
work, could have accounted for the following incident. One of his
publishers paid a visit to Aldworth and, crossing the lawn to greet
the poet, was assailed by fierce shouts of "Go away" etc. Such was
his surprise, that the visitor turned and fled!

Tennyson's interest in children was also recalled by Mr.
Sadler, an old man who as a child went to the village school

at Northchapel. This school was held in a village hall now used by the Women's Institute, and was attended by about a hundred children, who were taught by a headmaster called Ridgewell. One morning, during a lesson, the door opened to admit Lord Tennyson, dressed as usual in his black wide-awake hat and long cloak. He spoke a few words to the children after greeting the headmaster, but unfortunately my old informant could not remember any of the remarks.

Still another man recalls that as a boy he was taken by his father, J. Madgwick, a carpenter, to Aldworth. Old John Madgwick, still remembered by many in the town, a small apple-cheeked countryman with a little goatee beard, went off in search of Lord Tennyson, leaving his son in the garden. Shortly afterwards, Lord Tennyson could be seen at the other end of the garden on the arm of John Madgwick who was escorting his employer to a new job of carpentry. At that moment two American visitors appeared from behind the shrubberies and offered the boy £20 for his father, if he would help them to meet the poet. This take-over bid, however, was not successful.

A signalman, Webber, at Haslemere, said that in his time Lord Tennyson did not often travel by train. Having arrived from Farringford in the Isle of Wight at the end of May, he remained at Aldworth till October, with few visits only to London. He did, however, remember that his Lordship made visits to the Rectory where the family was frequently entertained.

Still another old lady remembered seeing the Tennyson boys riding in through Haslemere on their ponies to share a tutor with another family in Grayswood Road.

The staff at Aldworth were old retainers and, as such, gradually tapered off by age, so that a story told by Tennyson to Fred Harrison can be understood. A Flyman brought an American pilgrim to the barred gate of Aldworth who on parting refused to call the poet great "because he only kep' one man."

Those who felt that sometimes there was an ungracious vein in evidence may be reassured by the following tale. During convalescence from an illness, his nurse came to him to tell him that it was time for bed. "Go away and learn Latin," said he irritably to the nurse. She left the room at once, but shortly after, returned, and as the old man looked up, she said quietly, "Tempus fugit"—he smiled and at once went off to his room.

It was about this time that his nurse found him very melancholic and took him gently to task. "Mr. Tennyson, you ought to be ashamed of yourself for grumbling. You ought to express your gratitude for recovery from your bad illness by giving the world something of your poetry." He took the reproof well and retired, but in half an hour he came back into the sitting-room and showed her "Crossing the Bar."

Haslemere was becoming a popular place. A play had been put on at the Adelphi Theatre, London, called "The Bells of Hasle-mere." The Church had sixty more applications for seats than the Churchwardens, exercising their greatest ingenuity, could find.

A decision was taken to enlarge the church, and in 1888 a new South Aisle to hold a further 120 people was built. At this date a large number of people arrived at the Church by carriage, which returned later to pick them up.

There was some discussion at this time as to the propriety of planting trees along the High Street on either side, but a largely attended Vestry Meeting voted against it. In contrast to the wonderful weather of the Jubilee year, July 11th 1888 is noted as the worst July day for at least sixty years—the temperature was the lowest on record and not only rain but snow fell.

One small enterprise was born safely in spite of the unsatisfactory weather. At Inval near his house, Dr. Jonathan Hutchinson had had a log hut built in 1888, in which he arranged and collected all sorts of specimens to form a private museum. He continued to develop this work and in 1895 he had built on farm land above East Street in Haslemere a one-storied Museum (now the Council Offices). From all over the world specimens of all kinds, live and dead, arrived at Haslemere Station for this Museum.

CHAPTER IV

Now Praise Famous Men

HUTCHINSON (MUSEUM), MACDONALD, HUNTER, SHAW
CHANDLER — HIGH STREET

The next decade saw proof of the statement made in the last chapter that there was an awakening in the air. For some time past evening entertainments in the town had been a desideratum, and had been provided by several groups. A Choral Society which had been started in the town, with the Rector as President, and the schoolmaster Barkshire as Conductor, appears to have continued with varying degrees of success and popularity from its foundation in 1874.

The Church of England Temperance Society had mixed its propaganda with speeches on a variety of topics, while from 1878 a series, usually six to eight, of winter entertainments, was offered at the White Horse Assembly rooms. It is well to notice that all these gatherings were the product of direct organisation or work, and were not merely an aural exercise on disc, tape or box.

A revival of the weaving industry which in earlier centuries had played a considerable part in the life of Haslemere townsfolk was promoted by Mr. Joseph King in a specially built picturesque wooden building in Foundry Road. A year or two later he was joined by Godfrey Blount, who fostered a Tapestry industry at his own house on Southlands (now Weydown Road) and later in Foundry Road.

Blount also revived for a time an interest in Morris dancing. This must have played a part in the pastimes of the earlier forefathers and mothers of Haslemere, for a field above Foundry Road was known in the middle ages as Morris Field.

Towards the latter part of this decade came a strong interest in theatrical performances. As will have been learned from earlier remarks, there had been penny readings—charades, short plays, etc., given as part of the programmes of earlier entertainments. Following several years of reading of some of Shakespeare's plays, it was decided to give a series of full-dress performances. The first of these was "As You Like It" which received a great welcome when played in the Assembly Rooms. Midway between these cultural activities and plain education, grew the Haslemere Microscope and Natural History Society. This Society was begun by Mr. Rayner Storr and at first was housed in an Educational Hall which had been built in 1893 in Foundry or Gashouse Road. This

road was so called because it led from the Station to the Gas
Works (built 1869).

Working parallel, it might be said, with the Natural History
Society, was the private Museum of Dr. Jonathan Hutchinson, at
which he gave Sunday afternoon lectures, and demonstrations,
where possible, of his material. This was in every way an inspired
move. The nearness to the town encouraged greater interest in
and use of the Museum which the founder intended as a live
exhibition of nature and history. More detailed description of
this museum and its development will be found in other writings,
but the methods then advocated and adopted have since formed
a firm basis for the more progressive museums all over the world.
Only a short year or two passed before Dr. Hutchinson found
the need for a whole-time Curator. He was fortunate in meeting
with and gaining the whole-hearted co-operation of a young
teacher, E. W. Swanton, who from earliest youth had always
hoped for a life devoted to such work. Their association lasted for
many fruitful years.

One further cultural interest was gratified by the formation
of a Society of Artists which under one or other name has continued to attract great support and has given outlet to and training
of the desire to paint or draw in many residents to the present day.

A tale exists of 1897 in relation to the Postal Service. At
that time the Postal Office was close to the milestone on Broadway at Mr. Charman's shop. During a night in October, at 2.45
a.m. the mail cart had come from Midhurst en route for Godalming, and the mail cart drivers went into the office to collect the
mail. Tired with waiting, for perhaps with the cold night the
drivers may have remained longer than usual for a hot drink, the
two horses moved off, first at a walk, and then at a trot up the
sloping High Street. Shortly after, the two drivers came out of the
post office to continue their journey but found no van. Hastily
they procured two fresh horses from the nearby stables and set
out after the runaways, expecting to overtake an upturned mail
cart with perhaps damaged horse-flesh. They continued their
journey all the way to Godalming where, to their relief and
amazement, they found the mail-cart waiting beside the Post
Office, the van intact, and the horses sweating but otherwise
sound. It was an extraordinary piece of equine intelligence and
memory as well as good fortune that had brought the mail cart
safely through the eight miles at night from Haslemere to Godalming.

For some years past, seating in the Church had been allocated
to individual persons or families who paid rent for the retention
of their seats. This method which had been in force since 1870
(the date of the rebuilding of the Church) had provided a satis-

factory income to those officials responsible for the upkeep and
maintenance of the fabric of the building and the churchyard. In
1899, however, the new Rector, Rev. Aitken, found the tight
seating plan too un-christian to tolerate, and objected to the
method whereby late coming seat holders could eject previously
installed worshippers. The Church Council was persuaded to
modify the right to arranged seating, and to permit free seating
after the organ began the voluntary. It was not till 1917 that
the principle of completely free seating was accepted.

Until 1898 Offertories had only been collected at Holy Communion, or at other services for very special objects, but in April
1899 it was decided that the Church Rate should be discontinued
and that all Church expenses should be met from regular offertories.

A less desirable exhibition of community life received a
rebuke from the Churchwardens. In the Parish magazine for
August they begged to call attention to the annoyance caused to
people attending services by persons walking, talking and smoking
in the Churchyard. They urged that "there should be quiet in
the Churchyard during the time of divine service. It is not a
recreation ground, but is open for reverent use by the
parishioners."

A Cottage Hospital was built on the edge of the common at
the northern side of Shepherds Hill through the generosity of
surviving members of the old local family of Penfold. The growth
of the district over the past twenty years had shown the need
for adequate nursing in a properly equipped building. In June 1898
the new hospital was opened with 4 beds, under the care of
Miss Johnson, the first matron. From the first there was full
occupancy of the beds, so that within a few years extension of
patient beds and staff accommodation was required and provided.
For those who never knew those days, a doctor who worked
there was told of a case of typhlitis as appendicitis was then
called. It had only recently become normal to operate on such
cases in the acute phase; prior to this time, a patient was housed in
a medical ward till recovery from the attack should take place
or, as in not a few other cases, perforation. It was at this latter
stage that the desperately ill person was transferred to a surgeon
in a last forlorn hope. However, on one occasion an acute case
was seen in the Hindhead area. The decision was taken to remove
the patient to hospital for operation. A message was sent on foot
to the Haslemere Ambulance Station which then boasted a
stretcher which could be mounted on a wheeled chassis. This was
solemnly pushed up to Hindhead by a squad of Ambulance men,
and the patient removed in the same way back to the Cottage
Hospital. The patient survived this time lag, the crude transport

and the subsequent operation. Some folk then were tough, mighty tough.

The epilogue must not be omitted, for the illness occurred on a Sunday. When the doctor arrived at the Hospital and announced that he intended to operate on the new patient, he was met by this remark from the Matron, "But you know, Doctor, we never operate on Sunday." But for once at least the Matron met her master, and a successful operation followed.

At the same date a horse carriage overturned on Hatch Hill towards Churt, with some suspected serious injuries to a lady who had been returning to her house in Crondall. After examination, a doctor who had been called to the accident went down to Churt Post Office where, by telegraph, he summoned the horse ambulance from Guildford. In due course, which amounted to about two and a half hours over the hilly road, the ambulance arrived, picked up the injured woman and proceeded with the doctor still in attendance all the way to Crondall, where a proper handover to the medical advisor of the injured person took place.

Nowadays much of this episode would have taken up about half an hour, and would have been done with far more comfort for patient and doctor. In the case above related, four and a half hours elapsed between accident and arrival at the patient's bed, while for the doctor, six hours of his day had been occupied.

Education in its sterner aspect grew apace in these years in the nineties. In what used to be called the Lecture Hall, —actually the old Congregational Church in Lower Street—a Mr. Joseph Swindells advertised and started a Grammar School. His wife taught the girls and younger boys, himself would deal with the older boys. He advertised that "firm discipline is maintained throughout the school." I have, however, met a few survivors of his discipline who did not harbour any grudges at his methods.

It was early in this decade also that free education became available to all; the old penny a week contribution was abolished. Opportunity was taken at that time to form a local penny bank to encourage the thrifty deposition of the pennies previously set aside to pay the child's school fee. This bank received a mention a few times in the Parish magazine, but then a blank. Was there a run on the bank for a household need, or did it continue its initial success quietly like any other well-behaved bank? No accounts, no pack drill!

A few years later in 1898 National Schools were built to accommodate in a central position the increasing number of children. Miss Hesse very kindly made available one and a half acres of land. Previously, older children had been accommodated at Church Hill in the old school originally built by her father, the

Rev. Hesse, and subsequently enlarged four times, while the infants were taught at the old Town or Market Hall.

Having reached the turn of the century, we must stop for a breather to take stock. Perhaps we could foregather at the old Swan Inn as we did a couple of hundred years ago* or if it is a fine day, we might sit up on the fields of Half Moon Farm.

The climate outside Haslemere was rather threatening and lowering. The war in South Africa had been stuttering along for a year and the strength of the Boer resistance had been an unwelcome reality to the slowly awakening British Government. It was all so far away that the country at large, including its government, could not bring to focus any features of the war except the major events of loss or gain. The papers could even then write of our gallant men storming impossible positions with a cheer, while all around them were decimated, and of the gallantry with which the wounded or defeated enemy were treated. But, as usual, only those who fought, survived or died, knew the real horror and beastliness of the war, added to, then, by diseases such as typhoid, dysentery, tetanus, etc.

At home the increasing casualty list notified to those who read them, of the loss of useful and intelligent men—mainly the best, fittest mentally and physically, of their generation, who were to fertilise the sterile ground of the African Veldt, rather than carry civilisation forward at a faster rate. In Haslemere these lists were small, and the impact of war therefore small and individual, but much support was given to subscription lists for wounded, prisoners or relatives.

The Old Queen had entered the last year of her amazing span of rule. Her tenure of the throne had from the local point of view practically covered the years between the loss of Haslemere's borough status and the achievement of Parish Council government. The Queen had been a focus of devoted discipline in living and growth. Many people have objected to discipline as found in the armed forces, but a little reflection will show that these same disciplines interpreted with moderate intelligence and infected with a little enthusiasm would always win battles. Here in Haslemere were now, and had been for the past twenty to thirty years, an increasing number of intelligent and successful people who had caught some of that disciplined infection. They further had the means and the will to manage or lead others to similar ways of life.

At this time the recently appointed Rector of the Parish was a man who was able to give a lead to, and inspire fresh support for the various developing needs of the growing community.

---

*(See Haslemere in History)

Canon Aitken had been appointed to this parish of Haslemere at the retirement of the preceding incumbent, Etheridge. Mr. Etheridge had covered the first twenty nine years of the new Parish of Haslemere and certainly had a great record of progress. He had seen the complete rebuilding of the Church, the addition of a South Aisle, new organ and peal of bells, new Rectory and the enlargement four times of the National Schools. The number of Easter Communicants had increased by five times. In addition he had sponsored and managed a number of the charities and organisations mentioned earlier. His successor, Mr. Aitken, was no doubt grateful for the achievements of his predecessor, and was spurred on and encouraged thereby to maximum endeavours.

In addition to unflagging energy of body, Mr. Aitken seems to have had inexhaustible funds of inspiration and great winsomeness and tact in his dealings with the whole parish. His whole life here and his work could be summed up in a little poem which he quoted in the Parish Magazine for July 1901—"A Preacher's Soliloquy" :

> "There was a time full well I know
> When I had not yet seen you so,
> But now as through the streets I go
> There seems no face so shapeless, so
> Forlorn, but that there's something there
> That like the heavens doth declare
> The glory of the Great All-Fair.
> And so mine own each one I call
> And so I dare to love you all."

Before he had been in Haslemere many years, everyone knew that the last two lines of the verse were very true and they reciprocated his love, even where opinions in detail differed. By May 1899 he had been stressing to the local Friendly Societies the need to discuss Old Age Pensions and Workmen's cottages. In 1900 he told the Parish Council that for an ordinary cottage in East Street there were over thirty applicants—young people if they wanted to marry had to leave the parish. The new houses in Underwood Road were all occupied before they were dry or fit for habitation. More cottages would still be needed for the workmen on the newly developing estates at Derby Road, Museum Hill and elsewhere.

He was able to boast gladly of two hundred and thirty seven children and twenty-four teachers at his Sunday School. The Parish had recently been enlarged by the inclusion of a long strip of Thursley Parish which had always intruded into the vitals of Haslemere. The population had been one thousand three hundred and was now over two thousand five hundred. To welcome the

newcomers he envisaged and worked to form a new parish* and
encouraged what was already in process—the development of the
new parishes at Grayswood and Camelsdale.

It will be rewarding now to survey the scene around as we
sit perched on the hill, overlooking the town which housed such
forward-looking men as Jonathan Hutchinson, Stewart Hodgson,
George Aitken and Robert Hunter.

In the town below us we should see the spread of small houses
along the north side of Lower Street and the development of shops
around The Folly. The Folly was a tall thin house on the north
side of the narrow entry to Lower Street, opposite what is now
a pharmacy. Originally built about 1790, as a small private house,
it was soon christened "The Folly" for reasons which are not now
evident. It was let, for many years, to a succession of tenants, and
passed into a sort of limbo about the date of the accession of Queen
Victoria. More recently, about 1875 it was bought by a Mr.
Ebenezer Gammon as a shop for about £200. The Gammons till
then had been living in a cottage at the top of Shepherds Hill, and
Sunday by Sunday could be seen with their pony and trap going
to Northchapel where they attended a Coaklers'† meeting.

After the arrival of their first baby, Mrs. Gammon again
assisted in the shop, her baby behind the counter in a cradle which
she rocked with a foot while coping with a customer. As the
business grew, the Gammons moved away and a manager was
appointed who lived over the shop. In due course two daughters
were born to the manager and his wife. One of the daughters loved
and married against the wishes of her parents. The baby which
later announced itself was an embarrassment to the young couple
who went on an urgent visit to a relation. The thought of grand-
parental disapproval aroused so much anxiety in the pair that they
decided on a rather unusual way of planting the baby. The father
took the child to London in a parcel, engaged a special messenger
and sent the baby through the post, as the daily papers later
described it, to Charing Cross Hospital. The plan was not successful in the way hoped for. The baby survived, its parents were
traced, and the subsequent publicity led to a family re-union.

About the turn of the century, the original shop at The Folly
was enlarged and extended by the conversion of an adjacent store
and a grain store, which had belonged till his death to Mr. H.
Hale of the Old Malthouse. The extensions were made by a builder
named Reuben Smith, one of the founders of a firm which was
absorbed later by a large firm called Privett's.

A very old lady whose early childhood was spent in Haslemere has given me an interesting description of the little town

---

†Small religious sect.   *St. Christopher's.

about 1880. She lived at "The Folly" now part of a flourishing shop, then a large living room screened with fine mesh wire frame and a cellar beneath, leading back from the front door, a passage past a pump before the tiny back garden. The deep well contained excellent drinking water although it was within a few yards of the local slaughter house. One of their neighbours was a well-known Corn Chandler, stout, with a face like the rising sun, who spent hours leaning over his shop door at the foot of Shepherds Hill greeting all and sundry. The old lady recalled the attractive confectionery shop (now a chemist) just across the way, the square bay window packed with most delicious meat pies, cakes and buns. Great excitement was always brought to the town by the through traffic. On Goodwood Race days, sitting in the upstairs window, she had a close view of the stream of mainly horse-drawn traffic, hansom cabs, growlers, wagonettes, costers carts with pearly kings and ladies with ostrich feather hats, dog carts, caravans, an occasional bus, and very many bicycles. This went on all day and half the night.

Another regular journey which interested her was that of an old couple who lived at the top of Shepherds Hill. Sunday by Sunday, wet or fine, the old people set off early to attend the Coaklers meeting house at Northchapel. The old wife wearing a close fitting black bonnet and a shawl round her shoulders sat in the donkey cart while her husband walked the five miles by her side. Every week a countryman from Lodsworth came into the town with supplies of fresh fruit or vegetables which he sold from his cart.

At the beginning of the High Street we should see Frank Gibb's new shop and the butcher next door, built in 1892, both of which dwarfed the remaining buildings at that corner.

The Swan Hotel had found it necessary to enlarge, and hung its frontage forward. The Workmen's Institute also still looked fresh and new, though tiled in keeping with most of its neighbours. The next block of shops, called The Broadway, extended the whole frontage of a property on which there had been previously a plan for traditional stone faced private house. Its appearance may have given joy to the eye of the builder, but the great majority of people averted their eyes in horror from the twin minarets. How came it that the Parish Council had allowed the builder to carry out his frontage to the old railings? A firm decision on this point at the start of their first year of office would have created a precedent which would have, sooner or later, to be set in the Town. The other side of the High Street did not differ materially from its appearance one hundred or two hundred years before. Perhaps a few details, such as the trees beside The Lodge,*

*Then the name of the Haslemere Museum.

The Old Forge, High Street, Haslemere, now National Provincial Bank and others.

Aldworth, Blackdown. Former summer house of Lord Tennyson, poet laureate.

Above: Haslemere High Street c. 1896, before major alterations on the South East Side of the street.

Left: An old Broomsquire and his wife c. 1870. Nanny and Boddy Hill, Stoney Bottom, Grayshott.

The Local Motor Bus 1906
Passengers on this occasion included a school-master and several
well-known residents.

Haslemere High Street c. 1868, before the construction of West
Street. Left foreground, a public water standpipe.

Blackdown. In centre is the road junction where Aldworth drive advances to the bottom right of picture; bottom left to Roundhurst by the Smugglers Hollow. Note almost entire absence of trees.

Haslemere High Street c. 1890.

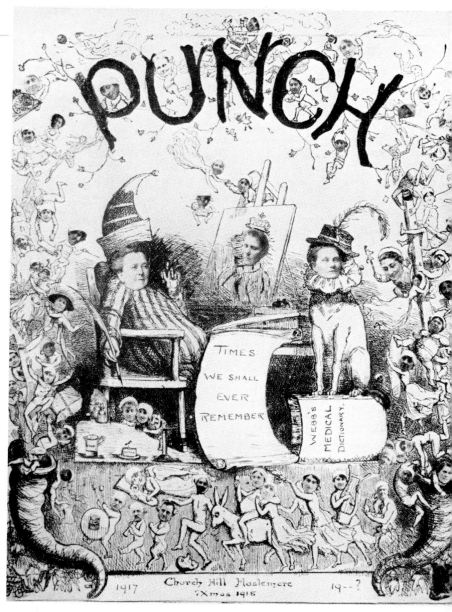

This card was made at Christmas 1918. The faces are those of then living workers at the Church Hill War Hospital. The coroneted head is the Superintendent, Mrs. Stables. Three doctors are bottom left, Ardagh, Winstanley, Roger Hutchinson.

View looking East from Old Malt House, at foot of Shepherds Hill. The Folly is adjacent to Gammons shop (now Neil Ross). Pastry shop (now demolished) ivy covered. Note street lamp on house.

Market Place at Jubilee of Queen Victoria 1889.

1886 Town Map of Haslemere.

This map, similar to earlier Borough Maps of 1722, 35, 75 and 1814, drawn by John Clark, was found during repairs to the doorway of the Comrades Club, with other papers.

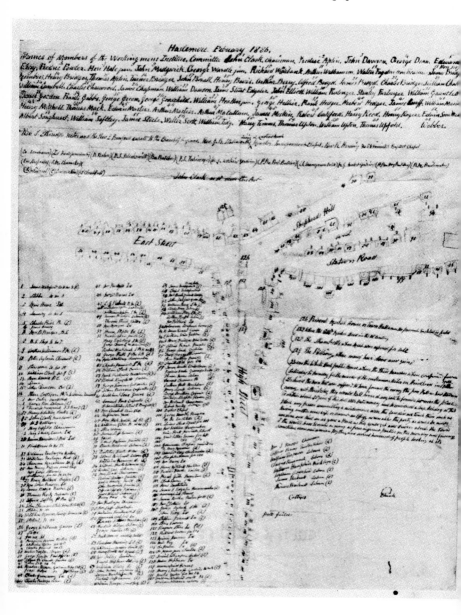

a few trees in front of the shops from the butcher to Mrs. Bridger's three-gabled business, one or two lamp posts and a water stand pipe will have been swept away. Looking to the east, a few houses were creeping up the new road called Museum Hill, but beyond Thursley End, the only house before the cottages on Haste Hill was the very plain Police Station. To the south, up and over the hill, there were no houses apart from Whitwell Hatch and Hilltop Farm, till Scotland Lane where a few cottages had recently been built. To the north, only Tanhouse, as Oaklands was then called, broke the green of the fields as far as the Church, apart from two cottages close to the railway. Away to the west if we could see round the corner, there were still only a few scattered houses on the slope of Clayhill, and on the irregular green at the foot of Farnham Lane was still the Jubilee water pump. This pump was one of several which had been installed round the town either in that form or as stand pipes with water delivered from nearby springs, owing to the generosity of the late Mr. Stewart Hodgson. Even at this date wells were the chief source of water supply to the houses, great or small, of the district, and provided the wells were at a sufficient distance from houses (which they never were) or from cesspits (which they often were not), the water might be good and potable. Many illnesses, however, were rife in those days, such as diptheria and typhoid and its cousins, which are infrequent today for sanitary and allied reasons. But it was not till 1907 that a public water works supplying unlimited water to the houses was built on the slope of Blackdown above Chase Farm.

Rising over the roofs of the west side of High Street, the bell tower of the New Schools could be seen, surmounting a large red brick building only completed this year. The novelty of the building had attracted an absolutely one hundred per cent attendance for a few days, but a month or two later parents were urged in the Parish magazine to make an effort to maintain full attendance.

George Macdonald, LL.D, who lived for a few years at St. George's Wood (built by his architect brother) was a remarkable writer, lecturer, poet and mystic. His Highland ancestry and upbringing endowed him with mental and spiritual energy which animated a compelling eloquence when he preached or lectured.

He was one of the magic Victorian circle of Ruskin, Carlyle, Dickens, Trollope, Thackeray and Macaulay, to pick out a few only of those with whom he was on the most friendly and respected terms. He received a Civil List pension and the gift from eminent friends and admirers, of a large villa in Italy.

His work was immensely valued and successful, his novels grossly pirated, were eagerly read all over America, equal in popularity with those of Dickens and Thackeray.

In his day his literary reputation ranked with the highest throughout the English speaking world.

About the turn of the century, Dr. George Macdonald often drove down into the town from his new home along the Grayswood Road draped in a scarlet cloak, which revealed a white serge suit, and with a bearded face topped by a large grey felt hat he presented an ensemble which would surely please the most progressive of modern tailors. The town was also frequently enlivened by the arrival of a smart four-in-hand driven down the High Street by a Mr. Harman who had come to live at Grayswood Place. He was so charmed by his surroundings that he presented a church to his parish at Grayswood. Unfortunately for him, after the consecration of the church, his wife was the first parishioner to be buried in the churchyard.

From the memory of an old resident, one of the most trying visitations of life was, as previously mentioned, the prevalence of dust. Road surfaces were still primitive and many authorities had not learned to make a well bound surface. A further cause for trouble for the new made roads was the hill slopes on which heavy rainfall, or the use of brake skid pans on carts, caused the surface to be wasted or broken away, with consequent mud and finally dust.

In May 1901 the local fair attracted nothing to the Market, but the occasion was celebrated by over two thousand people at 8.30 p.m. in the Town Square, where all forms of catch-penny and amusement were to be found. Swings, swing boats, "cokernut" shies, Aunt Sallies, shooting galleries. Much of this equipment needed fixing in the roads, and therefore hacked up a possibly previously hard surface. Small wonder that popular outcry grew to a petition by fifty odd people that something be done about good road surfacing, even in 1906. Over the next few years, hopping from field to field, via Town meadow to Clayhill, the fair finally came to rest on the common land now known as St. Christopher's Green.

Reference has been made earlier to attempts by certain well disposed persons to interest the fingers, intelligence and spare time of local people in art and craft industries. For some years these endeavours met with a fair measure of success.

All these endeavours had the object of employment of leisure or spare time, or of stimulating an interest in work which brought reward not only in a cash sale, but in the creation of beauty in function. Not every case, however, had high thoughts always; a section of the Town whose concern was a special skill was highlighted in the local Police Courts. In March of this new century year, three men were charged with having permitted certain unlawful games of chance—to wit, Shovehalfpenny and Tipit at the White Horse, Swan and Good Intent, and Shovehalfpenny and Coddam at the White Lion. All the Inns are still flourishing except the Good Intent which, after nearly a century of use as licensed premises has reverted to private ownership. At one of these Inns in the course of some alterations, the house cesspit was found under the dining room.

If you had turned the pages of the Visitors' Book in one of these Inns, you might then have read the following:

"Some praise their food and some their beer,
But I praise thee, fair Haslemere.
How sweet, foul air, foul streets, to find
We've left in London, far behind.
But if you want good beef, good beer,
I bid you come to Haslemere."

Before we leave our vantage point on the hill-top, we shall catch the echo of a remark made just as King Edward VII came to the throne: "Yes, Haslemere is a very pleasant place for the people who have plenty of money," and in the month of May that could be true.

"Soon will the high mid-summer pomps come in.
Soon will the musk carnations break and swell,
Soon shall we have gold-dusted snapdragon,
Sweet William with his homely cottage smell,
And stocks in fragrant blow!
Roses that down the alleys shine afar,
And open jasmine-muffled lattices,
And groups under the dreaming garden trees,
And the full moon and the white evening star."

Arnold.

And in the many lovely gardens, for be it remembered that gardens were in plenty, with generous and devoted attention, garden games and garden parties played a large part in the social life of the summer.

Much of this way of life continued with the intermission of World War I until World War II, though by then the glories were somewhat dimmed by greater taxation, the prevalence of motor cars and a fiercer competitive spirit in games. Nevertheless, to those who never knew such ways of life, the past will seem scarcely credible, and perhaps boring. This last would seem an ironic thought to the Edwardians, as they may, from elsewhere, regard the frantic attempts to escape from boredom of many of the later Elizabethans.

Horses and carriages, horses and dogcarts, hacking to visit or for pleasure—these were the delights of leisured mornings, or a happy afternoon calling. Parties of friends or clubs driving for picnics or meetings in two or four horse brakes, tradesvans from massive shires to the gipsy's bony little pony, horses even for the army for cavalry or transport—horses everywhere, and so pervasive were they that the unit of power for railway, marine or stationary engine, was a horse power.

At this date were saddlers in the town, with their smells of leather. At one time, of course, tanneries had been a commonplace in the town, but now no leather was produced except chamois leather at New Mill*. Down in the town where the Westminster Bank is to-day, there was Mr. Purkis, the cornchandler, ready to supply equine needs. Note his name—we are not so far from the New Forest where eight hundred years earlier, one "Purkiss" a woodcutter, carried home in his cart the dead body of William Rufus. Our roots are pretty deep in the countryside if one looks for them. The Purkis family had come to Haslemere in 1867 and had lived at Gorse Cottage, Petworth Road. Mr. Purkis had at one time been steward to the late Mr. Stewart Hodgson.

If he had walked the High Street of Haslemere in 1903, a visitor might have wondered just how deep the roots of Haslemere really were. If he had walked into the local Museum he would have met a very delightful Curator, who would have helped to resolve that problem. He had that morning received a pottery urn, admittedly broken, but complete enough to announce the presence of Roman influence. A gardener, while making a hedge in a new garden between Beech Road and Grayswood Road, had dug this urn whole but, leaving it out overnight, frost had cracked it. By arrangement with the landowner, a careful examination was made of the ground for fifty yards around. More pottery was found, much in an undamaged state, which accounted for a number of burials. Two years later, the development of a nearby building site produced more burial urns and evidence of what was described as a possible cremation area. The pottery has been re-examined, and is stated to be Romano-British of 40-80 A.D. and 80-120 A.D. The amount of urns would suggest the probability of a large farm or villa in the neighbourhood, probably at a distance of four to five hundred yards. But no sign of building has been found, though at Chiddingfold, only twenty years earlier, had been found the foundations of a large country farmhouse and its associated debris. The Museum was enriched also in this latter year by the operations sponsored by Allen Chandler round the dewponds at Blackdown, where a great quantity of worked flints were found of the mesolithic period. Many others had been found, in a scattered way, on all the greensand hills and farm fields of the neighbourhood.

So fast was development speeding again, that the commons round Haslemere and Hindhead were threatened with building

*Near Critchmere.

projects. Haslemere was fortunate up to this period in having had as Chairman of its Parish Council, Sir Robert Hunter, Solicitor to the General Post Office. Sir Robert had, for many years previously, been a great fighter for the commons and footpaths of the countryside, at first in the immediate neighbourhood of London, and later on a wider scale. He had taken an active part in the legal defence of many of the commons, and had succeeded in preserving their status against greedy developers. He had been, as previously mentioned, one of the original founders of the National Trust with Octavia Hill and Canon Rawnsley. It is to them, and their example, and to the few like-minded, that the public of Britain in general, and not merely of this small area, owe the immense tracts of England which are still available to country-lovers and free to all.

Around Haslemere, therefore, his mantle, helped by the efforts of others of like mind, spread a zone of unspoiled and unspoilable common and a tracery of open spaces. A standard of building was set to match the traditional methods of other days and to retain at least something of the craving for garden flowers or vegetables which is necessary to the spirit of most Britons.

We may recall that much of the development in Hindhead and Grayshott which had taken place during the previous half a century had been on common-land. There had been a few older houses such as Grayshott House, Grayshott Farm, the Old Huts Hotel, Seven Thorns Inn, a farm or two in Whitmore Vale and some scattered cottages, but the main surge of development had begun about 1890. Within ten years Hindhead could be described by a writer of the time as one of the most fashionable health resorts within forty miles of London. A good deal of unrest spread through the more thoughtful residents, and by 1902 the Haslemere Commons Preservation Society, which had originally functioned from 1884 to 1895, was revived, and under a new and representative leadership, saved a large part of what is now left of the nearby common-lands for posterity. Their two chief aims were announced—To protect local beauty spots, and to support the local Council in securing local rights and to urge them to put into force any powers they might have to maintain the beauty of the neighbourhood.

Looking back to 1885, among the earlier settlers in Hindhead was a Mr. F. Jackson, late of Hampstead, who acquired some sixty odd acres of land from Mr. James Baker of (Old) Frensham Hall. On this he built The Grange, in which he was living by 1895, at the corner of what is now Headley Road. His neighbour in The Huts direction was Mr. A. J. Balfour. He also sold various plots of land to the Russell family, and to a Mr. R. A. Townshend.

On his way to Haslemere in June 1898, Bernard Shaw had strolled into the Strand Registry Office with a Miss Charlotte

Frances Payne Townshend, and without fuss or ceremony they were married. Their honeymoon was spent at Pitfold House, lent them for the occasion by the parents of Lord Beveridge, a comfortable small house on the edge of the moor overlooking Critchmere. They later moved into the house called Blencathra, now St. Edmund's School, which Mrs. Shaw leased from her relations.

At Pitfold, during what sounds like a playful honeymoon, Shaw had several minor accidents, producing fractures of bones, attributed by his local medical advisers to poor blood, due to insufficient meat in his diet. A dispute over this diet after a third accident, produced the remark from him, "Death would be better than cannibalism." After a short change of air in the Isle of Wight, they returned to live at Blencathra.

At this time Grayshott as a village was slowly spreading out from its nucleus by the church, but was nowhere near the Shaw's house, though Hindhead was built as far as Tower Road. The local press of the time reported the attendance of Mr. and Mrs. Shaw at a series of four musical concerts given by well known artistes in the Hindhead Hall (now the Congregational Hall). Shaw, himself, took a leading part in the formation of a brass band at Grayshott.

Sir F. Pollock was then living at Hindhead Copse, and a performance of "As You Like It" was given in his garden during that summer. Shaw commented favourably on the acting, but not on the stage props, which he said should be described as "As You Don't Like It."

He did not consider a local dramatic society was competent to perform one of his plays, though a few years later he relented, so that a Haslemere company was the second in the country to produce his "You Never Can Tell."

More accidents followed in the summer of 1899 while fooling about with an early bicycle, and after a few months in a house on the Hog's Back, the Shaws rented Blackdown Cottage to the south of Haslemere during part of 1900. Here was every incentive to writing, isolation, a wonderful wide and long view over the Weald, and an unspoiled heath and countryside. However, he left the Hindhead district because, he said, of the time consumed in travel to and from London. This surely could only have been a part of his reason, for in 1905 he settled at Ayot St. Lawrence.

He had often been seen driving about Hindhead in a carriage and pair, and, critics of his socialism (there) said, dressed in a suit of pyjamas. There may have been an element of truth in this suggestion, for he appeared to have spent a considerable amount of time in near attachment to a sick bed.

It must have been about this time that Arnold Dolmetsch stayed with the Shaws, and had an introduction to the lovely countryside in which he later settled.

One person with whom Shaw crossed swords was the Grayshott village schoolmistress. Knowing of his love of nature, he was asked by her, while on a visit to the local school, to give the children a talk on that subject.

His roving eye caught a notice on the school wall advertising the close season for game, and he read out some of the headings. He then began his comments, and drew parallel for some of the apparent anomalies in other laws, based on false premises, and showed how young folk suffered in this way from the mandates of their elders. He declared to them that the first duty of a child was to disobey its parents, and the behests of adults in general. These remarks delivered perhaps in puckish humour to point a paradox delighted the children who, of course, took them at face value. The schoolmistress, however, rebuked him and protested, quite correctly, that she had the entire responsibility for the children at school all round the year, and that such remarks as his would take many weeks for her to efface!

Coincident with the death of the old Queen Victoria early in 1901, and consequent on the retirement of Sir Robert Hunter from his position as Chairman of the Parish Council, Allen Chandler was elected to this responsible, but scarcely enviable position. He guided the deliberations of a very mixed Council with much persistence and skill for the next decade. His experience which he had gained by serving also on the Hambledon District Council was of value in the direction of this fraction of the Union of Parishes. It was largely due to his initiative and skill that Urban District status was achieved by Haslemere in 1913. Owing to the constant and rapid increase in population, by influx as well as by natural causes, problems of housing, roads, sanitation, organisations, water and other public service supplies, all tested the temper, patience and ingenuity of all residents, including—not least—the Councillors. When some years later, in 1907, Arthur Parsons (Solicitor) died, who had given much public service to his home town, a friend wrote as follows:—"Many a long evening was spent in the back parlour of Peter Aylwin (The Chemist) trying in a primitive way to keep the village sweet and clean, trying too to interpret long letters of criticism which seldom failed to be a prelude to our proceedings."

These remarks were probably a gross understatement, for during the years from 1901 to 1905 the population was to rise from two thousand to three thousand persons.

CHAPTER V

And Those that have no Remembrance

DISAPPEARANCE — NEW CHURCH — SUFFRAGETTES
ROYAL VISIT — SCREAMING HORSE — CONAN DOYLE

A few items of purely local interest may be inserted here. Two more artistic ventures were started shortly after the Coronation of King Edward VII in 1902. A weaving house at Green Bushes was opened in Foundry Road by a Mr. Luther Hooper, and a pottery at Hammer by Mr. Radley Young. These projects were in a sense commercial, but were also a sort of mission on behalf of the fast dying out local crafts, and to give gainful employment to a section of the public who could not find a living in the newer industrial world. In the following year a wood working industry was started by Romney Green in Foundry Meadow. In the local paper of the day a hopeful correspondent proposed to build an electric tramway between Haslemere and Farnham.

The needs of the increasing population seemed to have impelled the appointment of a Town Crier once again, a post which had lapsed many years before. Possibly this need arose from the undoubted round of social activity of those days, not all of which was selfish, but often in pursuit of the care of the less well endowed section of the population. For though social strata were definitely demarcated and maintained in places like Haslemere, care was taken by many well-disposed persons to ameliorate conditions of hardship. The causes of those hardships were to remain for another forty to fifty years before their turn came for attention. The first remedy of those hardships was the bad one of doles (at best only an emergency prop) provided by the surplus incomes obtained by relatively high business gains set against a persistently low wage level. Two wars and a great economic recession were needed to drive home the lessons of the value of approximately full employment standards.

The old churchyard had now reached saturation point, and a new area was acquired and dedicated on the other side of the field track north-west of the church. Within a year or so the track was widened and extended, and later was further developed as Derby Road.

In 1903 a new church was consecrated as St. Christophers at Weyhill. For some years before this date mission services had been held in a small galvanised iron room in Foundry—now Kings—

Road. These had been conducted by a Rev. Leake, who became in 1902 the first vicar of Grayswood. The Choirmaster and organist was J. W. Whitcher, the Clerk of the Parish Council.

This new church in Weyhill had become necessary owing to the great spread of building along Kings Road and towards Shottermill. The Rev. Watson, who became priest-in-charge of St. Christophers said in later years that in 1902 there were very few houses between the church and Lion Green, one or two old cottages near the bridge over the stream beyond the Fair Ground and none on the left—the south side of Clayhill (Weyhill), as one comes up from the railway bridge. The mission hall had drawn a congregation of twenty-five persons, but as soon as it was built St. Christophers Church was near filled, especially on Sunday evenings. At the same date, however, the Rector of Haslemere, whose church was filled on Sunday mornings, made further complaint of the smallness (about forty persons) of the evening congregation.

The Sunday Schools were a joint service and were held in the Church Schools in Chestnut Avenue with an average of one hundred and eighty children. This joint service continued till 1911 when it was removed to St. Christophers.

In 1903 the church made a great change in its illumination; hitherto flaring gas jets, possibly by this date fitted with fish-tail burners, provided a fair degree of flickering light. Now these burners were scrapped, to be replaced by what were known as incandescent burners. Many will remember this brilliant lighting with its unaccountable ways of creating difficulties. The early mantles were very fragile indeed and might be split by careless fitting even from the start; the mantle supports were also extremely brittle, and the glass cylinders were originally made of glass which seemed to take pleasure in cracking with the least draught. The new installation, therefore, while in general giving a much improved light, would have been a ready source of criticism and chit-chat.

The Daily News of August 1903 in a comment on the strange disappearance of a lady doctor from a London Hospital adds a comment on a parallel incident. Over thirty years earlier a farmer named Williamson who lived at or near Haslemere left his house on a fine sunny day to cross a big meadow. His intention was to give further instructions to one of his farm workers on his duties on the other side of the field. He had left his wife, baby in arms, at the doorway looking out after her husband as he went away over the field, whistling and singing. At about half the distance across the field he suddenly vanished. No bush, hedge, ditch or well was known or visible which might have hidden him. The amazed wife, screaming "He has gone. What an awful thing" fell unconscious to the ground. Two neighbours who had been standing with her also were witness to this disappearance, and the shock to them was so great that they could not work for several weeks after. The wife, thus apparently so suddenly widowed, on recovery to consciousness was found to have lost her reason.

Further comment appeared in the Daily News of September 5th suggesting that so relatively near an event must be well remembered by many local persons. The letter asked for more information.

So far we have no further printed information, but search has been made in local registry and parish records for note of the death of a Williamson at or about 1867/70, but without success.

On consideration, this absence of official information is not to be wondered at, for without a body there could be no medical certificate or even a registered burial. Much questioning has been done of elderly people who might have been alive at that date or within twenty years of that time. One elderly lady whose mother had died young recalled that her father would frequently warn her if she were going out on to the common, to be careful or she might disappear like that farmer did. More she could not say. An old man who lived in the village of Hammer to the west of Haslemere, in the course of a conversation at his home, pointed with his thumb over his shoulder, the indicated direction being up over Bramshott Common, where he said there had been a farmer, Williamson. Another elderly lady did not remember having heard of the incident, but stated that a farmer, Williamson once lived at Pitfold Farm, who had no connection with Professor Williamson who lived, twenty years later, at Pitfold House.

Of slighter interest, but such as to draw several indignant letters to the local newspaper, was the mention of a line of small posts along the frontage of the house called Causewayside (just below the Georgian Hotel). One of the local doctors lived here and placed his line of posts along what he felt was his own curtilage, but traditionalists wrote at once complaining of possible obstruction or risk to passers-by. The backwoodsmen won.

The whole town was agog with news of the visit on the 3rd November 1903 of King Edward VII to Midhurst where he would lay the foundation stone of the new Sanatorium above Henley Hill. The King came as far as Haslemere by train, from which he travelled in an open landau with four horses. His route lay along Foundry or Gas-house Road, as it was sometimes called, but was renamed for the future as Kings Road.

The type of housing along that road attracted the comment from him that he had always heard of Haslemere as a pretty town, but now was disappointed. At Fernhurst, a large troop of children gave him a very enthusiastic demonstration, at which the King waved his hand and also cried "Hurrah, hurrah."

During the year the Ancient Order of Foresters Club had met at Hindhead to discuss a scheme for Old Age Pensions which had been submitted by the Executive Council of Sheffield. After some discussion a vote was taken which was unanimously against any state-aided pension scheme. Perhaps the Club felt a little over-confident in the stability of life, for on August Bank Holiday more than one thousand visitors had come to Haslemere, and there had been a notable cricket week.

The condition of the roads has been referred to before, and an attempt was made at first to mitigate the nuisance of dust by watering. In the main this was an inadequate remedy, for though there was actually plenty of water underground, in practice there was only well water in supply. Where sufficient water was applied intense criticism became vocal, because of the consequent mud and slush. Repairs to roads were haphazard, and mainly consisted in rough dumping, to be worn in later by the users. Attempts were made to improve this last nuisance of mud by means of scraping and so on, until about 1909 tarred pavements and road surfaces were recommended. This again was not at first a sovereign remedy, for the tar remained tacky, and stuck as often to the traveller as to the surface of the ground. Gradually, of course, improvement took place, but it was not till after World War I that tar macadam roads became the dangerous but smooth race tracks that are now provided for a nomadic, wheeled, population.

A dispute which lasted for the best part of three years broke out over a suggested road widening at Penfolds corner. This road junction of Lower Street, Tanners Lane and Station Road at that date had a small triangle of grassy waste land between the three roads. The first part of Station Road was a bottle neck, and was not merely reputedly a danger spot, but the site of accidents.

Correspondence passed between land-owner, Parish Council and District Council, and as fast as one point in dispute was apparently settled, another dilemma was presented. Ultimately the point in dispute rested on a demand for an unlimited pure water supply in return for land concession. Agreement was reached coincident with the completion of the generous Blackdown Water Scheme.

A new road was made at this time leading from the High Street to the new Schools below Pathfields, and within a year or two complaints were being received by the school authorities and by the Parish Council as to the long detour needed to go from the schools to the west end of the Parish. A proposal to the land-owner was made to carry a footpath from Tanners Lane across the higher ground of the intervening fields to the road leading to the

new schools. The suggestion was not received kindly and no
development took place until 1908 after renewed efforts at negotia-
tion.

In spite of the efforts of many progressive and enlightened
residents, there were obviously well entrenched last-ditchers. These
last-ditchers have a way of dying—frequently of natural causes
in their own ditches—which thus become a convenient bridge
for the progress of others. It happened here. First of all, this footpath through the water meadows which crossed one of the many
tributaries of the Wey by a small footpath, was gained by the
death of the land-owner, but not till 1911 was the long-delayed
dream of Mr. Aitken to provide more cottage accommodation
realised in the building of the Bridge Road and Fieldway cottages
by a voluntary group, under his leadership, which called itself
the Haslemere Tenants Association. The road now known as
Bridge Road, from Tanners Lane to Chestnut Avenue, was then
flanked by the houses of the new garden suburb.

Klondyke Cottages at Grayswood which had been built before
the turn of the century, were sited in an area which called forth
much criticism. Little had been done for the drainage of the area,
which had been cut about by building operations and, as usual,
the battlefield (English for builders' gardens) was strewn with
the wreckage of the said operations. It was a sad business for
those involved, for though Grayswood was administered from the
Haslemere area, the drainage was largely the responsibility, willing or otherwise, of an adjoining parish. It was all good grist for
the local papers.   .

Some local irresponsibility was given notice in the Surrey
Advertiser in January 1903, when the landlord of the Wheatsheaf
Inn was brought before the Justices to explain what was meant
by a police charge of "a lively night." He declared that the Inn
was an old and respected family business, and had been in his
family for one hundred and fifty years and more. The rumpus
was probably a celebration of the news that the licence was to
be transferred from the old Inn (now a private house beside the
petrol station) to a new building across the road. To save trans-
ferring good old liquor across the road, the patrons were evidently
doing their best to ensure transit by consumption. The new
premises were opened in 1904. After this disturbance, which
placed Grayswood squarely in the public eye, a policeman, their
first, P.c. May, was stationed in the village.

During this decade, more of the medium-to-large size house
was being built, just along Derby Road, though only Trantlebec
was visible before 1916—along the Grayswood Road from 1903,
Beech Road 1905, Weydown Road, Half Moon Estate, Hill Road,
Courtsmount and Petworth Road and Three Gates Lane. By the

First World War most building land available for such houses had been absorbed, and that type of development remained static for many years.

The great need for more cottage or small properties was to remain with slight mitigations for many years. Small speculative builders and some larger firms put up rows and even individual small houses wherever they could buy land in small parcels. Pathfields cottages (built in 1873 and still standing in 1963) were an imaginative but nightmare example of the poorer kind of private enterprise. Popes Mead and Western Terrace were two outstanding examples of the profit motive against the barest requisites of decency for a small family. Small wonder that the Rector Aitken, as usual spokesman of the sound but unheeded minority, made violent criticism of lassitude in respect of building developments which practically prohibited young people from marrying and raising a family locally.

As noted before, it was not till 1911 that he was able to form a strong committee which resulted in the building of many of the houses in Bridge Road, and all Fieldway. These houses were built by a Tenants Committee to then modern and convenient designs and bore a sufficient relation to the traditional homes of the district, and were let at rents which did not seek a lurid profit.

Beyond the west side of the parish, above Shottermill, there was living at Pitfold House, a family called Beveridge. In 1894, when his parents returned from India, William, the late Lord Beveridge, then fifteen years of age, came with them to live at Pitfold House. As a young man he began to take an interest in social problems of which, by 1905, unemployment was paramount. Local district committees were set up in many towns. The unemployment in many areas was seasonal rather than round the year and by 1908 Haslemere was faced with such a problem. In December of that year a local Unemployment Fund was started, to make a guarantee fund from which to pay for found labour. The Chairman and founder of this committee was Sir Algernon Methuen, then head of the well-known publishing business, closely supported by Sir Richard Garton of Lythe Hill. A register of unemployed men was compiled and employers were asked to provide work; any incurred expenditure to be borne by the guarantee fund. By February of the following year, work had been found for one hundred unemployed men, the committee meeting fortnightly at the Workmen's Institute.

Young Beveridge was closely associated with this Committee in addition to his London work, and by July 1909 a scheme for insurance against unemployment by workmen was worked out by a local committee on which he sat. For the contribution of 4d. a week, the unemployed man would receive ten shillings a week benefit. This scheme was used as a pilot measure for that which received the assent of Parliament in 1911. A new spirit was evidently moving in Haslemere which would then be in the van of social progress. One wonders whether Cobbett would still have thought and spoken of Haslemere as a sink of iniquity.

During 1908 a rising politician came to address the electorate of Haslemere. A debate had been arranged between Ramsay Mac-Donald and St. Loe Strachey. The meeting was presided over by the Bishop of Guildford, who opened the proceedings with an address of fifteen minutes. He was followed by Ramsay MacDonald, who spun words into daisy chains for the next thirty minutes. Mr. St. Loe Strachey, who followed for the next thirty minutes admitted that his command of language could not equal that of the pre-ceding speaker. He then proceeded to demolish the arguments of his opponent. Fifteen minutes of each in turn followed, of further explanations, and then a last five minute salvo from the two heroes. The Bishop then wound up all the threads of argument to a satisfactory cat's-cradle, and the audience, such as were still awake, were then free to stagger out into the fresher air of Hasle-mere.

This meeting was probably against the background of the burning question of women's suffrage. A month later, two suffra-gettes held a meeting in Haslemere High Street, which was attended by fifteen hundred persons. The speaker stood under the old chestnut tree, while at the far end of the Broadway, Bridger's Band played stirring music as an accompaniment. Against this band and also the rowdyism of a number of hecklers, the speaker persisted (one almost said manfully). At later dates other meet-ings were held in various parts of the district where order pre-vailed, in the School Hall, in Town Meadow and even at Gray-shott.

During the past ten years, politics had increasingly occupied the minds and hopes of many local people. Socialism had been a growing force in the larger towns and in 1898 Bernard Shaw had lectured to the Microscope Society in Haslemere, "Why I am a Socialist." Later in that summer he married a wealthy lady of Hindhead, after which the honeymoon was spent at Pitfold House, the home of the Beveridge family, whence he emerged to try to convert Haslemere. No great compulsion was felt, according to reports of that date, to follow his political prescription, but in 1903 a branch business of the Co-operative Society was opened in Lower Street, where it remained until 1908, when the present premises were erected on Weyhill.

These years also saw the emergence of a great Liberal majority at the election of December 1905. Till then there had been a strong Conservative interest in the Guildford constituency. The Liberal programme swept like a strong breeze through the dusty corridors of Conservatism. Many idols were overthrown, among them being Mr. Brodrick, later Lord Middleton, who for many years had been returned by his Surrey supporters. Now, however, a champion was found in Haslemere, a daughter of Sir Robert Hunter, who spoke eloquently, persuasively and skilfully in the Liberal interest on many platforms in and around Haslemere. Comment from London Newspress was very favourable, and spoke of the Haslemere lady orator. Perhaps years previously this lady may have listened to a young barrister during the journey from London. A carriage had been sent from the meeting which he was to address and, as his host accompanied him down the platform to the station exit, they were approached and accosted by two heavily muffled men from the other end of the train. "Are you Mr. Asquith?" said one of the newcomers to the young barrister. On being answered in the affirmative, "May we join you in your carriage to the meeting; I represent The Times, and my friend here, The Daily News?" Off then trundled the carriage to the meeting which Mr. Asquith addressed and from which he left an hour later to return by the nine o'clock train to London.

Switching now from the sublime to the more commonplace, council elections came and went annually with regularity. The selection of candidates was made at an open parish meeting when candidates could be seen and questioned. On one occasion either bad weather or illness or both reasons prevented many of the usual residents from attending. The opportunity was seized by a small group to proceed to election of various of their members. Just as voting was beginning by a show of hands, one of the minority demanded a vote by ballot. As no preparation had been made for such an advanced procedure, the meeting had to be adjourned, thus giving hope to friends of absentees.

On another occasion at an election, held at the Town Hall, one of the candidates had arrived by carriage. Suddenly the unfortunate horse which had stood patiently for some time was seen to begin to shiver. After a short time during which pacification proved fruitless, the horse began to shriek violently, finally collapsing on to the ground, still shrieking. The crowd gathered closer round, with much proffered advice, but nothing practical emerged from the wordiness till one bystander knelt down by the horse, and applying his mouth to the horse's ear, he also shrieked loudly. At once the horse ceased making a noise and stood up in the shafts again, apparently perfectly composed and well. Perhaps the unfortunate horse had fallen asleep and had had a nightmare of what was to happen only a year later when the new Haslemere and Hindhead motor bus was greatly privileged by permission to stand in the old triangle in front of the Town Hall. A horse bus, owned by C. J. Covey, had previously run from Haslemere to Shottermill since 1900.

One other event of considerable interest stirred the whole of the Haslemere folk. In August 1905 the French Fleet paid a friendly visit to England and lay for a time in the Channel off Spithead. There was a move to cement and advertise the friendship between England and France at a time of international tension over Morocco. French officers were invited to London and there feted; they had previously been asked whom they would care to meet. The one above all others of those chosen was Sir Arthur Conan Doyle, then living at the house which he had built (now the Undershaw Hotel) at Hindhead near the crossroads.

The return journey from London of the French officers was to be made via Hindhead to Portsmouth. On the day in question as the cars bearing the French officers arrived near the crossroads, they passed through lines of our naval and military men, duly bemedalled, while the cars were pelted with flowers by a number of charming girls. This enthusiastic reception cheered the slightly anxious spirits of the Frenchmen who had been wondering what sort of reception awaited them so far from the Metropolis. To a man they all stood up and shouted "Magnifique, magnifique" as they turned into the drive of Undershaw. Here they passed under a leafy archway across which spread a banner inscribed "Bien-venue." After debouching from their cars they were greeted by a huge man with a heavy Napoleonic moustache, head crowned by a small straw hat and dressed in a lounge suit. Four bands discreetly placed in the grounds added to the joy of the afternoon, while the French in their long blue coats and white uniform hats were taken in hand by a number of ladies with leg-of-mutton sleeves and carrying lacy parasols, and feasted in a huge marquee. A good time was enjoyed by all, and the visitors left regretfully, but knowing now that Conan Doyle was the greatest Englishman of them all.

CHAPTER VI

Politics – High and Low

There had been, since 1898, a small sewerage plant in Foundry Road (later Kings Road). From that date the East side of the High Street and some of Lower Street had graduated from cesspits to water closets. This scheme in time included most of the town proper, and extension of the system was recommended in 1907 following an equivocal report of the Hambledon Union Medical Officer of Health. His report stated that "the town water supply is obtained from Pile Well. It is supplied to the public by means of stand pipes fixed into the streets, to which there is a constant supply. Storage by reservoir and of filtration, none. Quality doubtful, defects too many to mention. There is also small source of supply in Mrs. Hodgson's meadow. Sewerage is supplied for the town proper and for College Hill. The sewage is treated in double contact beds. All house drains are ventilated and sewers are ventilated by tall shafts and are flushed by means of the water cart once every fortnight." This last paragraph contains perhaps the germ of the whole argument, but in spite of the report and the flushing of the drains, the tall ventilating shafts must have been, even so, fairly strong witnesses.

It was not till 1914 that a more comprehensive scheme was given to the town. Even as late as 1925 there was still influential support from certain quarters as to the merit of cesspit or bucket with its certain advantage for land cultivation, as against expense of new methods.

The very adequate supply of water from Blackdown which was brought to the town in 1907 now assisted those who wished the town drainage to be carried rapidly from residences, much as Hercules found assistance from the river, so that a new and improved sewage works was constructed along Foundry Road.

Not all Haslemere parents were stern, even if they were careful for the happiness of their family. In 1906 a girl of eighteen years of age entered the service of the Tennyson family at Aldworth. Her father was a gardener at Frensham Hall, then the home of the Dowager Lady Cawdor. Aldworth at that date was the summer home of the second Lord Tennyson and his family. When the maidservant took her day off she found her own way down Blackdown Lane—as it was then called—and through Haslemere to her home. But at night, she was in later life happy to recall, her father accompanied her back to Aldworth.

At that time there was an indoor staff of ten maids under the control of a butler called Waters. The Aldworth Servants Hall was too small for any kind of social activity, but at Farringford the young Tennyson boys of sixteen to eighteen years of age would often smuggle themselves into the kitchen and jig the young maids round with the male staff, when the butler arranged a dance. She remembered how the big table was moved to the end of the room, thus producing a miniature stage on which Waters the butler settled himself, to play his melodeon as a dance band.

Whenever the household was at Haslemere, those of the staff who were not on duty were driven in on Sunday to Haslemere Church in the wagonette with Lord and Lady Tennyson. The maids all wore little bonnets, and with their natural country freshness heightened by the drive, must have formed a charming picture. The family and their staff occupied the pews in the North Aisle close by the Galahad window.

On one of these journeys one of the young maids recounts how she found herself seated by the side of Lord Tennyson. Shortly after starting the drive he noticed that she was modestly sitting away from him in a rather cramped position, and invited her to spread herself more comfortably.

A strong committee was formed by the Rev. Aitken in 1908 to commemorate the centenary of the birth of the Poet Laureate, the first Lord Tennyson. Plans were envisaged for a pageant incorporating scenes from many of his works, the whole event to be run by a famous pageant master, assisted by well-known artistes. A public meeting was held to discuss the scheme, and to go into ways and means. Strong opposition developed, and the promoters of the pageant were defeated on the ground of cost—a petty triumph for a petty caucus.

The conditions of some of the town pavements was giving rise to some adverse comment. With the influx of new residents there had, of course come a new category of shoppers. Many of these who may have driven up to the town, left their carriages for the more intimate duties of the bargains and inspection. Such persons unaccustomed to country town roads and paths found the irregularities a sore discomfort for walking in fashionable shoes. The worst offenders at road level were apparently the cobbles which stretched up to and along the fronts of many of the older buildings. These practical units for raising a path from the surrounding mud or water were given many names, but a local paper summed up general distaste with an article headed "Petrified kidneys." A smooth pathway of asphalt or concrete was urged, but received no official blessing for about forty years.

The Church of St. Bartholomew had received the gift of a memorial window to Lord Tennyson, a representation of Galahad by Burne-Jones, placed in the North Aisle opposite the South door, where it is noted and admired by many visitors to the Church. At this date, also, two new bells were placed in the Church, making a full peal of eight bells. Twenty years later Major Hesse brought the peal up to ten bells, and was instrumental in forming a strong company of bell-ringers.

On Weyhill, Sir Harry Waechter of Ramsters, near Chidding-fold, bought land fronting on St. Christopher's Green and the Wey-hill Road, and built a Drill Hall for the training and exercising of Territorial troops.

So much building development was now taking place that the Haslemere Preservation Society was reformed. It will be remembered that this Society had originated in 1882 with a threat to the common land at Hindhead, but had ceased to be necessary as a watchdog about 1895, when Sir Robert Hunter, as Chairman of the newly formed Parish Council was alert, and able to instigate proper action for the protection of the countryside.

Perhaps the enthusiasm of the newly revived society led to the gift of three drinking fountains in the town—one at the foot of Museum Hill, one close by the station yard entrance, and one in the High Street. In those dusty summers, rendered increasingly troublesome by a growing motor traffic on roads as yet not acquainted with tar macadam, this provision of water must have been welcome.

The case of the Haslemere Preservation Society to watch local development was thrown into relief by a comment (which follows) from The Times of March 1909 in regard to Bath: "The authorities of a beautiful city ought to take a pride in its beauty; one of their main duties is to preserve that beauty against decay and private greed." Have we lost the aesthetic conscience which our fore-fathers possessed?

No roadway existed even at this date from West Street to Tanners Lane, but since the local Post Office had moved into West Street from the High Street in 1906, further new building from the High Street back towards the School Road had tended to produce a better surface on the road to the schools.

At last the Post Office's wanderings had come to a standstill. Back in the 18th century, letter post had been brought on horseback to the White Horse Inn, but about 1790 mail was dealt with at the butcher's shop of John Luff, in the High Street. About the turn of the century, Mr. Timm's shop (now Phillips) was the Post Office, and about mid-century, Miss Upton's old house, which preceded Dewhurst's business. During this half-century at least some of the mail would have been brought by the coach from London to Chichester, which arrived at 11.30 a.m. every morning except Sunday. The office then moved to Lambert's, a chemist at what is now Three Limes, and after twenty years to East Street to Mr. Jolliffe, now the china shop premises. Back once more to the High Street to a house next to Westminster Bank, then once more to the Three Limes—Aylwin, another chemist—and then to a shop next to the Swan Hotel (now the Institute). One last visit for three years to Mr. Reeves (the East part of Riley and Whishaw's) and by 1895 safely back again in the High Street at what is now a bookshop, lastly in 1906 to West Street where, after two years of peace, the Postal Authorities felt reasonably safe, and by 1908 the first telephone service for the area was inaugurated, the first telephone operator being Mrs. Moon (née Miss Dean) of Verandah Cottage in Tanners Lane, who was proud to open with fourteen subscribers.

The following year a small house was built in the upper part of Tanners Lane as a Children's Convalescent Home. This home, called St. Mary's, fostered by the Rector as a home for children sent by the Invalid Children's Aid Association, had started in a small house in Meadow Vale. The children, dressed in scarlet cloaks for outdoor wear, added a cheerful touch of colour to the little town, and they were entertained and asked to many private homes.

A step forward in local lighting was made by the opening of an electricity supply station, and in the following year, 1911, the Parish Church was equipped with the new lighting.

There were still many anomalies in the style of road and road service, in spite of the increase in the number of cars and bicycles. One very acute difficulty was always present along the main Hindhead Road. At the point where the road breaks off to Critchmere the main road narrowed for one hundred and fifty yards to less than twelve feet wide. It was the usual practice for vehicles coming from one direction to wait for traffic from the opposite direction. Beneath the hedge bank at this point, a stretch of highway waste had been encroached on by a small house in which, at this date, lived an old lady who, incidentally, sold sweets and toys for children, in an adjoining shed. This road was subsequently widened when the boundaries of Haslemere were enlarged.

A new means of amusement had arrived in Haslemere. Until now a magic lantern with perhaps slides in colour, as well as monochrome, had been the height of entertainment, apart from the occasional plays produced by enthusiastic amateur talent. But now the moving picture came to ensnare the free hours of an increasing number of the public, and to begin the removal of the joy of participating actively in entertainment. A Mr. Hoy opened the first cinematograph show in a shed behind the White Horse Hotel. A little later he moved, with the growing demand, to a room at Weyhill. The success of this venture encouraged another business man, Mr. Oldershaw, to open a second cinema, which was called the Empire. This cinema was supplanted by the Regal of Weyhill which, after the Great War, was enlarged and continued in action till 1938.

The next year, 1913, was fateful, not only for England in the wider sphere of world politics, but for Haslemere in local politics. The Parish Council which had sat in control, or more or less in control, since 1894, made application for, and received with great pride, the status of an Urban District.

Mr. Whitcher, who had taken the first minutes of the original Parish Council, presided as Chairman at the first meeting of the Urban District Council. It was resolved that as there was no business before the meeting, the Council should adjourn to the White Horse Hotel!

One of the prime movers towards the new status was Mr. Allen Chandler of Kimbers, whose skilled advocacy and influence had assisted and led the Parish Council for many years. He became the first Chairman of the new Urban District Council.

The population of Haslemere had now reached nearly three thousand, since an extensive piece of Thursley which stretched from the present Recreation Ground and Petworth Road over the hill to Weyhill and up Tanners Lane, was now included in the Urban District Council area. This new urban zone constituted a fairly compact drainage area, improved the rateable value, and probably encouraged the County Council in their grant of new powers. At that date the local rate was eight shillings in the pound.

The winding up of the Parish Council came at a time when an era was ending. A tornado was brewing in mid-Europe which in its future course was to sweep away many past traditions, and put a brake on human progress in international comity.

As if they knew it, and were agreed to leave with the change, several prominent Haslemere people died; Jonathan Hutchinson in June, Francis Harrison in July, Frank Gibbs in July, Barclay Day in July, Robert Hunter in November and Thomas Upfold in April of 1914.

A year later, in the shadow of the Great War, a building project came to fruition by the generosity of the late Mr. Barclay Day in the gift to the town of the Haslemere Hall. This has proved of immense value as a site for lectures, dances, concerts and entertainments of all kinds. It was also to prove of value in the war years as a canteen for neighbouring or billeted troops.

Many of these men who may still survive will remember the full sized billiard table in the new Haslemere Hall, others will have revelled in the hot baths provided at the Congregational Hall.

Enthusiasm for the support of the war effort was whipped into a frenzy by such posters as portrayed an enormous "Kitchener" whose eyes followed every viewer, and the caption "Your King and Country needs you," cartoons of the Raemeker's type, showing war horrors of all kinds against non-combatants and, of course, the incredible saga of the retreat of the Old Contemptibles from Mons. All these impelled the youth of Great Britain and her Colonies to enter voluntarily, and in vast numbers, the portals of the greatest holocaust which the world had seen to date. To anticipate a little, never let it be forgotten that on the first day alone of the Somme battle of 1916, more than twenty thousand men were killed and missing, with nearly double that number wounded.

By the end of 1914, it was on record that out of a population of about four thousand persons, more than two hundred men were serving in the various forces.

As the autumn wore on, many refugees from Belgium, soldiers and families, came to Haslemere, where the troops were welcomed into private houses, and rooms or housing was found for the families.

Our own troops were lodged in the town for shorter or longer periods, either during training or en route for Europe. Need for greater accommodation led to the building of hutted camps at Bramshott and on several stretches of Milford and adjacent commons. Early in 1915 Canadian troops occupied the Bramshott camp, and many friendships then formed, led to intermarriage and later emigration to Canada. A war help committee was set up to devise and direct the many activities of the non-combatant public in support of the war effort, an early feature being an Information Bureau.

The Parish Nurse, Miss Twidell, resigned in order to undertake active duty with the forces, and was replaced by Mrs. Branscombe and Miss Watkins, two nurses now being considered necessary to cope with the increased population.

On January 1st 1915 the Military Church Parade was held at the Parish Church, which was filled with five hundred men from Bedfords, Gordon Highlanders and Black Watch.

The need for accommodation for wounded men had outstripped the normal provision in military hospitals. A hospital was quickly organised at High Rough of fifty beds, at the upper end of Farnham Lane, and a hospital of twenty-five beds at Grayshott Convent under the control of the Cambridge Hospital, Aldershot, from September 1915 to January 1919. This was an extension of a hospital on Frensham Hill. At Courtsmount and elsewhere in Haslemere, the Red Cross set up workrooms where local members and helpers could prepare and roll bandages, dressings, bed equipment, etc. All these occupations, together with the absence of so many residents on their proper affairs elsewhere, precluded much use of the Recreation Ground. Cricket and football languished, apart from such games as could be supported by neighbouring troops. For a time, in March, the Devon regiment was quartered in the town before proceeding abroad.

The Battle of Loos occurred in the summer, and Festubert in September, bringing a flood of new wounded. Again, a new Red Cross hospital was opened at Hilders, Shottermill.

In the midst of all this international conflict, the needs of the home public were not forgotten, in this area at least. At the far end of Hindhead, the Woodcock Inn was opened early in 1916 by the Surrey Public House Trust, who doubtless had noted the increased traffic along the Farnham Road.

As the third year of the war came round, the demands of the fighting forces removed and absorbed man power. To take the place of some of those thus lost to the home front, women and even children were recruited to help in hay harvesting, and later in a more organised way on the land. In this neighbourhood, four pence an hour was the reward for ordinary help, with a penny increase to five pence as skill in harvesting was acquired.

A second Red Cross workroom was opened at Caudebec on Museum Hill, while the Rectory maintained a splint room which had thirty members.

One local figure, old George Timms died in August, at the considerable age of eighty-six years. Perhaps one of the reasons for his survival had been his occupation in the mid-nineteenth century. In his youth he had been the local postman, and had taken the local letters to Liphook. He walked these three miles every night, and according to Miss Harrison who left a diary, stayed the night at Liphook, and returned with the next day's mail at 5.45 a.m. in the morning. This practice must have ceased in

1860, by which time the new railway had just put Haslemere on the railway map.

A most striking and interesting oecumenical rapprochement took place in the autumn, Haslemere had received several Serbian refugees earlier in the war, and a child of one of the families died at the local Cottage Hospital, then at the top of Shepherds Hill. To the great joy of the parents, a priest of the Greek Orthodox Church was contacted, and on December 9th, Father Nicholas Velmorovic took the funeral service, complete with the beautiful rites of the Greek Church, at the Parish Church. This was one of the unexpected fruits of the war, and was most welcome to all thinking persons. The breadth of view shown in the treatment of the death of the Serbian child may have prompted a new project at the Parish Church. Seating, which since 1868 had been allotted to church members on a rental system, which, incidentally, had covered some of the church expense, was now, in 1917, made free to all. Since Canon Aitken had been rector in 1897, the seating, though rented, had at least been free after the Voluntary had started. But no doubt slightly later regular churchgoers, who had found themselves supplanted by squatters, would have begun their morning service in a spirit not entirely in accord with the opening prayers. From this date onward, and only from this date, were regular collections made by the sidesmen, instead of, as in past years, as almsgiving at Communion Services, or on certain special occasions. It goes without saying that the collections were needed in place of the previous pew rents to support the year-to-year expenses of the Church.

The refugees had now fallen from an early seventy in number to twenty-eight, but other needs were growing with the Paschendaele offensive, which had steam-rollered through its muddy death bath, after the incredible mistakes and miscalculations, and deathless heroism of the Somme offensive.

In March a further convalescent hospital was opened at Church Hill, now Peperham House. Of this there is an interesting memento reproduced in this book, a replica of a cover of Punch, cleverly turned into a series of photographic cartoons of the Matron, Doctors and nurses of the Home.

One family, who in fact were in a sense refugees, came to Haslemere to settle. Arnold Dolmetsch and his wife, who had for some years prior to the war lived in France, decided to make their home in a corner of England which they had known earlier, when visiting friends. Among their friends had been George Bernard Shaw. Arnold Dolmetsch was a craftsman as well as a practising musician. Like many others he found pleasure in the study of his own craft in the British Museum, and opened a new world of music to an eager public. As is not uncommon, the public did not at first realise that they were eager. Novelty often creates opposition and coldness, but Arnold Dolmetsch pursued his discovery with untiring keenness, giving concerts and lectures on both sides of the Atlantic. His later life will be noted in due course.

The set back of March 1918 was recognised by few as the last major convulsion of the enemy. Everyone at home had now became involved closely in the war either by the loss of relative or friend, or by the united action necessary to support the home front on a smoothly working basis. This was achieved in spite of a close food rationing system, blackout, travel difficulties and shortages of all clothing or working materials. Various societies came into being with the aim of preventing future wars, and their ideas and ideals so widely spread, that a League of Nations when suggested later, found ready acceptance.

As the year wore on, the news of Allied successes brought much relief to the spirits of those working at home, a relief diminished, unfortunately by the figures of the casualty columns. When November 11th broke, the news of the Armistice arrived early in Grayswood, with a telegram from her husband to Lady Atkinson Willes of The Stroud, Grayswood. It was not till 12.40 p.m. that the Post Office was able to issue an official confirmation.

In the evening a special thanksgiving service for the cessation of hostilities took place at the Parish Church, which was also attended by the Chairman and Councillors of the Urban District Council, and many Railway staff, Post Office and Fire Brigade members.

The Convalescent Hospital at Church Hill was early on the list of the War Effort organisations to be disbanded, while in recognition of her services during the two years of activity, the Matron, Miss Davenport, was awarded the R.R.C. She was not allowed to remain at leisure, and was quickly induced to become Matron at the Cottage Hospital on Shepherds Hill, following the retirement of the first Matron, Miss Hargreaves.

It may be of interest to recall the list of major voluntary organisations which had assisted the war effort, and stiffened the will of those who had perforce to move in the background: Auxiliary Medical Hospitals at Hilders, Grayshott, High Rough, and Church Hill (closed 1919), some of whose V.A.D. personnel have since worked at the local Cottage hospital, War Savings; War Help; War Pensions Committees; two Red Cross workrooms; Food Control; Waste Paper Collection and a Soldiers' Canteen in St. Christopher's Hall.

The great influenza pandemic arrived in England in October and caused, among other distress, the closing of local schools for some weeks from early November and again in the New Year.

Christmas celebrations, though still on a subdued scale, were enjoyed with a great spirit of relaxation. The Haslemere Pantomime under Miss K. Chandler was revived to the great joy of young people of all ages, and to the great satisfaction of all who visited it. In effect, the pantomime, "The Copper Castle" said the world is standing upright again, and ready to face the future with a smile, after huddling in trenches and ruined homes.

The later spring brought a fall of six inches of snow to the Surrey Hills, but within a week or so one local observer was noting the many nightingales singing by day in the copses near Northchapel.

One considerable record deserves a special note—the Waste Paper Committee had since October 1917 collected and sold sixteen and a half tons of waste paper. This, after sale and deduction of costs of collection and transport, left a useful balance of £112 to the local Red Cross work.

With the May number of the Church magazine there was enclosed a printed referendum form, the subject being the desirability, or not, of providing a Church War Memorial. Three answers were possible—a direct negative, a recasting and rehanging of the church bells and, lastly, other suggestions. After some discussion, however, it was considered unwise to open such a fund at that time. In the town a public meeting was conducted in harmony, for once, as to a Haslemere War Memorial, and a Committee of fifteen members was chosen to consider proposals which were then made, and report on a later occasion. Certain people expressed the opinion that a sum of £12,000 at least should be raised in order to supply a worthy memorial.

Not everyone at this time felt able to rejoice as the Peace Celebrations approached. In Haslemere there had been a successful Comrades Club which had been strongly supported in the Haslemere Hall and a Soldiers' Canteen at St. Christophers Hall. In May, however, the Canadian troops who had been stationed at Bramshott Camp were under fresh orders—to return to Canada. This migration caused much distress to two hundred local maidens who had helped (wo)manfully to ease the war duties of the troops. Reunion at a later date—in many cases by marriage—and emigration to Canada, eased many heartaches and solved many problems.

Still younger and more adventurous folk sought to continue the risks and thrills of the war years in more allegedly peaceful ways. These ways, however, wrung a cry of anguish from one (at least) Haslemere resident who complained that "thirty motor cars and motor bicycles an hour are now tearing up and down our High Street, and the Grayswood Road had become apparently a speed track."

Undeterred, however, by these thoughts, a clergyman used for the first time his beautiful new motorbike to come from Portsmouth to Haslemere to conduct a service, and to stay a few days here (perchance to recover from the journey). He arrived without mishap, but we are not told how late. The paragraph recording this ends, "We hope to visit him in the future, but at present fares accumulate and trains decay. Travel is only for the rich."

1914 - 1918

So young they were, so strong and well
Until the bitter summons fell
Too young to die ....
....
But never more will any see
The old secure felicity
The kindness that made us glad
Before the world went mad.
They'll never hear another bird
Another gay or living word,
Those men who lie so cold and lone
Far in a country not their own,
Those men who died for you and me
That England still might sheltered be.
And all our lives go on the same
(Although to live is almost shame).

E. V. Lucas

We will remember.

CHAPTER VII

Growth and Explosions

In 1917 the Rector, Canon Aitken, had found it necessary to resign his living for a less strenuous parish. He had, just prior to the War, announced his impending removal, but had been persuaded to continue at a time when so many young men were needed as front line chaplains. He had thus remained at his post and had continued, in every sphere, his encouragement and support for every worthwhile project. He served his Church as was only to be expected, and his country also, not only in private life, but also as a local Councillor for the public weal. After his appointment to a parish in London, he was only permitted to work for another two years, when he died in harness. The great sorrow and attendance at his funeral, which took place in Haslemere, only served to emphasise and declare the respect and love and appreciation of the people among whom he had lived and had served for twenty years.

Since the middle of the nineteenth century, Haslemere had been fortunate in her leading men, and a resident of 1917 might well have wondered if that good fortune could persist, and have wished for a crystal ball. There were signs which might have given hope. The Clerk of the Urban District Council, Arthur Whitcher, had now been in office for over thirty years. Looking back over the previous twenty odd years, he could remember the successes and the difficulties, not lessened by the War; though during the fighting period the difficulties had been as much physical as spiritual. If he had been asked to risk a prophecy, he might have thought hopefully of the united spirit of the War years. But deep in his thoughts he would have wished for a renewal of wise leadership, backed perhaps by some of his accumulated experience. And, in this view of the future, he would have been correct.

For the next few years, a local businessman, James Edgeler, assisted the town to settle back into a regular peace programme. James Edgeler had been born in Haslemere in 1848, and had been a harnessmaker in Haslemere High Street. As a boy he had seen horses and sheep tied or penned up around the White Horse Hotel, and pigs in front of the Swan Hotel, on market days. He had played around the Guy Fawkes bonfire which, in those days, was built and lighted on the site of the present War Memorial, till the doors of the Swan Inn were scorched. Now he guided the young Haslemere Council from the dark days of 1916 to the temporarily more calm waters of 1920, with the wisdom and experience gained through a long life of service to the town.

The new Rector, Walter Wragge, who had lived since his arrival in Tudor Cottage, High Street, was given a new Rectory in Derby Road. The old Rectory, now called Sadlers, was felt to be on a scale too grand for the post war economic life. In the following year the curate was rehoused in the Glebe Cottage in Derby Road, but nearer his Church.

A welcome invasion in these war years, but of a peaceful kind was the Dolmetsch family, who came to live in Haslemere about Christmas 1917. They had previously been staying in Thursley in the cottage of an old friend, Mrs. Beatrice Horne. While there, they made the acquaintance of some French Canadian soldiers to whom they extended hospitality on Sundays, both musical and, when possible, dietetic. Later in the same year, having already satisfied themselves that south-west Surrey was a desirable countryside in which to have a settled home, they found, as they said, the perfect house, "Jesses." Their kindness to the Witley camp was well repaid over the move to Haslemere. Winter ice and snow covered the roads, but the Canadian Commandant rose to the occasion, and offered them transport. To the foot of Grayswood Hill, by Rookmer Bridge came several units of horse-drawn transport. The hill proved too steep for the horses to negotiate, so a halt was made, greatly to the delight of the children, while the horses were re-shod with shoes adequate for the slippery slope. They remember with joy the happiness of dancing round smith and horses, while the shoes were made and fitted, so that the last section of the journey to "Jesses" in Haslemere was relieved of tension.

Their next few years were spent, apart from the usual musical tours at home and abroad, in the development of more musical research, and the extension of the workshops for making the many types of old musical instruments. A small orchestra was formed with the co-operation of the girls' school then at St. George's Wood, and a second orchestra at Bedales, Petersfield, and these varying activities paralleled the growth of the family Dolmetsch until 1924—but we must not journey too far.

Early in 1920 further discussion began as to a fitting War Memorial, and a Committee was set up to organise a fund and to make recommendations. During the following year the Committee recommended that a Cross, suitably inscribed with the names of those who had died, should be placed in the Town Broadway.. A recommendation was received from the Comrades of the Great War that as the lease of the Recreation Ground by

Pound Corner was finishing, a large piece of ground should be bought with the money surplus to the requirements of the memorial. This piece of ground should be for a recreation ground for Haslemere people in thankfulness for the safe return of many who had served with the Forces.

One proposal which was refused by the Charity Commissioners had been to encroach on or acquire a part of Lion Green for the erection of a Memorial Hall. This was prevented by the restatement of the Enclosure Act of 1845, when it had been designated as a recreation ground and open space.

Not all decisions of the local authority were as sound, for in April of the same year plans for the new shop front of a business situated in one of the narrowest parts of the High Street were passed which allowed an actual encroachment on the highway. Twenty-five years earlier in some rebuilding on the Broadway the new buildings were permitted to come forward on to the front of the old garden fence. Such mistakes may have been tolerable in times which scarcely recognised building lines, and when traffic was sparse. But how do we reconcile the buildings at the corner of West Street, handsome though some will consider them, which have replaced the old Angel Inn, and covered its surprising little garden bordering the pavement.

As regards the War Memorial, the stone cross (Inigo Triggs), in the Town, proved no stumbling block, but it took from February until August for the Council to be receptive to the suggestion of a thank-offering field, even though land of adequate size to the new needs had been offered at reasonable cost to the Memorial Committee. Even then there were two dissentients. But in due course, Sir Algernon Methuen, as Chairman of the Haslemere War Memorial Committee handed over to the Hon. Richard Denman, Chairman of the Urban District Council, the following Memorial Scheme:

(a) A Cross in High Street to perpetuate the memory of those sixty-two Haslemere men who had lost their lives in the War.

(b) The deeds of the Water Tower Field (now Recreation Gound) which the Committee had bought from the Hutchinson Estate Trustees, for the purpose of a recreation ground for Haslemere, as a thank-offering for the services of those men who had fought, and those who had died.

During the following two years, this ground received careful attention and preparation, and in 1922 the last game of cricket was played at Pound Corner.

Need for more open space had become evident, for the old football field had been covered in 1899 by the New Church Schools, and players had had to use the rather small Pound

Corner Recreation Ground, where bowls were played also in the
north-east corner.

Hockey enthusiasts had spread in Haslemere with the number
of young people growing up in the newly built homes during the
past twenty years. These found a suitable site at the top of Shepherds Hill on what is now the Half Moon Estate. Within a few
years, however, building demands again proved insatiable, and the
new ground provided by the War Memorial Committee was gratefully made use of for hockey as for the older games.

A popular tennis club had been started near Pound Corner
Nurseries beyond the house called "Olivers." Hard courts and
grass courts were available and kept in first class condition by an
active club, which flourished there for the next decade.

Accommodation for sick persons had now also become inadequate. The routine of life and health had been severely disrupted
by the War. The strain imposed on the civil population, as well
as the wounds sustained in mind or body by those who had
fought, demanded more need for hospitalisation. The Cottage Hospital on Shepherds Hill given by the generosity of the Penfold
family was unsuitable for the needed enlargement. A strong committee to raise funds for a new hospital was quickly formed, and
a fresh site was looked for. The end of the Pound Corner lease to
the Recreation Committee was the fortunate opportunity for
those seeking to build a new hospital. Plans were soon drawn up
for a building in brick and tile, though one farseeing doctor on
the Committee begged that it should be built of wood. His reason
for this was that in ten to twenty years, extensions would be
required, or new ideas incorporated. To do this in stone or brick
might prove costly or impracticable, but a wooden building could
always be burnt down and a start made on a clean and modern
type of design. He was, of course, correct in his estimate of the
future as regards hospital needs, but the novelty of his idea was
too much for the solid but well meaning traditionalists—and we
are still suffering. The new hospital was opened by Viscount Cave,
C.M.G., in January 1923, and Matron Davenport with nursing staff
came proudly down from Shepherds Hill to take charge. Haslemere was again fortunate that she was able to remain as Matron
till 1927. Ably supported by the House and Medical Committees,
she set the pattern which has since persisted and, indeed, been
insisted on, that the patient is a person and not just a bed
number. In the years since its opening, many people from other
areas have been patients, and have found time or desire to comment on the care and attention given, apart from any question
of skill.

The local council was not allowed to lag behind in the competition for building land. In spite of the wish to commemorate

the sacrifices of the war years, in April 1919 the keenest card in the local election programme was that of housing. There was a very general anxiety that not only should proper housing be provided for the returning troops, but that there should be housing as a charge on the rates for young people with low incomes. The old council which had sat unchanged for four years was of the opinion, by ten votes to two, in spite of a largely supported public petition, that the housing situation was adequate to the needs of the town. When in April 1919 an election was held, seven housing candidates were nominated and elected, leaving the Anti-Homes at the bottom of the poll. A scheme for building fifty-two new houses was prepared, and after some little difficulty as to siting, land was found bordering on High Lane, on the old Church Hill Farm. Mr. Clapham Lander of Letchworth was the Architect.

A further small piece of land was found at the corner of West Street, opposite the then Depot yard, and in front of where the Police Station would later stand, for a gift from the War Trophy Committee. The Urban District Council had accepted a German field gun from this Committee and, as a sign of victory, and a reminder of war, arranged that the gun should be manhandled by the Comrades of the Great War to this site. Here it remained as a signal warning, until memories had faded, when it was disposed of, and a flowering cherry planted instead, under which in 1941, a large gander, the mascot of the N.F.S. maintained vigilant watch and sentry parade, much as his ancestors of the Roman "Capitol" which two thousand five hundred years earlier had given warning of an invasion by ancestors of the same race as those defeated in the war of 1914-1918.

All the ferment of growth and building which was trying to froth over in these post-war years, determined the County Police to secure a site and build an adequate modern Police House with accommodation for staff and delinquents. This site was found at the end of West Street, which had been properly surfaced and made up some three to four years earlier, and a satisfactory and pleasing building was erected in stone, adjacent to the yard of the already existing Fire Station.

The old Police Station, on the Petworth Road, was re-christened rather poorly, and gradually brought into use as a private residence, but it now proudly bears the name of "Old Coppers" in allusion, presumably, to its original occupants.

Even in these post-war days of rapid growth, some rugged individualists managed to struggle on. One old broom-squire would drive into the town on occasion, in his pony trap, stopping here and there for a personal tank filling. Of course sooner rather than later some little hitch occurred in his pleasant outing, and his temper, usually on the short side, would suddenly fracture. Down

from his seat he would leap, offering battle to all and sundry. It
is perhaps as well that the ubiquitous cine-camera was not then
available to demonstrate to his future not undistinguished descendants, how uninhibited neo-Georgian life could be.

In his later years this same old man was overtaken by
influenza, and the ensuing bronchitis confined even him to his
bed. A message reached his doctor to call, "but," went on the note
from his wife, "if I am out, be careful how you go into his
room." Fate was kind, and on making the call, the doctor found
Madam at home in her little kitchen. A short account of the
past few days closed with "Be careful how you go in his room"
as the doctor mounted the stairs. Knocking on the bedroom door
was answered by a fierce "Oo's that?" to which the reply "The
doctor" brought no "come in." Another knock and again "Oo's
that" followed unmistakably by two clicks. Again the reply "The
doctor, you know who he is" and quietly the handle of the door
was turned, the door gently pushed open, while the visitor was
keyed up to duck under the bed at the slightest sign of any movement. Fortunately the light was good enough for the doctor to
be recognised, and the hammers of the twelve bore gun which
had just previously been cocked, were let quickly down. "Oh, it's
you, is it? I thought it were," but the last word was lost in the
noise of putting the gun down. Gratefully the doctor sat on the
foot of the bed, there being no chair, and another visitor coming
in at that moment might have been hard put to guess which was
the real patient!

During the next ten years, Haslemere was trying to settle
back into a pattern of life not much dissimilar from that before
the war.

On the outskirts of Haslemere, Grayswood had been growing in the previous quarter of a century, and now could reckon
about one hundred and twenty five houses. Shottermill had been,
at the beginning of the century, little more than a cluster near
the Shottermill ponds, Lion Lane, a small scatter along Weyhill,
besides a terrace along Sturt Road, and a sprinkling of houses up
the valley towards Hindhead. Now Shottermill could show about
three hundred houses, with a concentration of small shops along
Weyhill.

The Recreation Ground in Shottermill, bought by public subscription in 1909, still maintained its ground conditions by the subscriptions of the clubs who played there, which included cricket,
football, hockey and tennis. It is interesting to read that in 1920
the product of a penny rate for Haslemere in the assessable pound
would produce £94 10s.; the rate levied was at 10s., being made
up to 5/2 general rate and 4/10 poor rate.

A little more private building was possible on the previous scale in the lanes and new roads round the town, but it was not for some years that land which had been held jealously, either for agriculture or personal amenity, came into the building market. Haslemere was still a town with short tentacles spreading out into fields and lanes.

Sports clubs of all kinds resumed their pre-war activity, cricket, football, tennis, bowls, rifle shooting. Bridge parties formed an easy method of evening entertainment, while the more ardent experts enclosed themselves behind curtained windows to play with greater concentration, even during the afternoons.

It was about this time that, on a holiday in the West of England, a visitor to the Library of one of the local learned societies, noticed an occasional murmured vocal sound which appeared to come from a screen enclosing an area in front of the open fire. Cautious investigation via a cracked hinge-line revealed a table of bridge enthusiasts oblivious to all except the game in hand.

The social art of "calling" recovered much of its one-time importance. For those who may be unaware of this game, we will briefly go over the rules. "A" comes to live with his family in the delightful countryside of Haslemere. He may or may not be a churchgoer, but gossip from many sources will circulate from the know-alls to those less fortunate. A good deal of information will thus be available to the would-be caller. The first move comes from the caller, Mrs. B., who, between the hours of three and five p.m. will leave by hand on to the salver offered by the staff of the called-on, one card for herself and two cards for her husband. After a reasonable lapse of time, similar acknowledgment of this call is made by Mrs. "A" at the house of each person who has called on her. This is the end of the first round.

The second round is played within the house of Mr. and Mrs. "A." The caller will have noted from Mrs. "A"s card not only her address and title, if any, but also the hour and day at which she will be "At Home" to callers. The caller, shall we say, Mrs. "B" enters Mrs. "A"s house, gives her name, places her visiting cards on the salver, and is duly announced by the member of the house staff. In the drawing room Mrs. "A" is ready to receive one or more callers, and at a set hour will ring the bell for tea for any caller who may be present at that time.

The third round is played by Mrs. "A" herself at the door of the late caller, etc. After these preliminary rounds, the acquaintance might ripen into full recognition via dinner or garden parties, and at other social functions.

If Mrs. "A" is fortunate enough to have friends in the district, this part of the game is easy, or even if mutual acquaintances can readily be found. But hard might be the lot of the unfortunate family who just arrived because they thought Haslemere looked a pleasant place.

Such a couple once followed this course and enjoyed an enviable house and garden, furnished in most careful taste. One caller, a member of a long-established local family, began an inquisition. Where do you come from? Did you know anyone in Haslemere before you came? Why did you come to Haslemere? ... and so on. This did not provide a good introduction to ease the path of the next caller, and in this case the newcomers moved elsewhere before two years had passed.

For those who were tolerant, tough or well recommended, life in Haslemere became easy, amusing and pleasant. One of these pleasantries was the Pantomime which, having restarted, was a constant interest to many people with their families from September to January. It was a hoped-for hallmark for parents, as well as the child who might be asked to take part in the Pantomime. Dresses to be made up, after bundles of material were passed by Miss K. Chandler to the proud mother, the book of words more or less perfect (more perfect if you wished to be asked again), and the exciting prospect that you might be lucky enough to become one of the regulars. For, of course, this pantomime had to have a background of teenagers and a few older characters, most of whom had graduated on from the years since the turn of the century.

The Gilbert and Sullivan performances were again a source of great interest among those who had good voices and were active enough for the necessary dances.

Both the Pantomime and the Gilbert and Sullivan plays—a week each—received strong public support and played to packed houses.

One London impresario who had come for a long week-end at one of the greater houses in the district, on hearing that a local pantomime was playing to full houses, was unbelieving. His host tried vainly to convince him that no seats would be available, and the Londoner drove to the Haslemere Hall. Here he was told "Sorry, no seats for sale, no return tickets for sale, no standing room." However, at that moment the conductor of the orchestra, Mr. W. E. Muir, happened to come by the Ticket Office and recognised the impresario. He was able, happily, to arrange a seat for the visitor, whose appreciation afterwards was only spoiled by a remark that it wasn't Pantomime. Nor was it, in the London or common sense; it was a fairy play; but it was and remained the Haslemere Pantomime till the Second World War. Advertisement played no part in the success of these remarkable pantomimes, as the press photographer of one of the large daily illustrated papers learned. He had been sent down to take some photographic records of a dress rehearsal and after the rehearsal had got under way, he set up his apparatus, which then was more cumbersome than now, and needed a stand. By bad luck he had placed the camera in the main gangway, and was extremely surprised to find himself being tersely told by a little lady in indoor shoes and a short skirt to take his apparatus from the gangway. He tried to explain that he represented the Daily ...... and had been instructed to take photographs for the Press. "Well," said she, "You must take your apparatus elsewhere, for I need to move up and down," and off she went to bring order elsewhere. The photographer was eventually persuaded that if he wanted any photographs he had better do as instructed, that none really cared, least of all Miss Chandler, whether any were taken for the Press in that way, and that the pantomime would still go on from success to success whatever he did.

Other activities, such as concerts and other acting groups had only partial success, for creeping in on to the public notice was the B.B.C. and, of course, a gradually improving cinematography.

The growth of post-war Haslemere had now reached the point of a demand for a more considerable water supply than that which had flowed from the reservoir in Chase Lane. This soft water had been pleasant and satisfying to drink either by itself, or with other added ingredients, and had been praised by women for kindness to skin in washing person or materials. A new source was found at no distance from the pumping station in Camelsdale, and in plentiful supply. The only drawback was that it received from some unrecognised source a mild contamination from time to time. This fault was easily corrected by the measured addition of chlorine to the water supply. Many and loud were the complaints which have not even yet ceased in some quarters which appreciate water as water, at this uncouth spoiling of a previously pleasant liquid.

The older generation was loud in their outcry against the weakness of the present day, muttering that they had been brought up on wells in which analysts certainly found considerable fouling, and they were none the worse for it, etc. This went on for some years till a fateful week-end laid an uncounted number of people in the water supply area, low—very low. For some reason the usual dose of chlorine had not been added to the water tanks, so that a perhaps larger dose than usual of dirt organisms came untreated into the household supplies, with the result that there was an explosive outbreak of enteritis. This convinced most unbelievers of the need for purification of drinking water.

CHAPTER VIII

Social Ferment

COUNTRY TOWN STILL — STRIKES — MOTORS — SLUMP
ENLARGED U.D.C. — JAZZ

To one young couple who came to live in Haslemere in 1925 the whole prospect was pleasing. A small country town surrounded on every side by miles of literally unspoiled country, and a great number of welcoming, even if critical, homes. They had been fortunate, perhaps, for they were sponsored into the community by one of the oldest resident families. The welcome was overwhelming in respect of the calling fetish to which reference has already been made. Over a hundred cards came over the doorstep, and a little calculation will prove that someone would have a busy time for a few months at least, apart from her usual household duties. However, it was all good fun in the circumstances, and a considerable step from the casual ring-up now, after a still more casual meeting at a cocktail party. "Hello, darling! Will you and Jimmy come round to drinks next Friday or Friday sennight—we are expecting a few others along." You may, or may not, recognise again your host and hostess after a brief encounter at the original party which will be quite impersonal, except between a few old friends who will be glued comfortably together in a dim corner. The amount of noise engendered by good hospitality will tell you on entry how far the party has proceeded. But in 1925 such receptions or gatherings were nearly ten years ahead—for one thing, cars were not always owner driven, nor reliable enough. Now the cars are vastly more reliable than many of their drivers, particularly at the close of a cocktail party.

The High Street was not then cluttered up with Ministry of Transport notices in their staring red, white, yellow and black notices of fearful warning, but so infrequently or irregularly noticed or enforced, that the minor penalties imposed scarcely act as a consistent deterrent.

The menace of the parking problem had barely arisen, for most of the shops in the town, except the smaller, had regular delivery services every day, so that a minimum of time was needed to shop. Even the pharmacies were able to provide a boy on a bicycle for medicine distribution.

There was no garage with garish petrol notices, nor any large multiple store. A few shops appeared on the pavement opposite the Georgian Hotel, which had so become following the death of Mr. H. W. Mozley in 1919. A small butcher's shop with private house attached was sympathetic to the eye where modern plate-glass fronted stores offer wines and provisions for sale. The corner of West Street was still graced by a pair of Elizabethan cottages set behind flower packed little front gardens below the senior doctor's house at Causewayside. The remainder of the square, apart from the disappearance of the Kings Arms Inn and of Deas provision store close by Lloyds Bank, has not changed much, except as before remarked, in the vulgarity of the spate of present directions to do this or that, or go here or there. If the planners could only do a little basic thinking, it might be possible to abolish much of the accumulation of cheap and strident advertising.

Away from the town, Grayswood Road as far as the Beeches, was still without a footpath to reach the pleasant villas which bordered the north side, though this amenity was provided a year later.

Three Gates Lane had no development on the south side, apart from the old established Meadfields and Manor House and Redcot, while from Sadlers, only Red House and The Towers broke the field on the north; and down the steep hill, Grayswood Place and Highlands, were alone in looking out over the Weald.

Along East Street,* or Petworth Road, as it was beginning to be called, no house could be found from the Congregational Manse to Gorse Cottage at the top of Almshouse Hill. The frontages on perhaps a half of Derby Road and Weydown Road had been developed. The lower stretch of Bunch Lane had been partly built on, but Farnham Lane was a harbour of large properties, and was spoken of, rightfully or otherwise, as Millionaire's Lane.

Cricket was slightly under a cloud for various reasons, perhaps one of them was that the pitches were not beyond reproach. Marl, a free gift from a well-wisher, was supplied a year or so later in such quantity that a too plumb condition was reached.

The Tennis Club near the Hospital attracted many who earlier might have graduated into cricket, and the various larger properties in the district offered pleasant dalliance, on often surprisingly first-class courts, over a cup of tea, and at a less strenuous pace than was usual at the Club.

Mlle. Lenglen, G. L. Patterson and W. Tilden were the public idols of the day for all who held a tennis racquet. Small wonder that there were secessions from a game which demanded suppression of self for the good of the team. This lesson had perhaps been too hardly pressed or learned in the long war years, and a recoil from control and a wish for self expression was understandable.

---

*Once called Cow Street.

A small sign of the times might have been noticed in 1926 when the local council decided to sell the old horse mower, and acquire a motor type.

A landmark for the Council staff was that the principle of a State Contributory Compulsory Superannuation Scheme was adopted by this Council. To Council staff whose moderate salaries barely permitted any savings against the uncertain future, this scheme must have been, and continues to be, a wonderful lifebelt and ultimate safe anchorage.

A great deal of the time of the councillors was taken by road improvement schemes. Various private roads were accepted by the Council after having been brought up to standard requirements, and improvements were made at certain corners, as at Dene End, Beech Road and Bridge Road; together with the new idea of the placing of white lines on the road at other corners for control or guidance of traffic, which was increasing at a rate faster than the ability of the road network to absorb it.

The General Strike at this time was the third of a series of protests by wage earners, in mining, railway and again mining organisations. These two industries had fallen far behind in adopting new ways and means, consistent with the needs of the public, and such business methods as would ensure an adequate wage for their employees.

In the field of building development, local authorities at this date were recommended to set up committees which should prepare planning schemes for their own area. This was an attempt to find out what was possible or desirable from the local point of view in areas under review. The schemes so derived were to be integrated by a body at county level, at which level permission for development must be sought. The idea while being a step forward, lacked one thing at this date—an agreed and relatively uniform policy. Neighbouring authorities, for differing reasons, might easily have diametrically opposite views on development, and while each set of plans taken by themselves were a practical answer to a problem, yet much absurdity could be produced, as where one authority wished to retain as much unspoiled country as possible, while the adjacent authority believed in a heavy building or works programme. These problems are still coming forward, especially with the urgent housing demand in the south-east.of England.

This extra work decided the Council to move from the Upper Room of the Town Hall in the High Street, to the recently vacated buildings of the late Sir Jonathan Hutchinson's Museum.

The growth of interest in this Museum had set the Committee and Curator a problem—how to house the new gifts to the Museum. The answer was found in the large house in the High

Street which belonged to the Hesse family, who had moved across
to Olivers on the death of their aunt, the previous owner. A strong
committee of Museum supporters soon found the necessary money
for buying the property, which not only could house the material,
but also the Curator, and was blessed with a few acres of formal
garden looking out over Collards Farm valley to the east. The
change-over was made in the late summer of 1926. Three years
later, after a number of alterations in the buildings, the Town
Council moved to the old Museum.

A desire by some people at least to retain some of the more
beautiful features of the district was evidenced by the gift of a
small piece of meadow by the railway below the Parish Church.
A contemporary comment said, "Its acquisition will preserve for
posterity one of the most perfect bits of scenery in the district.
It is a free gift with no restrictions, and could well be used for a
playground for very young children to whose school it lies near."
To the cost of laying it out a sum of £125 accompanied the land
gift.

As the houses crept out along the lanes around the town, it
became necessary to extend the sewerage system into Farnham
and Three Gates Lanes and the Weydown Road area and, of
course, with the provision of these extra services, there was a
consequent shadow of rate increase. The objection to the increase
became stridently vocal in the formation of a Ratepayers Association which, by 1930, had a fighting strength of over five hundred
members. At a local election which took place then, seven out of
the twelve possible seats were won by Association nominees. Just
prior to the election it had occurred to a few persons to restart
a Perambulation of the Borough Bounds. This was of purely anti-
quarian interest, for out of the thirty bound stones which had
been seen in 1813, now only five could be discovered. Beating the
bounds by bouncing a boy on the boundstones for the sake of
good memory had fallen into disuse long before, but as recently
as 1905 there was a disputed right of way at Hindhead, an enquiry
on which had spread over six months. One piece of evidence was
offered by an old man who remembered being bounced at a certain
spot on the land in dispute. This actually was not good evidence
for the stone in question was merely a parish boundary, and gave
no support to a footpath right. It is only rarely, nowadays, that
the evidence of the old succeeds over documented registration.

The following year, 1932, saw the great World Slump, but
it appears to have affected this part of Surrey to a slight extent
only at certain levels, apart from some small modifications in life.
At about this time, a local senior bank official was heard to
remark, "I never knew the value or extent of overdrafts till I
came here." This may have been a bit rhetorical, but for people

with a satisfactory capital reserve, at certain times and levels of bank rate, an overdraft could be useful as well as fashionable. Certain really wealthy benefactors were rumoured to finance their benefactions by means of overdrafts. So does the tongue of tittle tattle wag, and who knows when he puts his hand out in the dark whether he catches the snake by the head or the tail.

In other walks of life, the pressure of unemployment caused great distress, and the anticipations of certain forward looking persons were realised. To relieve in some degrees the lot of the local unemployed, Mr. G. Whitfield formed an Unemployment Committee in the autumn to consider ways and means of finding financial help and employment. Haslemere was once again writing a page of history, as had been the case in 1909, when the first Labour Exchange and Unemployment Committee (in England) had been formed by a group of local benefactors.

Work was found in the cleaning out of Sickle Mill pond at a cost of £1,000. In the first two months in 1932, two thousand cubic yards of silt were removed in the expectation of improved water storage for driving the turbines of the Waste Destructor at the Mill. Before refilling with water in June, the empty pond site was recorded by official photography.

Possibly with a view to ameliorating the labour situation, the provision of a Town Swimming Pool was demanded, both privately and by a Council sub-committee. Discussion led to the recommendation of such a pool, to be placed on part of the Council's Bunch Lane land, and Mr. Rex Chandler's design, within the woods on that site, was commended. Failing acceptance of this plan, an alternative site at No. 2 Sewage Works, when available, in Sickle Field, was suggested.

One major decision at that time was that no swimming pool should be built which did not harmonise well with local amenities, and that it should be worthy of the town. A year later the Bunch Lane site was dropped because of development covenants, which, at that time, were usually respected.

After three public enquiries held by the County Council as to the continuance to, or withdrawal from Haslemere Council of Urban District powers, a decision was made by the County Council in favour of a renewal of their Urban status, with an increased boundary.

The year 1933/34 thus introduced Haslemere to new partners —Hindhead and Shottermill, and from then their fortunes were linked together. About a hundred years earlier, a small guide book to this district could only write: "The Hindhead hills are approached from Haslemere at a point where there are a few small cottages and a public house called 'The Huts.' At this little wayside inn would stop coaches and wagons for slight refreshment, and to pick up bundles of heather and birch brooms which were made by the owner of the inn and his friends, the local broom squires.

Shortly afterwards as land, previously commonland, became available for building, two well-known families, I'Anson and Whitaker settled in what afterwards became the village of Grayshott, to be followed for a short summer visit by Lord Tennyson in 1866. Professor Tyndall built himself a house near the Huts Corner in 1870. All these people wrote so enthusiastically of the good air and wonderful open countryside, that within ten years Hindhead was considered a valuable health resort.

Since those days, very considerable development has taken place in Hindhead from the Huts corner to beyond Beacon Hill, and in Grayshott from the Portsmouth road along and on both sides of the Headley Road as far as Ludshott Common.

A great deal of the earlier development was in comfortable residential properties, with two large and a number of smaller hotels. By 1933 all these exhibitions of cushioned living were still maintained and even increasing. Churches to meet requirements had been built: St. Albans at Hindhead and St. Lukes at Grayshott, though an earlier dedication for the Grayshott Church had been St. John, for at that time Grayshott was considered almost in the wilderness.

Following on the fateful but welcome decision that Haslemere should retain its Urban status, it was recommended that there should be an extension of the district boundary to include not only Hindhead, but the parishes of Shottermill, and parts of Churt and Thursley. This extended the district area from 2,263 acres to 5,571 acres, and the population from 5,100 to 10,817 persons. There was a consequent revision of representation in the next newly constituted Urban District Council.

In order to compete with the expected increase in service demand, the sewerage works which had existed in Kings Road for over thirty years were transferred to the valley between Shottermill and Hammer, where there was adequate space away from the main development in housing.

The successful result of the enquiry which took place in 1933 as to the future status of Haslemere was due largely to the efficient presentation of the case for Haslemere by the then Chairman, Mr. W. H. Lowe of Church Hill* and Mr. A. J. Whitcher, the Clerk to the Council, whose wealth of knowledge of the town spreading over forty years was invaluable.

With all this new land which had been included in the Urban District boundary, problems of amenity in regard to building sites arose very quickly.

---

* Now Peperham House.

The effects of the World Slump were now wearing off, at least in parts of England, and a new government in 1935 heralded hopes of progress, in spite of the high rate of unemployment in England, and the thinly veiled German bluster and threat over the Continent. America's deep concern for her own economic recovery did not apparently allow her to have conscious awareness of any future European crisis, and she maintained that insular aloofness from world problems which had marked her policies before and through so much of the first World War.

In Haslemere a new store appeared, functional in style, but unsympathetic to its neighbours, a forerunner of the Council flats which, though needed as housing, were planted in a sort of horror contrast at the foot of a curving sweep of seventeenth century cottages. These and other housing developments on land which was now being released for building purposes by owners who had no liking for agriculture, or any other sort of culture, stirred the conscience of a number of country lovers and respecters.

Sir Richard Garton, who had lived at Lythe Hill since 1902 and, although a keen man of business, had acted at home as a friendly squire, died in 1934. Among his many gifts to his town— his as Lord of the Manor—had been, first, a steam fire engine in 1907 and then a motor fire engine in 1934; considerable support for the hospital rebuilding—later, several of its extensions were his personal gift; the parish church also had cause to thank him for a Tower Screen. At his death his 2,000 acre Lythe Hill estate came on to the market, and soon afterwards it was learned that the land on either side of the famous and beautiful Tennysons Lane was in the hands of a builder. At once a strong committee was formed, headed by Lt. Col. and Mrs. Hume whose enthusiasm for the preservation of a decent country and its beauty led to the immediate reforming of the Haslemere Preservation Society. This Society had gone into retirement at the start of the late war, but now came into action again. The necessary fund to meet the cost of saving most of Tennysons Lane was raised partly by local subscription, and partly as the result of an article and letters in the London Press. At a later date, the rescued Lane which had been entrusted to the Haslemere Preservation Society, was transferred to the local Blackdown Committee of the National Trust for permanent safekeeping.

A municipal burial ground had, after some debate, been decided on, and located at Shottermill, and was consecrated in June 1934 by the Bishop of Guildford.

Further works programme at this time included the development of the Eight Acres area to the north-west of Beacon Hill. It had been found difficult to acquire land for council building nearer

Haslemere, and this new housing estate, though five miles from the centre of Haslemere, helped to fill a painful vacuum in the local housing programme. Bus services were conveniently near, bicycles were still in common use, motor cars via Morris Motors were now the playthings of the general public, and lastly, petrol was still only 1/6d per gallon.

By 1935 the Council took a breather, and looked around at their new estates at Border Road, Pitfold Avenue, Sunvale and Eight Acres. In order to break the monotony of brickwork, a programme of tree planting was undertaken, and the old trees in Chestnut Avenue whose roots had begun to disturb the footway, were removed and replaced.

The B.B.C. which had progressed beyond the chrysalis form of 2LO was now broadcasting much of the music which had become popular since the American invasion towards the end of the 1914-18 war. This was one of the more popular but less valuable legacies, but it has persisted, while regressing to a more primitive type of beat, accompanied by a nasal noise derived from a German Band dual instrument, such a noise as could be expected from a cross between a bassoon and a clarinet—I refer to a multi-stop sound-factory called Saxophone.

In a lecture given many years ago at Haslemere on the Development of Design from Utility by an A.R.I.B.A., he remarked, as illustration, that the tom-tom of the savage is the ancestor of the Military Band. Had he lived till now, he might have been able to moralise on what is becoming more obvious, that Development does not always progress in a straight line, and that a circular course returns the pilgrim or the savage to the point from which he started out. We can say with a fair degree of truth nowadays, "This is where we came in." We are back again with the tom-toms, the cow-horns—the cymbals and the hip waggle stomp.

From this time onward could be heard, quietly at first, but there for those with ears, the wheezes of the frustrated, the moans of the angry young men, and of carping critics and iconoclastic writers and playwrights.

Is all this nervous irritability and unstability a real sign of the times, or is it a mere end product of noise, car and cycle popping, plane engines, tom-tom throbbing, and the drug of rhythm, as was so well evidenced in the films record of the royal tour of West Africa? Is there never a moment sufficiently free from noise for a voice to be heard "Be still and know . . ."?

All through the previous twelve years had run a silver thread of pure music. There had been, of course, the mixed concerts of the Musical Society of Miss Bristow, supported by many

well-known artists. The Haslemere Players had since 1905 produced annually a Gilbert and Sullivan opera. But since 1925,
offered annually by the family of Arnold Dolmetsch, there had
been a festival, for which was displayed a growing appreciation
of early music, by a broadening section of the musical public.

To this music there was need to listen. There was no assault
on the ears by the many synthetic overtones provided in more
modern instruments. There was no brass and no drum. The
rhythm was given by the throb of the viol or the skill of the
performer on the solo instrument. Needless to say the appeal was
lost on many who were already demanding more and more noise
—even Mark Hambourg was admired for his piano crashing
ability. But appreciation of the older music as interpreted by the
Dolmetsch family and their disciples grew steadily, even to the
point of music writing by modern composers for the older instruments. It was, however, not till after the second world war that
the Festival began to receive the financial support of the Arts
Council, since when the festivals have grown in stature, interest
and appreciation, year by year.

CHAPTER IX

To War Again

RAIL ELECTRIFICATION — CAR CONGESTION
EUROPEAN UNCERTAINTIES — WAR — SELF SERVICE

Following urgent representation for a better rail service from Portsmouth to London, the then Southern Railway electrified this important link between the coast and the Metropolis. As has been often remarked before, the picturesque and, at the same time striking, appearance of a steam train either at rest or in motion, was lost. No one looks twice at the electric worms as they slide through the countryside, or thinks of having a chat with the unfortunate driver who sits in isolation at the front of his vehicle, pushing a little lever round and round, or pressing a knob. To see a giant express steaming quietly at ease at the platform and awaiting signal from the guard, was to see coiled power. A shrill whistle, a nod from the stoker as he watched the signal flag waved by the guard, and with a long hiss of released steam from the valve, the first enormous puff of smoke rose from the funnel and the giant driving wheels began to move round. What a thrill for the small boy, and many older boys, to hear the sudden puff, puff, puff, if the grip on the rail was not maintained at first, until gradually with even snort the train moved grandly from the station.

Now, no flag wags; either a whistle or handwave from the platform porter, the slamming of a few doors, and a reptile moves away with a rising moan. No, in spite of engine soot and tunnel smells, those were the days, when, as a steam express roared through a countryside, people would turn to watch it out of sight, much as they would have done a hunt in full cry.

It, however, became possible to organise better train schedules and at first there were several fast trains per hour from Haslemere which did the trip to London in or just under the hour. From now on, Haslemere and the district round enjoyed a fresh invasion of those whose business was in London, and who did not object to the distance of forty miles, either on the grounds of time or cost. The station yard morning and evening began a process of car-parking with more or less skill, rather like a football scrum, which continues with ever increasing congestion.

A referee, or should one call him only a touch judge, stands on the touch line (pavement) on behalf of the buses and cars which growing ever larger compete with varying degree of success for the limited space in the station yard.

A special source of attraction to the would-be new resident was the amount of National Trust land which, in the nearby area, had already been given or subscribed for. There was now a total of over fifteen hundred acres of open common land and woods where those who could come to live in Haslemere might walk or ride (on horseback) or even just stand and stare. The fact that these lands could not be built on or desecrated increased the attraction of this part of south-west Surrey to those who admired amenity. Practically the whole of the Hindhead Common with Marley Common and woods, and, at a little distance, Ludshott Common, were all free to ramble over. Thus was saved the cream of the Surrey hills, largely by the generosity and public spirit of a few people who cared not only for beauty in the abstract, but that that beauty should be shared, stared at, and enjoyed by as many people as possible. To the south lay five hundred acres of Blackdown, placed in the safe keeping of the National Trust by the generosity of Mr. E. K. Hunter.

If building had taken place over such areas of outstanding beauty, only a few persons could have benefitted and, as time went on, greater density of building would have led to a reduction of such choice settings and vistas, as may have previously charmed the few.

The National Trust deserves not only the good wishes and thanks of all country lovers—and that is, I still believe, eighty per cent of the English nation—but also their very active support.

A few lines earlier, I did write "could not be desecrated" but with the depositing of more and more litter, even up to cars, lorries and refrigerators, on the commons, those words need some modification. Why does the English race tolerate this astounding exhibition of laziness and bad taste?

The lower end of Shepherds Hill had already been spoiled by the removal of the two lowest cottages and their replacement by a cinema, now defunct, and later a completely out-of-keeping block of shops and flats. The loss of these cottages had triggered the removal of Walter Tyndale, the artist, from his home at the corner of Hill Road, the approach up Shepherds Hill having entranced him from the artist's viewpoint.

Now the old Malthouse at the junction of Shepherds Hill with Lower Street was condemned as unsafe, and as an obstruction to traffic, which, ever increasing, moved to and from the junction. When it was pulled down, a number of small coins of dates from Charles II onwards was the only treasure trove, though in the seventeenth century brandy and tobacco had been sold there. The irregular area which remained was grassed over and suitably enclosed, but the blank end of the flats remains, an inharmonious feature, in spite of the efforts of the local surveyor to shroud it with Virginia creeper.

The celebrations of the Royal Silver Jubilee were given due attention not only by the local authority, but by all residents. The town sprouted flags, etc. from windows of houses and shops lining the main streets, while at Pound Corner, on both sides of the Town Hall, at Weyhill, at Lion Green and Junction Place, large arches were built, covered with greenery and flowers. Children and others were given silver-plated teaspoons embossed with date and royal heads, medals, and a tea-party.

A proposal to demolish the Town Hall, replace it and the whole triangle where cars parked, in the centre of the High Street, with a shrubbery, was turned down by the local Council after letters in the paper, for and against, had been received and digested. The relatively new (then) idea of a roundabout was canvassed and fortunately dismissed—fortunately, I say, for in the light of subsequent experience, most road authorities now recognise that a roundabout is a hindrance rather than otherwise, being so often a free-for-all, the thruster winning. The fact of the existence of the Town Hall, and inability to see through or across it, tends to induce more care in those who pass it. While the appearance, as then quoted, at the end of the Town of the buildings beyond the south side of the Town Hall would not give any pleasure to point to the Town scene.

With all the re-awakened social life and improvements in the standards of living since the world slump ten years earlier, few persons could be found to listen to the bubblings of the cauldron of world affairs.

Unfortunately the political scene was occupied by a bunch of relative nonentities—pipe dreamers—political nostrum mongers —good clubmen and a jaunty rather second rate salesmanship. The men of vision like Winston Churchill could only snipe from the wings of a stage full of strutting fools. Cassandra in the days of Troy saw the shape of the future, but none heeded her foreboding. In 1930 to 1940 history was repeating itself. Reports from Continental centres appeared to be disregarded or pigeonholed. Whenever public criticism of government inactivity in the face of mounting Nazi insolence became audible, the bland father figure belching his own smoke-screen, was propelled into publicity to soothe the fractious British family. Lulled into a near torpid cynicism, Britain maundered her way to the threshold of disaster. It is almost ludicrous to recall that eventually a whole country might trust that an umbrella could stave off destiny.

One of the subjects over which much council time and talk had been spent, and which had provoked supporting or irritated comment in the local press, was the matter of a swimming pool.

First mooted in 1931 with the backing of the Chamber of Trade, and by Miss Chandler, the Urban District Council was slowly inoculated with the idea. Discussions and propositions for and against went on from 1934 to 1939, with on the average fifty per cent of the electorate for or against, i.e. of those who troubled to vote. The Ministry of Health approved a £10,000 plan for the lay-out of Camelsdale fields, with certain economy modifications. At this point in May 1939, in spite of great support from the Co-operative Society and various youth organisations, the Council passed a motion rescinding all previous resolutions by an adverse vote. However, an ad hoc Committee was nominated in view of much public unrest, which submitted a scheme for a smaller pool on a site in Bunch Lane. In October 1939 the whole scheme was postponed till after the war.

In September 1939, with the declaration of war by Hitler, plans which had been waiting in cold storage for the evacuation of children and mothers from London to safer areas, were put into operation. On the first week-end in September twenty special trains unloaded nearly eight thousand children and helpers at Haslemere station. Of this number about two thousand were to be settled in the surrounding area. The Haslemere Hall was taken into use as a distributing office, and during the day all were found temporary homes within a six mile radius. The pattern of distribution and reception in the Haslemere area did not differ from that which prevailed in other safe reception areas. After a little shyness, the majority of newcomers bedded down happily in their new homes. The eyes of many folk were opened to the ways of living of people from other areas. Some children, though not from well-to-do homes had never shared in household chores, or even cleaned their own shoes; money in several cases had been supplied to children to go out and have a street shoe shine.

The country was, to the children, usually a great joy, though fruit orchards and, occasionally, gardens provided overmuch temptation. As for adults, many deeply missed the delights or lures of London lights and, in spite of comfortable billets, returned to their old homes as the war proceeded in an apparently peaceful way. To such people it was unthinkable to live a few miles out in the country, two or three miles from the nearest fried fish shop, cinema, pub or lighted street corner. It is likely after the real rough stuff began over London from 1940 onwards, that many of those who had thus gone home, sought shelter in the wider countryside again.

On a lovely morning in September soon after 7 a.m. in 1939, an air raid warning brought people from their beds. A faint but steady drone came gradually overhead where to the naked eye only a blue sky with slight wisps of steam trails could be seen.

Through field glasses, however, were revealed hundreds of aeroplanes, the larger proceeding in a mass with small planes circling the centre mass like a number of sheepdogs. As they passed beyond the town, faint poppings were heard of the machine gun fire, and a few cartridge cases gave the town a first baptism of war rain.

By October, eighty per cent of those evacuated to Haslemere still remained, and the swollen population was further increased when the Admiralty moved two departments from Portsmouth to work at a large house on the outskirts of Haslemere, called Lythe Hill. Here in the relative peace of south-west Surrey, much of the radar equipment which kept Britain ahead in the air, and on the sea, was developed.

The Local Defence Volunteers got away to an enthusiastic start. Even while the broadcast was in progress asking for volunteers, the first name came over the telephone at the local Police Station, while other names were offered during the night. The Hospital nearly doubled its potential accommodation by the acquisition of further beds. Nursing would have been a heavy and difficult problem if these beds had had to be erected, owing to the restriction of space between adjacent beds.

The usual war-time organisations came into being under the spate of government instructions.

Distribution of gas masks, food rationing and coal rationing offices were opened. Air raid shelters, a warden system and posts were selected and manned. The usual difficulties were encountered over black-out systems which took some weeks at least to adjust. The chief local power lay in the hands of the Big Three—the Chairman of the Council, the Surveyor, and the Clerk—though an enormous amount of work devolved on the Health and Sanitary officials.

In the case of serious trouble such as a heavy air raid or invasion, the Big Three would have had to assume complete responsibility in the area.

The winters were severe after the start of the active war in 1940; much snow lay to a depth of feet in 1941 and 1942 for weeks before the limited work parties could clear the roads properly. Evening social activities were considerably reduced with the diminution of fuel supplies, the difficulty of walking in the dark, and the need for concentration on the war effort.

As the war progressed, a small tip and run raid spread a few light bombs along the upper part of Three Gates Lane without damage, except for a small hole in the corner of a garden. Two further raids produced some moderate damage across the upper part of the High Street, but fortunately no direct house hits.

During 1942, British Restaurants were opened at Weyhill and Beacon Hill, Hindhead, which continued to serve the public till

1946, while a cash and carry meals service was started for agricultural workers. The general population endured the nuisance of blackout, both within their own homes and in moving about outdoors after dark. As the night raids on London and the Midlands were stepped up by the Germans, air raid warnings brought wardens to their beats and, at first, many people to their shelters, until they acquired a certain cynical philosophy.

Many public services suffered a near crippling loss of many of their regular staff, not least the nursing and medical, whose services were necessary in the bombed areas or overseas.

The great fire raids on London in 1941 were visible from Haslemere at night as a strong glow in the north-west sky, though from Hindhead, the extra four hundred feet in height made the sky on the horizon a lurid sea of fire. The local fire brigade, as with many other home county units, was attached for duty to the London area.

Some alarm, shock and sorrow was caused by the crashing of one of our own planes on to the road by the Holy Cross Hospital wall, with the death of its crew. Parts of the engine fell through the roof of the Rex Cinema, causing damage to the structure, but no panic to the audience which was sparse at that hour.

A number of German planes crashed in the immediate area—Grayswood, Roundhurst, Fernhurst, Marley and just beyond Northchapel. The only fatal casualty to Civil Defence was the result of a fast homing German plane which dropped its stick of bombs across the High Street from north-west to south-east. One bomb exploding outside an ambulance station, killed a woman driver, Marion Clarke, who happened to have just left the building. Her co-driver was wounded.

The same night the crew of four of a German bomber in difficulties baled out round Haslemere. Two parachuted to safety, one to land, somewhat burned, in the grounds of a large house near Shottermill Ponds, and a second man, who was found wandering, but still combative near the railway line towards Liphook. The remaining two of the crew of that bomber landed fatally, with unopened parachutes.

Another German raider, hotly pursued by a Spitfire, was in such a hurry to get home safely that he unloaded a couple of oil drums and other loads, near Boxalland Farm, just over the Sussex border. A double decker bus nearly received the unwanted present, but pulled up and assisted the farmer to put out the flames which were threatening the nearby farm buildings. A noisy night followed with much to and from air traffic, for Haslemere was on the general route from the Continent to the Midlands. The farmer and his wife retired for the night, as was their war time habit, on to a mattress under the kitchen table. They dropped off to sleep eventually, but about two a.m. were awakened by a couple of gigantic explosions. No harm was done to the house, and it was only when morning came that the farmer found his farm yard and the next two fields littered with pieces of earth and bomb. Two fields away were two enormous craters made by delayed action bombs unloaded by the plane of the previous evening.

The pursuit by an English plane of a German raider caused it to unload over the Fernhurst Crossroads, with slight house and personal damage. A curious sidelight on official attitudes emerged after this event, when the Haslemere doctor who had visited Fernhurst immediately after the incident, and dealt with all casualties, received an official reprimand from the adjacent authority for trespass on to their sacred area.

In 1944 Haslemere had its only direct experience of a flying bomb which fell, once again, on the edge of Three Gates Lane only twenty yards from where the first bomb in the war had been dropped. On this occasion, however, much more extensive damage was done to property, but fortunately with little more than shock and a few scratches from broken widows to the immediate neighbours. An onlooker from the other side of the valley had watched the progress of the machine across the sky from the south, and noted the cessation of the engine beat and its fall into the hillside opposite. She turned to a visiting friend with a general comment, and suddenly realised that her husband, a doctor, was in one of those houses. In his turn, the doctor husband, had heard the approach of the flying bomb, had drawn the attention of a member of the household which he was about to leave after a visit, and then was aware of the absence of engine beat. Though no more than ten yards from the house, the explosion merely removed several windows on that side, while at least one member of the household claimed not to have heard anything. But two other houses nearby suffered extensive damage.

The end of the war on 19th May, 1945 was treated as a great Thanksgiving Day, and was marked by a Victory parade. But V.J. day on the 18th August later the same year brought a great sense of relief and relaxation, so that by the evening, the High Street was floodlit, and two thousand people massed around a huge bonfire which had been built in a concrete drum.

On the commons near Haslemere, there had been twenty-five thousand troops in Bramshott and Witley camps, as in the previous war, and the population of Haslemere had been swollen to fifteen thousand. These last figures dwindled to something under twelve thousand, as people and Government Departments returned to other areas.

This year was a year of portents, for on the 11th July, 2.27 inches of rain fell over one period in the day, and later there was a downpour of 3.1 inches, of which nearly one inch fell in half an hour. The widest part of the High Street was at one time completely covered by water nine inches deep in the centre of the road, which rushed away down West Street along the course of the old stream which now underlies the Post Office. In front of the Oaklands Hotel an inspection manhole was lifted up on an upsurge of water, and for several minutes balanced on top of a liquid pyramid. The roadway, under the bridge below the railway station, was for some time buried in water to a depth of five feet, several cars being trapped there.

The next year or two found organisations being wound up or re-started. Government policy and the need for rebuilding industry and housing on a peacetime footing tended towards full employment. One of the minor adjustments which, however, created much grumbling, was the continued absorption of female labour in various branches of industry. Strange to say, it became almost impossible to find domestic help, even help by the day was at a premium, and many promising family friendships were wrecked on the seduction of help from one home to another.

This, it could be said, was the beginning of the self-service programme. This is supposed to be excellent training for morale, moral fibre, know-how, or what-have-you, and is passing nowadays from the home into the business world. As a means of time wasting, the condemning of the average housewife to total house chores could not have been more successfully planned. The use of people in repetitive factory employment rather than the more varied occupations of the home could only be justified by the pleasure, if it be such, of working in a large group. What will be the shape of things, in the future, for those whose capabilities lie in this repetitive work, now that partial automation, and soon-to-be total automation, takes over complete production from blue print to finished article?

The next Election battle cry by a really progressive political party will certainly be—No Work, Automatic Pay.

As life moved into a more normal pattern, leisure occupations began to assert themselves. More books were being read, and to meet this need, a branch of the County Library, which had been housed at the Town Hall, was moved in 1947 to larger quarters in Weyhill. Looking back over the years, the first public library was opened in 1865 in Haslemere with books from Mudie's, London, and in 1874 a parish library with a children's section was started by the Rector for a membership cost of 2/6d. per year. The public library was moved from the White Horse Assembly Rooms in 1886 to The Workmen's Club, but did not long continue there. The parish library continued in the Town Hall till 1941, when its work was absorbed by the County Library, of which a branch had been started in 1926 and housed in the Town Hall in 1930. Since opening at Weyhill, the use by the public of the library facilties has in the past decade grown extensively, and the county network now costs a 5½d. rate (1962 rate).

Planning for housing and other development was in the immediate post-war years a matter of concern to those who had at heart the welfare of the whole countryside, as opposed to mere commercial advantage. To the proposal to allow the siting of fairly heavy industry in the Camelsdale area, the local Council turned a deaf ear, and stated their policy that only small service industries would be permitted round Haslemere. This was subsequently endorsed by the County Planning authority.

The new Town and Country Planning Act of 1947 placed a considerable degree of control of planning and, shortly after, advertising, in the hands of County Councils. To insure adequate coverage and the best use of local knowledge, the County Councils delegated much of their power to local authorities such as Urban Districts and Rural Districts. In this way, Planning Committees were constituted to consider the best use of land, and the distribution of housing and industry in their respective areas. Town maps with red, white and green areas were marked out on a five year basis, and conjoined with the National designations of Green Belts, Areas of outstanding Natural Beauty, and later on, the formation of National Parks, have attempted not always without success, to stem the urgent pressure of building in the commuter areas round London. There is little doubt that as time goes on greater density of housing, if not of building, will have to be permitted. People from the northern zone of England, from Scotland, from the West, Wales, Ireland and from overseas, are all attracted like moths to the Metropolis. Having sampled the accommodation, prices and amenities of the inner zones, they flee in numbers to the outer zones to live, in many cases, a precarious but London-attached existence. National planning and distribution of work and opportunity seems very slow and halting in its efforts to divert this spate of misguided humanity away from the south and south-eastern Home Counties. A new Pied Piper of London is needed.

In the same year, 1948, there was a further threat to the existence of the Town Hall, which was again over-ruled by commonsense. Had this been allowed, the proposal envisaged the removal of the War Memorial to the foot of Shepherds Hill, a roundabout in place of the Town Hall, and a regulation herring bone car park along the centre of the High Street.

For a time, car parking was permitted in the centre of the High Street, but the increase in the number of cars, compelled the authorities to devise some better scheme, if possible. Land at the west of the High Street was acquired by the Council for a two-acre car park to be entered from the High Street. The diversion only partially successful, of stationary cars was the subject of an immediate outcry from traders surrounding the High Street. It was evident, however, and still is, that one car placed against a business house for any length of time, successfully blocks the approach of any further customer, and most businesses would appear to thrive best on a succession of customers. Timed parking limits were the next suggestion of the back-room boys, but with few exceptions this has not proved of great benefit owing to the absence, or usual absence, of sufficient staff to supervise the time limits. In this regard a reasonable solution might well be in the construction of a tiered car park capable of accepting more cars off the congested roadways, even if a small charge were imposed towards maintenance.

The centre of the High Street was laid out as a green enclosure, with the War Memorial as a centrepiece, and is a welcome relief in the sea of surging traffic.

CHAPTER X

New Plans and Old

To enlighten public thought and opinion on the subject of the renewed threat of uncontrolled development to the English countryside, the Commons and Footpaths Preservations Association was given a platform by the British Broadcasting Corporation, and for the Association, Miss Dorothy Hunter, daughter of Sir Robert Hunter, spoke eloquently. Miss Hunter described the aims and work of the Association, and of the need for preserving, for all time, the heritage of great commons and open spaces, many of which were now being in part safeguarded by the creation of National Parks. In the course of her remarks which, as always, and as a daughter of her father, were pithy and powerful, she said, "The way to the country is a short cut to Health!" This is largely a truism, but in these days of urbanisation is being proved by the hundreds of thousands of people, who week-end by week-end, burst the seams of our main and country roads, and overflow on to the commons and open spaces saved by the forethought and work of early countryside conservationists.

In the following year, E. W. Swanton, A.L.S., Curator of Haslemere Museum, retired. For over fifty years he had guided and watched the development of the small museum, first in 1897 on Museum Hill, and later in the High Street. When he handed over his duties after a short interregnum to John Clegg in 1949, the Museum and its work had a very wide reputation. It was known more especially for the great insistence placed on education, both by specimen study in the Museum, in the laboratory, and in the open field. In common with other Museums, it held courses of lectures on subjects of interest to adults and children who wanted answers to the great question of "Why?"

Swanton's work in his special field of fungi, and in the Museum world in general, was recognised by the conferring on him of the O.B.E. The appointment of the new Curator and a competent and willing Assistant, Arthur L. Jewell, not only maintained the standards previously set, but inoculated the whole life of the Museum with a healthy dose of progress, re-organisation and re-display. The work of satisfying and training a wide public love of knowledge and nature has steadily increased, and as a result of the writing and broadcastings, both sound and television, of the Curator, the Museum set a pattern of display and function which many other museums have not been too proud to follow. As to activities outdoors, Haslemere is so far the only Museum which has a working programme of Field Ecology courses.

The local Council began a new housing project on the hill overlooking Sicklemill, and built a pleasantly laid out estate of eighty-eight houses, which later received commendation from the County Planning Officer. At Woolmer Hill, the hundred pre-fabricated houses which had been erected by the Admiralty during the war years had now lost most of their original tenants, and were quickly bought by the local council as an extension of the new housing programme.

This plan was extended in 1951 by acquiring the ninety-one houses which had been built by the Haslemere Tenants Society during the previous forty years. These houses had been built in a locally traditional style, the Fieldway and Bridge Road examples being brick and tiled, with some timbering. There was also a variation in size to accommodate different families. Those at Lion Mead were built of dark brick and tiled. The Marley Hanger development made possible by a gift of the land to the Council, lay in Sussex, and were of dark brick and tile, semi-detached, in a curve along a gently rising slope of Marley Common. These first experiments in local estate housing are pleasing to the eye; proper conformity in style being relieved by lack of uniformity in plan.

This year was marked for many by reason of the frequent and heavy rainfall which in the year totalled fifty-five inches, eighteen inches more than the average.

Dark autumn days led to discussions about street lighting and in 1952, after much debate, sodium lighting was chosen, partly because cheaper than other comparable forms of lighting, and partly by recommendation of that form of lighting by other authorities where it was in use. With a kindly thought for the appearance of the High Street, the Council avoided the over-use of lamp standards for the new lighting. Tactful approach to a number of house owners led to the fixing of some of the lamps to existing buildings. The scheme did not come into full opera-tion until 1955—but it brought four hundred and twenty concrete columns in its train.

In May 1951, the retiring Chairman of the Urban District Council made some valedictory comments extending back over the previous five years of his chairmanship. He noted that District Councils had not been able to lose much of the central controls which had been imposed as special war measures. He also felt that direction of affairs was growing more and more departmental and regional, and less and less a matter of local management. He asked if such local government as is left to a council is worthy of the attention of the ablest of the town's citizens, when less than twenty-five per cent of the ratepayers even trouble to exercise their vote. Speaking for himself, he was sure that there were still many important and interesting matters affecting not only the pockets, but the general amenities of the district, and the people's welfare, which still need most experienced brains at the local level.

As to pockets, the rates between 1946 and 1951 had advanced from 13/- to 18/- in the pound, and were likely to increase for reasons outside Council control. At that date the County precept was about 11/6 and of that amount, fifty per cent, 5/10½, was devoted to education.

In early 1952 Haslemere shared the nation's loss and grief at the death of King George VI. Thrust as he had been, fifteen years earlier, on a pinnacle, suddenly and only partly prepared, he had earned the love and trust of all the then Commonwealth of British Nations. The whole country admired him for the way he took up the burden of the Crown, tossed aside by one who rated personal feeling and desires above the call of the duty for which he had been trained, and for which, when it should come, many had had such high hopes. The examples and courage of King George VI, wonderfully supported by his wife Queen Elizabeth, shone like a beacon during the dreadful years 1939/45, and in his sharing the sorrows of London, his people were upheld in their loyalty to his courage and ideals.

A little over a year later, the Coronation of Queen Elizabeth II took place in a country which still was partly stunned by loss of the King, her father. Even the skies were unable to withhold their tribute to the past sovereign, and much rain fell, without, however, dampening the affectionate greeting of the crowds, which cheered the young Monarch on her return from her Coronation. From the whole country there was a vast upsurge of loyal feeling and support to the new Queen and her husband.

On the route of the procession were members of the local Haslemere St. John Ambulance and Red Cross detachments, who, though being thoroughly soaked while awaiting casualties, were satisfied to have shared the day's duties.

Local celebrations included a meal for the children, with the gift to each child of a commemorative mug. Rain prevented many of the celebrations which had been sited out of doors.

For the first time, through an excellent television broadcast, the whole nation was able to join in the whole Coronation service with the invited guests in Westminster Abbey.

This new marvel of television, as with sound broadcasting twenty years earlier, produced some unforeseen social results.

The programmes and public interest in them became a means of collecting families in their own homes again; to the disadvantage of professional or amateur entertainment of the more conservative variety. The tenuous but compelling, in many cases, contact with the outer world by picture and voice reproduction has limited to a considerable extent the social interchange of news and conversation which the guest or visitor used to bring. Only by deliberate selection of programme can the undoubted benefits of television be realised by a public avid for entertainment and reasonable instruction. This qualification is the more urgent as raised standards of living and shorter working hours offer extended leisure. However, such public societies as persist have undoubtedly raised their standards of entertainment in competition with the new household "sine qua non."

As the new medium approaches its tenth birthday, there are signs that this hoped-for selectivity in viewing and listening is being forced on the public willy-nilly by the spate of American canned or inferior grade programmes.

The Manorial rights and deeds of the Godalming Manor and Hundred, together with those of the Manor of Haslemere, came on to the market in the spring of 1953. Although most of the land rights were over strips of roadside waste, there were several areas of common land. These latter included 40 acres, well timbered, of Grayswood Common, several acres at Haste Hill, and at Weydown. There were also a number of boxes of deeds relevant to the history of the two manors, some of which dated from 1330. For good reasons, the Haslemere Urban District Council thought it worth while to conclude the bargain.

With this new mantle on their shoulders, the Council took the further step to request a grant of Arms from the College of Heralds for modern Haslemere. To round off the insignia of office, a badge for the Chairman was shortly afterwards acquired for wear on official duties.

This year also was one of signs and wonders in Haslemere, brought about by a Ministry of Transport order. Seventy odd large road parking signs were to be placed in and about the Urban District area, and work was rapidly begun to effect this. Devised apparently on an office table, the full scheme (the banded posts with, at first, mercifully shrouded heads) spread like a disease rash along the main streets. Disgust in the minds of many who cared for the natural beauty of Haslemere led to a wide popular protest. The local Preservation Society expressed its opinion at full strength, and sent a Letter of Protest, by the kindness of the local Member of Parliament, direct to the Minister of Transport. On this occasion action was rapid, and after further official inspection, the number of posts was reduced to forty-seven.

The observant visitor will, however, notice that many more posts have, since, sprouted in areas not originally nominated. This seems to be a result of the vast increase in the number of motor vehicles in use, and the determination of the motoring public not to walk. Some of these prohibitory signs might well be avoided if more of the general public could realise that a car is reasonably safe and no longer a traffic obstruction when stabled in a properly designed car park. Contrariwise, on a roadway, an empty static car is only a freight carriage in the wrong place and, as such, should be classable with litter. The multiplicity of road signs only tends to produce a blurred impact on motorists, much as cautionary tales by over-anxious parents lead to deafness, at least on that wave band, in the child hearer.

To the north of St. Bartholomew's Church and beyond the Kiln Field cottages, thirty-eight acres of land were now bought by the Council and developed comprehensively into a pleasantly laid out estate of some two hundred and fifty houses. A part of the development was specifically for elderly or single people; either as small flats at the ends of small sections of building, or in bungalows surrounding a large grassed open space, later used for recreational purposes by several junior clubs. A site was reserved for a village store, and some years later the opportunity so offered was taken up.

The amenity aspect in lay-out was respected, trees of previous growth being kept in the picture where possible at first, while other trees were planted.

The total appearance of the new development gave comfort to the many who had known that hillside as part of Church Hill or Peperham Farm.

In earlier ploughings many worked neolithic flint tools had been found, while from a garden by High Lane, flanking the new Estate, a Romano-British burial urn was brought by two keen-eyed boys, to the local museum. Haslemere may well be proud to have been a desired residential area for at least five thousand years. Under grass or corn, those acres had been a fitting background to the pleasant group of the old Church, sided by Church Hill House and Peperham Farm. Now the needs of the community were for housing rather than local food production, and the planning authority deserves much credit for this imaginative use of so much farm land, with the access roads laid in sweeping curves.

Down in the High Street, the old chestnut tree again came under fire. Certain roots, the course of some of which could be seen just below the surface of the footpath, were alleged to be a cause of damp or disturbance to a small nearby property, while the spread of branches was alleged to be a risk to traffic from age, length and weight. A small conference between the local authority and the Preservation Society met on the site with an expert tree adviser, who later reported that the tree itself was healthy and safe, though over one hundred and sixty years old. On his advice the offending roots were carefully removed. Finally, a Comprehensive Accident Policy was taken out by the Preservation Society, so that the great trusses of bloom may be expected to give annual pleasure to many thousands of people for another generation or two.

After many years of argument between adjoining authorities, a really inclusive scheme for the drainage of the Hindhead area was finally agreed in 1955. For more than forty years efforts had been made to find a satisfactory conclusion to the growing needs of an increasingly popular residential area. The practical results of each delay was, as is often the case, an enormous increase in the overall cost, due to wage rises, raw materials and increases in land values. The scheme was sent to the Minister in whose care it was to remain for the next five years, during which time, of course, the overall cost mounted still further. One cheerful aspect which was seen when the work finally began was the realisation that in the lapsed time certain legislation had been passed which gave power to the Ministry of Housing and Local Government and the County authority to make grants in such cases (as in the Hindhead scheme) where the sewerage operations had to be carried through a rural area. Much benefit thus accrued to the local rates, in a negative way, the overall rate cost which would have been about 8d. - 9d. being reduced to 4d.

The Council now turned its attention to the renting of Council properties, and to ensure that housing problems were dealt with fairly, and the local cost placed where it should belong, adopted the Differential Rent system. A basic rent level was fixed to ensure financial stability, and scope for maintenance and expansion within the scheme. The basic rent was related to a selected income level, while those tenants with incomes above or below this level were allocated increases or rebates in proportion to differences from the normal. It is only fair to say that after some initial scepticism, the scheme has been well received, and has maintained financial equilibrium, while giving scope for further building as need arose.

At this time, also, the Government relaxed a little in its grim demand for taxation. Powers were given to local authorities to grant on request, a fifty per cent relief of rates to certain charities. Such reliefs were extended to Museums, Educational establishments (non-profit making), Clergy houses, hospitals and though, in general, a wise and helpful benefit, in a few areas where many relief receiving institutions are settled, there has been a great loss to the local authority rating total. This loss is not easy to offset, and restricts the ability of such a locality to make proper improvements in its own area.

The old wooden buildings, built sixty years before as a Museum, which had also for the past thirty years housed the departments of the local Council, were now too cramped to permit proper efficiency. Council car parking was also a serious problem, restricted as the offices were, on a built-up and steep by-road.

It may amuse some readers to be reminded that when the Council first met in its Council Chambers, the door to that room was still, from its museum days, labelled "Fossil Room."

Consideration of the need led to a proposal for the acquiring of the house at Pound Corner, once the Rectory and now Sadlers. For various reasons this idea was abandoned. Shortly after, a small property facing Lion Green became vacant, and was bought by the Council for future development as Council Offices and Chambers. This was certainly to some people a move in the right direction, the site being much more central to the general area development.

In the year of 1957 the local Blackdown Committee of the National Trust was faced with an expensive problem. The old Shottermill ponds which had been given anonymously to the Preservation Society (who, in turn, transferred them for safe keeping to the National Trust) were suffering from age. Constructed originally some time in the sixteenth century, at least, as an adjunct to an Iron Mill, for the last one hundred and seventy five years as a corn mill, its dams were leaking, the sluices insufficient and the pond beds were silting up. An estimate for £3,000 was the bill presented to the local National Trust Committee, who quickly set to work to raise this large sum for repairs. With a deal of hard work, encouraged by generous and intelligent public support, the necessary target was passed, with a small surplus in hand for future needs. This fund is built up from time to time as the general balance or private generosity permit.

Many of the ponds which once bejewelled the countryside have disappeared or are silting up. A string of five ponds along Collards Valley are in their last stages. The old ponds below the Haslemere Parish Church of course disappeared with the building of the railway. A small pond below the Manor House, another by the old Windmill in Highercombe Road, and a third nearly opposite Mann's timber yards have been filled in. Of a string of ponds in Critchmere Vale, those from the Royal Oak southwards, have been built over. The lowest of these used to drive the wheel of New Mill, but is now a grass field by the side of the road to the Sewage Works. At Hammer, a scrub covered level area is all that remains of one of the feeders of the leat for the iron hammer and used to be called Woolmer Pond. The latest sacrifice to progress is that pond at Sickle Mill whose upper reaches are now an industrial site, while the lower three acres are being dried out.

These are a few of the many ponds which in many cases were made by our ancestors to pound up the generous local rainfall for use by water mills. Now these mills are supplanted by power brought from a distance at great cost and appalling defacement of landscape, while power failure (without warning) is still not unknown.

The swans which had enjoyed the Shottermill Ponds for many years, returned after the repairs and scouring, and their successors continue. Two pairs of ducks were placed on the ponds by the generosity of a nearby resident during the absence of the swans. This pair was supplemented by further gifts from two local schools whose ownership by the schools provided a large amount of immunity from sabotage, by the personal interest in their well-being.

It may have been the pleasure engendered by the sight of swans and ducks swimming comfortably on the rejuvenated ponds that brought forward the subject of swimming pools once again. Certainly an increasing number of private residents were building family pools on their own property. The Shottermill Primary School Parents Association, led by the Headmaster of the School, approved the principle of a bathing pool where the children from five to eleven years of age could be taught at least the rudiments of swimming, and realise that water could support a human body without much effort, but with much benefit. The plan was approved by authority at all levels, and with the co-operation of the local Medical Officer of Health, a satisfactory and pleasing swimming pool was built, largely by the muscles and brains of parents and friends, who also managed various fund raising schemes.

The success of this project started a discussion of plans for a local authority swimming pool once again. As before (twenty-five years earlier) many ideas were prescribed and as many objections were produced, until after many vicissitudes the skeleton of a scheme received financial approval from the Ministry, though the pay pause and national economy drive negatived the adoption of any loan temporarily. Popular opinion expressed by a postal poll was, as before, fairly evenly divided. There were the usual divisions of "Why should we do anything at all, especially if I don't share," the "Don't care what happens," "Too bored to reply, couldn't care less" group, and a reasonable proportion who saw fairly that some real benefit could accrue at least to the younger section of the population if a good lead were given.

There were still a few people who cared greatly for the surrounding commons and beauty spots, who were prepared to

buy such land as it came on to the market, not purely for personal
enjoyment, but to give pleasure to the many by the subsequent
transfer to the National Trust.

By 1950 the Trust properties in the immediate Haslemere area
of the bordering three counties of Surrey, Sussex and Hampshire
amounted to a little over three thousand acres. Within the next
few years a further one hundred acres in the Hindhead area and
sixty-five acres nearer Haslemere were preserved for ever as open
spaces by deed of gift to the National Trust.

These extensive open spaces are a delight to all who can
enjoy them, those people who are fortunate enough to live near
them, and those who come more and more each year to share
their quiet, varied and delightful features. For the local Committees of the National Trust, these large areas are a great responsibility, and their maintenance and protection from litter,
which year by year increases, and from fire risk, is a matter of
serious expense. It must not be overlooked that the Haslemere,
Midhurst and West Sussex Councils jointly gave land in the
beautiful Marleycombe Valley to the National Trust, and give
their moral and financial support to the local work which is being
done by voluntary committees for the oversight and care of these
priceless open spaces.

For the countryside at large, and not only in our own neighbourhood, the last few years have brought a new menace in the
erection of power lines and grids on immense steel pylons for the
supply and distribution of electricity by overhead cable. We learn
with some amazement that the only substitute, to date, for the
overhead cable, is the buried one which involves the use of
impregnated paper originally devised by Ferranti seventy years
ago. Perhaps this system which should now be receiving an
honourable old age pension may one day be replaced by a competent plastic insulation. Something along these lines has already
been achieved with the help of a new type of insulation whereby
current up to 11Kv can be used without insulators or segregation.

Shall we remember the ludicrous difficulties of introducing
the first turbine engine against official stupidity, and how a great
review was turned by a spurned new invention into a giggle. You
may read this for yourselves, but we are facing similar problems
today with the same entrenched official obstruction and self satisfaction. Wake up, England! as well as Haslemere, or you will be
living in a cocoon, not merely a cat's cradle.

In these last years, certain problems have obtruded themselves
very forcibly on public notice, most of which are a function of
planning. The south-east of England during the past half century
has become more and more attractive to people from other parts

of the world. The seaside resorts have hugely grown and become dropsied to the point of stagnation from road and service congestion. The formation of Green Belts, and open spaces has concentrated the pressure of new building into specified zones, which are reaching saturation. Much of this new local building is for the commuter residents whose occupations take them to London or the larger coastal towns. Industrial development is negligible and is limited to light industries. Land is thus a commodity in such short supply that much ingenuity is used to discover and develop, if possible, any likely or desirable sites, with the knowledge of great financial reward for the lucky speculator.

It is surprising, therefore, to find in the Haslemere district, as much community spirit as can be recognised by any who trouble to look beneath the surface with so many of the population spreading to a five to six mile radius of the railway station. Under a different economic set-up there might be scope for an even stronger corporate community spirit and life. A certain increase in industrial development of a non-heavy pattern would not negative the amenities of the locality, but give a firmer basis for the growth of a more stable and locally interested electorate.

There are still many people who look upon the district as a pleasant dormitory area, with reasonable shopping facilities and a better than average train service. None can disagree with this summing up, but it is leaving out some of the special desirable features in any residential landscape. An insistence on, or persistence in the dormitory way of life can never lead to more than a superficial interest in the common weal. Something or someone is needed to stimulate the production of community loyalties and interest. There is a faint stir in the air of forward movement again in our locality. For the last century, Haslemere has been waking out of its niche as a small country town to the responsibilities which face it as the active centre of a large residential and commuting area. There is a useful central co-ordinating body in its Urban District Council, now fifty years old, but still suffering from growing pains. Surrounding Haslemere is an amorphous group of little parishes which have lost any sense of direction which they may once have had under a beneficent (or otherwise) Manor House or priest.

The future will show whether Haslemere can accept leadership of some of these fringe villages, and help their development within an extension of the planning framework which has, in the main, proved beneficial to the present U.D.C. area. It may also be possible to see whether a large measure of decent tradition and amenity may be retained while permitting reasonable expansion for the total needs of the future.

Goodbye to all That

We have now come near our own day, a day of advertising ballyhoo, fiddling, fear both of present and the future, but of wonderful discovery, material achievement and challenge.

Can we step aside to a quiet place, if such can be found and listen; listen to the voices that never speak. The voices breathe of hope still for the human race, and that records of history show patterns of repeated anxieties, but that progress upwards towards an unseen goal has been constant, though uneven.

We can take note of the greater tendency to co-operate between nations as a practical measure for co-existence, instead of only in dire need. We see this again, in national life from Trade Unions to Oecumenical Conferences.

There is still a great measure of respect for cohesion in home life.

All these tendencies stem from a growth of the appreciation of collective responsibility for each other in all lands, with a somewhat slower recognition of personal responsibility.

The old leadership and control exercised by King, President or the ancient manorial lords has been largely replaced by the growth in stature of Parliament—the Voice of the People.

For a satisfactory efficiency in this form of government is required an interested and educated people.

In 1930 Bernard Shaw addressed a local gathering at Hill Farm, Camelsdale, then the home of Joseph King, M.P., to celebrate the elevation of two persons to the peerage. After some badinage as to the tragedy of the situation, he described Arthur Ponsonby as eminent, from having struggled out of the lap of Queen Victoria. The Labour Party had pitched him now, by the scruff of the neck, into the House of Lords, but there were compensations. He declared that the House of Lords was the only representative body in the country. A man was in the House of Lords because he was the son of his father, and that, be it said, was why any of them was in the country at all. Consequently the House of Lords did really represent them, whereas the House of Commons was a chamber of selected undesirables.

Hence my plea for an interested and educated people.

The fight is still on, against those who are merely power conscious, whether in combines, mass advertising for purely material ends, or finance manipulation.

The Press at its best, and this also applies to Broadcasting by sound or vision, has done much to spread knowledge, while such as Penicillin, blood transfusion, and the like, have transformed and removed many of the anxieties of former generations.

Enormous possibilities of progress in all phases of living are almost within reach.

Those, who having perhaps taken some note of past history, are now turned with vision straining into the future, may see approaching the bald-headed figure of Time. In 600 B.C. one of the Seven Sages of Greece said, "Seize Time by his forelock." It is no less true today for there is no hold on his bald occiput once time is past.

A little over a century ago, our journey started at the door of the then White House.

We can easily move today inside the fence under the chestnut tree which the old doctor knew so well—perhaps with his friendly ghost beside us. It would be interesting to see his appreciation of much that we find commonplace—steel horseless vehicles, hard roads, reasonably good pavements, and at night he would doubtless have approved street lighting. Many modern features within the houses would call for praise. I doubt, however, whether traffic increase and the accompanying noise, absence of staffing in his house, the imperative demand of the telephone, the rather out of scale presentation of merchandise would have produced any words of commendation.

For a few of our so-called amenities he would have expressed regret, but I think he would be well content to return again to his faithful Martha and Emma and to the ghostly memories of the quieter world he had served so faithfully.

HASLEMERE, FEBRUARY 1886

WORKING MEN'S INSTITUTE COMMITTEE

JOHN CLARKE   *Hon. Treasurer*
WALTER FOGDEN   *Chairman*
JAMES BRIDGER   *Hon. Secretary*

Altogether 62 members
and

Rev. S. Etheridge, rector
Rev. Benford, curate to the Church of England
Rev. G. B. Stallworthy, minister of Independent Chapel
Rev. R. Harding, minister of Baptist Chapel

Co. Coachman	MG. Market Gardener
Id. Independent	H.Bu. Hog Butcher
B. Baker	BM. Brickmaker.
BS. Blacksmith	Car. Carpenter
Bu. Butcher	SM. Shoemaker
FM. Fishmonger	(L) Liberal
WG. Working Gardener	(C) Conservative
P.Bu. Pork Butcher	(D) Doubtful
JS. Journeyman Smith	

John Clark (No. 18) made this out

East Side
High Street from Pound Corner
1 James Wakeford Co. to No. 3 (C)
2 Stables to No. 3
3 Miss Hesse, Id.
4 Laundry to No. 3
5 Charles Prior, B. (L)
6 Pent House
7 Mrs. B. Bridger, BS.
8 BS. shop to No. 7
9 Arthur Williamson, FM. (L)
10 Peter Aylwin, Chemist (C)
11 Storeroom to No. 10
12 William Clark, WG. (C)
13 Ben Woods, PC (C)
14 Lane
15 John Dawson, Car. (L)
16 Three Cottages
  (1) Mrs. Carter, small shop
  (2) George Roe, Laborer (L)
  (3) Frederick Madgwick, I Stone
    7 (L)
16½ William Quenell
17 Henry Whiting, Doctor (L)
18 John Clark, Newsagent (L)
19 Two cottages
  (1) Sary Upfold, Charwoman
  (2) Sary and Margaret Court, Id.
20 Misses Harrison and brother, Id.
21 Pent House to No. 22
22 William Furlonger's mother
23 William Furlonger, Bu. (L)
24 Duncan Macallum, MG. (L)
25 Mrs. Fanny Helyer, small shop
  Mrs. George Stenning
26 Gateway for Nos. 22, 23, 24
27 Henry Ballard, Draper (L)
28 Mrs. John Bridger, Id.
29 James Broyd, Barber (L)
30 Thomas Mack, Car. (C)

31 Alfred Softley, P.Bu. (L)
32 John Charman, White Horse Hotel
  (C)
33 Stabling to White Horse Hotel
34 William Mawer, Kings Arms Hotel
  (C)
35 Stabling to Kings Arms Hotel
36 George Welland, Grocer (L)

North Side of Petworth Road
37 Shops
  (1) For No. 61
  (2) Benjamin Brown, Tailor (D)
  (3) William Upton (No. 48)
  (4) Charles Pannell (No. 55)
38 Walter Fogden, Draper (L)
39 George Reeve, Post Office (C)
40 Albert Bicknell, Driver (C)
41 Bakery Shop to No. 66
42 Renton Brown, Gardener to No.
  120 (L)
  George Helyer, Gardener to Mr.
  Thomas (C)
43 Charles Greenaway, Id. (L)
44 Charles Bridger, Valuer (C)
45 Mrs. Forsyth, Id.
46 Mrs. W. Barns, Id.
47 C. G. Roberts, BM. (L)

South Side of Petworth Road
48 William Upton, Laborer (L)
  William Upton, SM. (L)
  Thomas Stent, Tailor (L)
49 Turner Bridger, Laborer (C)
50 Mrs. Morgan, Id.
51 Henry Steptoe, Id.
52 Fred Aplin, Painter (L)
  Henry Enticknap, SM. (D)
  George Dean, Co. to Mrs. Vale (C)
  Richard Windebank, IB. to No. 23

53 George Fulk, P.Bu. LB. (L)
54 Miss Westbury, Dressmaker
55 Charles Pannell, SM. (L)
56 William Clark, Carrier (L)
57 Mark Bicknell, Beerhouse (C)
58 Robert Kingshott, Gardener
59 George Tumme, Coal dealer (L)
60 John Burrows, Carpenter (L)
61 William Deas, Grocer (L)
62 Samuel Ford, Car. (L)
   Dr. Winslanley (L)
   Rev. E. Benford (C)
63 Mrs. Cambell, China Shop
64 Half Moon Yard
65 Hoir Hale, Malster at No. 82 (C)
66 William Gibbs, B. at No. 41 (C)

Shepherds Hill, South Side
67 Storerooms
68 James Luff, Carman (L)
69 Road
70 Robert Palmer, Painter (L)
71 Charles Bicknell, Laborer (L)

Shepherds Hill, North Side, Top
72 Butcher Searle, H.Bu. (L)
73 Albert Bicknell, Laborer (L)
   William Farminer, Laborer (L)
74 William Heath, Milkman (C)
75 Richard Gale, Laborer (L)
76 Mrs. Lovell, Charwoman
   Richard Bridger, Painter (L)
   Walter Horsley, Smith (D)
   John Madgwick, Painter (L)
   Alfred Upfold, Fishman (L)
   Jesse Boxall, Laborer (L)
   Henry Ford, Laborer (L)
77 Mrs. Furlonger, Charwoman
78 Mrs. Luff, Shopkeeper
79 William Smithers, BL. (L)
80 Hannah Oakford (Id.)
   Thomas Jones, Bricklayer (L)
81 Frederick Helyer, Laborer (C)
   George Trusler, Laborer (L)
82 Malt House used by No. 65

South Side of Lower Street, beginning
at foot of Shepherds Hill
83 Reuben Harding, LS. (L)
84 William Maides, Smith (C)
85 Henry Booth, Company agent (L)
86 Mrs. Jelly, Laundress
   Ernest Hepburn, Solicitor (L)
87 William Olden, B. (L)
88 John Moore, Laborer (L)
   James Huntingford, Laborer (L)
   Richard Luff, Carman (L)
   William Treagues, small shop (L)
89 James Madgwick, Beershop (L)
90 Mrs. Bush, Private Lodging
91 Chapel, Independent
92 John Oakford, Groom to No. 127
   (L)
93 William Berry, SM. (L)
   Charles Berry, Laborer (L)
94 William Stacey, SM. (L)
   Arthur Ruff, Laborer
   Mrs. Bicknell, Id.
94a Lawrence Longhurst, Farmer (L)
94b James Hammond, Groom (L)
94c William Wise, Gardener (L)
94d Henry Bridger, Stone Carter (L)

North Side of Lower Street
95 Albert Fagent, Printer (L)
96 George Searle, Gardener (L)
97 Margaret Denyer, Charwoman
   Dan Bridger, Painter
98 Smith's shop for No. 84
99 James Weeks, Clock Cleaner (L)
   Frederick Weeks, Groom for
   Thomas Moon, Laborer (L)
   Edward Charman, B. (L)
   Arthur Hall, Bricklayer (L)
   Henry Lovell, Laborer (L)
   George Smithers, Car. (L)
   William Slaughter
   Mrs. Bicknell, Charwoman (L)
   Robert Morley, Laborer (D)
100 Baptist Chapel
101 George Wardle of the Institute
   (L)
102 Lane, shed and yard for No. 101
103 Mrs. Weller, Dressmaker
   Miss Heath, Private School
104 Yard and storerooms for No. 65
105 Yard and storerooms for No. 65
106 Gammons, Drapery carried on by
   Henry Meadows (L)
107 Edward Eley, Clockmaker (L)
108 Slaughterhouse for No. 110
109 Mrs. Hersey, Id.
110 Henry Mitchell, Bu. (D)
   Frederick Fowler, Tailor (L)
111 Frank Taylor, Swan Inn (L)
112 Club Room, Swan Inn
113 New Institute

High Street, West
114 James S. Edgeler, Harnessmaker
   (L)
115 Unoccupied house
116 James Baker, Baker for No. 111
   (C)
117 Mrs. Clothier, Id.
118 George Leslock, SM. (L)
   John Tidy, Id.
119 Stephen Pannell, Id. (C)
120 Storerooms
121 Rayner Storr, Id. (D)
122 Billiard Room for No. 121
123 Misses Parsons, Id.
124 Miss Fory, Id.
125 Dr. Pearse, Id. (D)
126 Dr. Pearse's son, Doctor (L)
127 Josiah Whympher, Artist (L)
128 Miss Hepburn, Id.
129 Unoccupied house
130 Henry Chalcraft, Gardener to
   No. 3 (C)
131 Market garden for No. 24
132 William Welland, son to No. 36
   (L)
133 William Newman, Laborer (L)

Pathfields
   Mrs. J. Bridger
   Alfred Barns (L)
   William Tragmoor (L)
   David Remnant (L)
   William Hampshire (C)
   William Goodchild (L)
   James Bicknell (D)
   Thomas Bicknell (L)

INDEX